The Extens... the Fran...ise, ...1

HEINEMANN ADVANCED HISTORY

Heinemann Educational Publishers
Halley Court, Jordan Hill, Oxford, OX2 8EJ
a division of Reed Educational & Professional Publishing Ltd
Heinemann is a registered trademark of Reed Educational & Professional
Publishing Ltd

OXFORD MELBOURNE AUCKLAND
JOHANNESBURG BLANTYRE GABORONE
IBADAN PORTSMOUTH NH (USA) CHICAGO

© Bob Whitfield 2001

First published 2001

ISBN 0 435 32717 8
04
10 9 8 7 6 5 4

Designed, illustrated and typeset by Wyvern 21 Ltd, Bristol

Printed and bound in Great Britain by The Bath Press Ltd, Bath

Index compiled by Indexing Specialists, Hove

Photographic acknowledgements
The author and publisher would like to thank the following for
permission to reproduce photographs: Bridgeman Art Library: 159;
British Museum: 193; Mary Evans Picture Library: 31, 102, 125, 126,
132, 153, 156, 158, 162, 175, 182; Museum of London: 142 (both),
160.

Cover photograph: © Hulton Getty

Picture research by Elisabeth Savery

Written sources acknowledgements
The author and publisher gratefully acknowledge the following
publications from which written sources in the book are drawn. In some
sentences the wording or sentence has been simplified: Briggs, A. *The
Age of Improvement* (Longman, 1979): 273; Checkland, S. *The Rise of
the Industrial Society in England, 1815-85* (Longman, 1964): 224;
Evans, E. *Parliamentary Reform, 1770-1918* (Longman, 2000): 271;
Marwick, A. *Women At War, 1914-1918* (Fontana, 1977): 182;
Pearce, M. & Stewart, G. *British Political History, 1867-1995*
(Routledge, 1996): 273.

CONTENTS

HOW TO USE THIS BOOK

This book is divided into two sections. The AS section comprises two parts. The first, on The Great Reform Act of 1832, explains the reasons why the Reform Act was passed, what changes were made by the Act and the consequences of the Act for the political system. The second part of the AS section covers the story of the struggle for Votes for Women between 1867 and 1928. The summary questions at the end of each chapter will challenge the student to analyse, prioritise and explain key features of these subjects.

The A2 section of the book covers the period 1830–1931 and takes a thematic, analytical approach to the story of the transition to democracy in Britain. Students who are using this section of the book will need to read the AS sections first, in order to acquaint themselves with the outline of the story of the two key stages in the transition to democracy.

At the end of each part there are assessment exercises. These have been based on the new AS and A2 specifications. Guidance is given on how students should approach the different types of questions.

AS SECTION: PARLIAMENTARY REFORM, 1815–50

INTRODUCTION

The Great Reform Act, 1832

In 1832 Parliament, elected according to a set of rules that had not been changed since the seventeenth century, passed a Reform Act. Many MPs believed this Act would result in them losing their seats and would reduce the influence of the people they represented. This Act has been given the title of the Great Reform Act by many historians because it was the first such reform, although others argue that the Reform Act of 1832 actually changed very little and does not therefore deserve to be called 'Great'. There are a number of areas of controversy between historians surrounding the 1832 Reform Act and students are introduced to these debates through this book.

Social and economic change

Since the eighteenth century Britain had been experiencing social and economic changes with the growth of new manufacturing industries, the gradual shift of population from the countryside to the towns and the rise of nonconformity in religion. By the early nineteenth century a growing number of people were arguing that an electoral system that had been established at a time when the majority of people lived in the countryside, worked in agriculture and worshipped in the parish church, was increasingly out of touch with the changing reality of British society. The system produced MPs and government ministers who came mainly from the landowning classes and who had little knowledge of the worlds of commerce and manufacturing. Thus social and economic change led to pressure for reform, but the system was not without its defenders. It could be argued with some justification that landownership was still one of the most important economic interests in society and that the old, unreformed system was flexible enough to allow representatives of commercial and industrial interests to enter Parliament.

Pressure for change

Proposals to reform Parliament had been put forward as early as the 1770s, and a number of groups took up the cause of parliamentary reform in the late eighteenth century, both in Parliament itself and outside. By the 1790s, however, it was clear that an anti-reform majority existed in Parliament and that this view had the support of the majority of 'informed' opinion in the country. The situation in Parliament itself remained substantially unchanged until 1830 but pressure for reform from outside Parliament reached a peak in a wave of radical activity in the years 1815–20. Despite the failure of this movement to persuade government and Parliament to concede, some important progress had been made. New political organisations had been formed which were capable of mobilising popular support through establishing links between the economic distress of working people and the demand for popular representation in Parliament. When the issue of reform returned to the political agenda in 1830, radical political groups played a vital role in putting pressure on Parliament to pass the Reform Bill.

The crisis of reform

Historians have disagreed over the relative importance of different factors in the passing of the Reform Act. One school of thought emphasises the crucial role of pressure from outside Parliament in forcing reluctant MPs to pass the Reform Act. Riots in several cities in the autumn of 1831 and a threat to undermine the banking system in May 1832 heightened fears of a revolutionary situation developing if the Reform Bill was not passed. Talk of a revolutionary situation is largely discredited by historians writing recently and attention has shifted to the changing situation within Parliament itself. Between 1827 and 1830 the seemingly impregnable position of an anti-reform Tory government was undermined by a series of factors, with the result that a pro-reform Whig government was able to take office in 1830 and introduce a Reform Bill in 1831.

Even after the Whigs gained a majority in Parliament, however, opposition to reform within Parliament was so intense that pressure from outside was needed to force the Bill through. Explanations of the reasons why the Reform Act was passed in 1832 must, therefore, give due weight to the role of pressure from outside Parliament and to the complex changes in the parliamentary situation between 1827 and 1832.

The impact of reform

Many supporters of reform had exaggerated hopes of the changes that would follow a reform of Parliament. Opponents of reform had equally exaggerated fears about the dire consequences that would result. In the event, the Reform Act made many significant changes to the political system, some foreseen and others unforeseen, but there was much in the post-reform political system that was not changed. The aristocracy remained the dominant political and social class and many features of the pre-reform era persisted until long after the Reform Act was passed. Nevertheless, the years after 1832 did see significant changes to political parties and the beginnings of wider participation in politics by the middle classes. Between 1832 and 1850 there were also a number of further reforms that were at least indirectly linked to the passing of the Reform Act. Most notable among these reforms were the 1834 Poor Law Amendment Act and the 1835 Municipal Corporations Act. This period also witnessed the growth of pressure groups that were campaigning to persuade Parliament to enact further reforms, the most important of which were the Anti-Corn Law League and the Chartist movement. Thus, although the post-1832 scene retained many of the features of the unreformed parliamentary system, by 1850 the political landscape in Britain was very different from that which had existed in 1830.

CHAPTER 1

How was society changing?

WHAT WAS THE TRADITIONAL SOCIAL STRUCTURE?

The opponents of the reform of Parliament were attempting to preserve a society that had been gradually evolving over many centuries. This was a society in which most people lived in the countryside, where most communities were small scale, and where ownership of land was the basis of wealth and prestige. Apart from London, which had a population of almost 1 million in 1801, there were only seven towns with populations in excess of 50,000. For most of the people of Great Britain in the eighteenth century, the parish in which they were born was the limit of their horizon. The parish was the basic unit of local government; each parish was responsible for the upkeep of its roads, the maintenance of law and order and the care of the poor. In this society there were fine gradations of hierarchy and status, which everybody understood and most people accepted. Although in the eighteenth century the language of class began to be used to differentiate between different groups, most people were not conscious of **class** differences in the way that this would be understood today. Awareness of one's place within a hierarchy of **rank**, however, was very clearly understood. Landowners were conscious of belonging to a group that provided the social and political leadership within society, although there were clear distinctions of rank within landowning society. Merchants, bankers and lawyers belonged to the 'middle ranks' while farm labourers, craftsmen and domestic servants belonged to the 'lower orders'. Within this hierarchy, most landowners accepted that they owed a duty of care to the underprivileged, particularly to their servants and to the workers on their estates. In return they expected the 'lower orders' to show deference to them and to conform in matters of politics and religion.

Church of England

At a time when the vast majority of the population professed to believe in Christianity, membership of a common national church was one of the elements binding society together. The Church of England, or Anglican Church, was the established church. This meant that it was deeply embedded in the fabric of national life at all levels of society and that its position was enshrined in law. The monarch was head of the church. Bishops and archbishops sat in the House of Lords and were appointed by the government. The church controlled the universities of Oxford and Cambridge and many of the leading schools. All public and official ceremonies were conducted according to the doctrines of the Church of England. At a local level, the '**parson**' occupied a position in villages second only to that of the '**squire**'. Most clergymen owed their positions to local landowners who controlled appointments to 'church livings'; their incomes came mainly from **tithes**, a form of taxation on agricultural land which was enforceable by law. The parish church was the centre of village life, providing a place of worship for people of all classes and underlining, through the **seating arrangements** within the church, the social hierarchy within the community.

Town and country

Most people derived their incomes from agriculture, either directly or indirectly, and the pattern of life tended to revolve around the farming year. The state of the harvest, therefore, was of crucial importance to the well-being of the majority of the population. It is important to note, however, that this was not a static society. The growth of manufacturing and of foreign trade had enriched the manufacturers and merchants and also, to some extent, many landowners. Towns had been expanding during the second half of the eighteenth century, particularly leading seaports such as Liverpool and Bristol, but also centres of manufacturing such as Birmingham and Manchester. But at the beginning of the nineteenth century, leadership in society and political power still rested in the hands of the landowners. The landowning classes can broadly be divided into two groups, the aristocracy and the gentry.

The aristocracy. Membership of the aristocracy was reserved for some 200 of the wealthiest families in the land. Their wealth derived from landownership; some aristocratic families owned more than 10,000 acres of land and derived incomes from their estates, mostly from the rents paid by tenant farmers, of £50,000 per annum. Wealth alone, however, did not secure a place in the top rank of society. The possession of a title indicated an aristocrat's position within the social hierarchy, ranging from dukes at the top, through marquesses and earls to viscounts and barons. Wealth and status set these families apart from the rest of society, a position that was symbolised by the splendours of their great mansions and the extent of the parks that surrounded them. Chatsworth in Derbyshire, Castle Howard in Yorkshire and Blenheim Palace in Oxfordshire, all of which could rival the royal palaces of the time, were built as symbols of the power of the aristocrats who lived in them. At county and at national level they assumed the leadership in political matters and set the standards in taste and manners.

During the eighteenth century the aristocracy consolidated their position in society. Their incomes from rents were increasing as agriculture became more profitable. The rise in agricultural prices during the **French wars**, 1793–1815, was of particular benefit to the landowners who increased their incomes from rents by some 80 per cent during this period. Many landowners also benefited from the growth of industry and the expansion of cities. Since they owned the rights to any minerals found under their land, the growing demand for coal enabled landowners such as the Duke of Bridgewater to increase their wealth by investing in coal mines and canals. Other families, such as the Portlands, the Bedfords and the Grosvenors, were fortunate to own land in west London that increased in value as the city expanded and fashionable new suburbs were built.

The gentry. The landed gentry were a much larger group than the aristocracy – about 13,000 families could claim this status in 1780 – but occupied the next rank within the social hierarchy. Their wealth and status also derived from

KEY TERM

French wars Britain was at war with France for most of the period, 1793–1815. During these wars the French Emperor Napoleon attempted to defeat Britain by imposing an economic blockade, cutting the country off from trade with the continent. As European produce could not be imported into Britain, British farmers benefited from a rise in agricultural prices.

HEINEMANN ADVANCED HISTORY

landownership but their landholdings were much smaller. Estates ranged in size from about 300 acres up to about 3000 acres and incomes varied from about £250 a year for a northern gentleman farmer to about £2000 a year for a southern baronet. Such incomes could not fund a lifestyle as lavish as that of the aristocracy but, in most cases, would be sufficient to allow a leisured way of life in which the country gentleman would be able to play his part in the affairs of the county and the nation. Many served as Justices of the Peace with the power to dispense justice and oversee the administration of **poor relief**. Most Members of Parliament for county seats were country gentlemen. At a time when MPs were not paid a salary, country gentlemen were among the few who could afford the time and the expense of parliamentary duties.

Below the landowning classes in the social hierarchy came the farmers and the labourers.

The tenant farmers. During the eighteenth century the number of small farmers who were owner-occupiers of their land declined. By 1790 only about 10–15 per cent of the land in England was owner-occupied. The majority of farmland, therefore, was leased out to tenant farmers who needed to make a profit from their farms in order to pay their rents. Farming became an increasingly commercialised activity. This had the effect of stimulating improvements in efficiency and productivity through the increased use of fertilisers and the introduction of new farming methods. The growing population led to a steadily rising demand for food and, coupled with a general rise in food prices during the French wars, greater prosperity for farmers. Once the wars were over, however, the collapse of prices and the increasing burden of the poor rates bore down heavily on the tenant farmers.

Farm labourers. At the base of the social pyramid in the countryside were the farm labourers. 'Farm servants' were traditionally hired for a specific period, usually a year, which gave them some security, particularly as the contract was renewable. Many farm servants lived on the farm and ate at the same table as their employer. In this way relations between farmers and their labourers, despite the gap in their circumstances, were relatively close. Several factors were combining, however, to undermine the position of the labourer and to generate tensions in rural society. Rapid population growth was increasing competition for employment and driving down wages. The French wars brought higher food prices. After the wars, prices dropped but this increased the pressure on farmers to reduce wages. It is estimated that agricultural wages fell by one-third between 1814 and 1822 and in the 1830s typical farm wages in the South-West were as low as 8 shillings per week. Although many labourers' families could supplement their incomes through spinning and weaving in the home, the evidence of severe distress was unmistakable. Food riots were widespread in the 1790s and early 1800s and, after 1815 when distress became more general and more serious, farm labourers turned to rick-burning, cattle-maiming and the destruction of farm buildings as their weapons of protest.

The challenges to stability

Although rioting by the 'lower orders' was a regular feature of eighteenth-century life, the most striking feature of British society at this time was its stability. Aristocratic rule went largely unchallenged and, although there were some reverberations from the French Revolution at the end of the century, Britain did not experience the social upheavals that engulfed France. Although society was stable, however, it was not static and towards the end of the eighteenth century new forces in society were beginning to emerge which put the traditional hierarchical structure under severe strain. These new forces were as follows:

- The rapid growth of population and the shift of population from the countryside to the towns.
- The rise of new industries and the gradual shift to factory-based production.
- The growth of the middle classes.
- The emergence of the working classes.
- The rise of nonconformity in religion.

HOW WAS SOCIETY CHANGING?

Population growth

The unprecedented growth in the population was the most striking change in British society from the late eighteenth century onwards. In 1780 the population of England and Wales was about 7.5 million; by 1811 it had grown to over 10 million and by 1831 to nearly 14 million. The increase in population was particularly rapid in the 1810s and 1820s when growth rates of 18 per cent and 16 per cent respectively were recorded. All regions of the country experienced an increase but not in equal amounts. The region that consistently had the highest rate of growth was the North-West, followed by London and the North-East. Rural areas in the South and South-West, however, also recorded large increases.

Rapid population growth led some contemporaries to predict disaster. Foremost among these was the Reverend Thomas Malthus who in 1798 published his *Essay on the Principle of Population*. Malthus predicted that the population growth would outstrip the increase in the food supply and famine would be the inevitable result. He argued that the poor should be encouraged to exercise 'moral restraint' by putting off marriage until they could support a family, and that society should apply pressure to encourage this by restricting access to poor relief. Although Malthus's gloomy predictions did not come true, mainly as a result of the ability of British farmers to increase agricultural productivity, his views were very influential particularly with the middle and upper classes.

Growth of towns

The other most striking social change at this time was the rapid growth of towns, particularly in the north of England and the Midlands. In 1750 only about 15 per cent of the population lived in towns; by 1800 this figure had increased to 25 per cent and by 1851 to around 50 per cent. Early in the eighteenth century, London was the only really large town in Britain; only two other English towns, Bristol and Norwich, had more than 20,000 inhabitants. By 1801, London had grown to nearly 1 million inhabitants and there were seven towns with populations

KEY STATISTICS

Population of England and Wales, 1781–1851 (in 000s)

1781	7,587
1801	8,860
1811	10,102
1821	11,923
1831	13,815
1841	15,783
1851	17,818

in excess of 50,000. In 1851, London had grown to 2.3 million, there were four towns of over 200,000 people and a further 17 towns of over 50,000.

The growth of towns, 1801–51 (in 000s)

	1801	1811	1821	1831	1841	1851
London	959	1139	1379	1685	1948	2362
Bath	33	38	47	51	53	54
Birmingham	71	83	102	144	183	233
Bradford	13	16	26	44	67	104
Bristol	61	71	85	104	124	137
Leeds	53	63	84	123	152	172
Liverpool	82	104	138	202	286	376
Manchester	75	89	126	182	235	303
Newcastle	33	33	42	54	70	88
Norwich	36	37	50	61	62	68
Sheffield	46	53	65	92	111	135

Distribution of population

Until the eighteenth century, the most heavily populated areas of the country were the rich farm lands of the south and east of England. The largest towns, apart from London, were ports such as Bristol or traditional centres of the woollen industry such as Norwich. By the early nineteenth century, the distribution of population was beginning to change. The largest concentrations of population were appearing in South Lancashire, the West Riding of Yorkshire, the West Midlands and the north-east coast of England as well as the central belt of Scotland. These were the regions that contained most of the fastest growing towns. Manchester and Birmingham were among the most striking examples of this trend. Manchester, centre of the cotton industry, grew from a population of 75,000 in 1801 to 303,000 in 1851. Birmingham, where the main industries were engineering and the metal trades, grew from 71,000 in 1801 to 233,000 in 1851.

Some of the growth in town populations was the result of natural increase but much of it was due to migration from the countryside. Many of the people who swelled the populations of Manchester and the other growing industrial towns were moving away from the poverty of the countryside and were attracted by the prospect of earning higher wages in the factories. The majority of those who migrated from the countryside, however, did not move far from their places of birth. Most of the migrants moved to growing regional towns, usually within 20 or 30 miles of their birthplace.

Consequences of changes in population. These changes had far-reaching social and political consequences. The concentrations of large numbers of people in areas that had previously been villages or small towns led to an increase in social tensions and a breakdown in traditional social relationships. A hierarchical society required the 'lower orders' to show deference to their social superiors but this could only work in communities that were small-scale and stable. The squire and the parson, traditionally the sources of authority and influence in rural communities, could not exercise that same degree of influence in large and growing urban areas. The growth of towns also placed severe strain on the traditional structures of local government. A system based on the Justices of the Peace and the parish was ill-equipped to deal with the problems of policing, poor law administration, housing and sanitation that were an ever-increasing feature of life in the industrial towns.

Industrial change

Britain was the first country to experience the series of changes that have been called the industrial revolution. The change from a society that depended mainly on agriculture for generation of wealth to one that relied mainly on manufacturing, was a complex process which took place over a long period of time. During the period roughly between 1750 and 1850 the British economy experienced a series of changes which radically altered the production process in a number of industries and which had profound consequences for society. Those changes can be summarised as follows:

- The introduction of new machinery to speed up the manufacturing process. The invention of the spinning jenny (1764), water frame (1769), and the mule (1779) revolutionised the spinning process in cotton manufacture. The introduction of the power loom in the 1820s did the same for the weaving process.

- The use of water power and, later, steam power to drive the new machines had major consequences for the location of industry. The use of water power necessitated the location of factories in upland areas near fast-flowing streams. The use of steam power brought factories to the coalfield areas since the transport of bulky goods such as coal was difficult and expensive. The major industrial areas, therefore, were all located in or near the coal-mining areas. South Lancashire became the main centre of the cotton industry whilst West Yorkshire became the home of the woollen industry. Older centres of the textile industry, particularly the West Country towns in Gloucestershire, Somerset and Wiltshire, experienced a sharp decline in their prosperity.
- The introduction of large machinery and steam power necessitated the concentration of production into factories. The first water-powered factory was established at Cromford in Derbyshire by **Richard Arkwright**, the inventor of the water frame, in 1769. Its success led to the building of other large textile factories, many employing more than 2000 workers – a scale of operation which was unprecedented at the time. Large factories, or mills, became a familiar sight in the cotton towns of Manchester, Bolton, Oldham, Preston and Stockport and the woollen towns of Bradford, Halifax and Huddersfield.

The changes described above all concerned the textile industry. There are good reasons for this since the introduction of new machinery, the use of steam power and the concentration of production into factories were largely confined to the cotton and woollen industries during the early phase of the industrial revolution. Other industries expanded production and in some cases, such as the smelting of iron and steel, there were important technical innovations, but the concentration of production into large factories did not happen until much later in the nineteenth century. In the 1820s and 1830s people employed in the metal trades in Birmingham or the cutlery trade in Sheffield worked in small, specialised workshops and continued to use traditional handcraft methods of

A scene inside a textile factory around the end of the eighteenth century.

manufacture. As late as 1851 the typical employee did not work in a factory or use machinery. The two largest categories of employment in 1851 were agricultural labourers and domestic servants, a reminder of the limits of the changes that had been brought by industrialisation.

Effects of industrial changes. Although the industrial revolution did not transform British society overnight, the changes that began in the textile industry and gradually spread to other industries had a profound, long-term effect on society. These social changes in turn had an impact on the political life of the nation.

- The growth in the economy could only be sustained by exporting to overseas markets. In the 1840s the cotton industry provided over 70 per cent by value of total British exports. The growing reliance on foreign trade made the British economy more susceptible to fluctuations in overseas markets. The successive booms and slumps of the trade cycle led to periodic bouts of high unemployment in the industrial areas, leading to distress and unrest.
- In many industrial areas there was a growing separation between the classes. The factory system involved not only a division of labour but also an increasing gulf between the owners of capital and the workers engaged

in production. Conflicts of interest between employers and workers, over issues such as wages or hours of labour, were more open and more bitterly fought than in industries which were still based on small workshops where masters worked alongside their employees. Class conflict, therefore, was a growing feature of life in the textile towns of South Lancashire and West Yorkshire. In Birmingham, on the other hand, the prevalence of small workshops allowed an atmosphere of greater class co-operation to survive.

- The industrial revolution had its gainers and its losers. Men employed as spinners in the new cotton factories were relatively well paid; the women and children who worked alongside them fared much less well. Handcraft workers had mixed fortunes. In the late eighteenth century when the cotton industry was expanding rapidly, the weaving process was still largely done on traditional handlooms. The handloom weavers, therefore, benefited from an enormous increase in demand for their services. By the end of the French wars, the power loom was beginning to be adopted in factories and the handloom weavers increasingly found themselves with insufficient work. Wages were forced down in an effort to compete with the power looms and widespread distress among the handloom weavers was the result, particularly during periods of bad trade. Similar problems were experienced by the men who knitted stockings on handframes in the East Midlands.

The gradual transition from a largely agrarian society to an industrialised and urbanised one brought major changes to the social structure. Away from the industrial areas traditional social relationships in the villages and small towns survived well into the nineteenth century. In the growing industrial towns, however, a new class structure was taking shape and with this change came new problems.

The middle classes

The industrial revolution resulted in the growth in the size, wealth and status of the middle classes. People of the 'middle rank' had always been part of the traditional social structure. Farmers needed corn dealers and wool merchants to buy their produce and sell it on. Master craftsmen

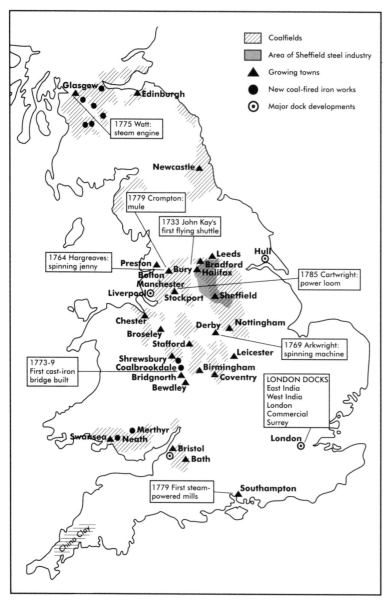

Map labels:
Coalfields
Area of Sheffield steel industry
Growing towns
New coal-fired iron works
Major dock developments

Glasgow
Edinburgh
1775 Watt: steam engine
Newcastle
1779 Crompton: mule
1733 John Kay's first flying shuttle
1764 Hargreaves: spinning jenny
Preston
Bolton
Bury
Manchester
Leeds
Bradford
Halifax
Hull
1785 Cartwright: power loom
Liverpool
Stockport
Sheffield
Chester
Broseley
Derby
Nottingham
Stafford
1769 Arkwright: spinning machine
Leicester
1773-9 First cast-iron bridge built
Shrewsbury
Coalbrookdale
Bridgnorth
Bewdley
Birmingham
Coventry
LONDON DOCKS
East India
West India
London
Commercial
Surrey
Merthyr
Swansea
Neath
Bristol
Bath
London
1779 First steam-powered mills
Southampton
China Clay

owned the small businesses that manufactured clothing, footwear, farm tools and household goods and the many other items which most people could not make for themselves. The services of professional men such as lawyers and doctors were always in demand, particularly from the landowners. During the eighteenth century the expansion of foreign trade provided unprecedented opportunities for merchants to earn higher profits from overseas ventures. Successful businessmen could use their wealth to purchase country estates, send their sons to the best schools and make marriage alliances with landowning families so that, over a period of time, the family could enter the ranks of the lesser gentry. Such a course of action was followed by many of the most successful entrepreneurs of the industrial revolution. Richard Arkwright, **Sir Robert Peel**, **Matthew Boulton**, **John Fielden**, **Samuel Whitbread** and **Abraham Darby** were among the many who followed this path.

Diversity. By the early nineteenth century the middle classes had become much more numerous. Using the 1816 income tax returns as a guide, Gash (1979) has estimated that there were over 160,000 persons belonging to the middle classes at that time; the 1831 census gave a figure of 214,000 persons belonging to the group described as 'capitalists, bankers, professional and other educated men'. Generalisations about their wealth, status and attitudes are very difficult to sustain since one of the most striking characteristics of the middle classes was their great diversity. An income of £50 a year was considered sufficient to support a middle-class lifestyle with careful economy; an income of £100–£200 a year was enough for a comfortable lifestyle, which would include the keeping of at least one servant. A minority, perhaps fewer than 5000, had incomes in excess of £1000 a year, a level of wealth that would place them on a par with the lesser gentry. Among the middle classes were people who had risen up from the lower classes and those who had moved down from the gentry. There were wide variations in education, occupation, religion and political outlook. It is not surprising, therefore, that the middle classes were not united in their aspirations or capable of acting together as a class.

Middle-class attitudes. Although generalisations about the middle classes are fraught with difficulty, it is possible to identify a number of characteristics of an emerging middle-class culture:

- Ownership of property was the basis of their security and their feeling of self-worth. Perceived threats to their property from a breakdown of political and social stability were viewed with as much alarm by the middle classes as they were by the landowners.

- Many businessmen had achieved their success through hard work, thrift, drive and ambition. The virtues of self-reliance were at the heart of middle-class culture.
- Middle-class people tended to look to government for a relaxation of the rules and regulations that they believed were obstacles in the way of business success. Many manufacturers wanted trade to be free from customs duties on imports and exports and for the government to take a **laissez-faire** approach to the regulation of business and commerce.
- As in their businesses, so in their attitude to government: they valued efficient administration and value for money. Taxes should be kept as low as possible and wasteful expenditure should be avoided.
- There was growing criticism of the existing system of government in which positions in the civil service were filled by patronage, allowing aristocratic ministers to use appointments to reward their supporters or favour their relatives – a system that led to inefficiency and incompetence in government.
- Views such as these were given a wider audience through the growth of local daily newspapers that catered mainly for a middle-class readership. Notable examples of these newspapers were the *Manchester Guardian* and the *Leeds Mercury*. The circulations of these newspapers ranged between 2000 and 5000 an issue, until the advent of the railways in the 1830s and 1840s enabled local newspapers to reach a wider regional and national readership.

KEY TERM

Laissez-faire is a term used to describe a policy of allowing people to make their own decisions about their social and economic activities, free from government interference or regulation.

The working classes

Like the middle classes, the working classes exhibited such wide variations in income, experiences, occupations and outlook that generalisations about them are fraught with difficulty. Contemporary observers tended to talk of the 'working classes' or the 'labouring classes' in recognition of the extraordinary diversity across this broad spectrum of society. Membership of the 'labouring classes' was based on involvement in manual labour and the earning of wages, rather than on income levels alone. A skilled craftsman could earn as much as £2 per week in the 1820s, giving him an income which was comparable to many middle-class incomes, but the fact that he earned his wages from manual labour rather than a salary from clerical or managerial work placed him in the labouring classes.

Within the working classes there were wide variations in income. Skilled craftsmen belonged to the so-called **aristocracy of labour.** Having served long apprenticeships to achieve the status of a craftsman (or artisan) they could exploit the shortage of qualified men within their trades to command higher wages than the labourers. An income of 30 shillings per week in the 1830s placed a man in the 'aristocracy of labour'. Coal miners and cotton spinners earned on average about 24 shillings per week. Most adult male workers in unskilled labouring jobs were paid less than £1 per week, but even they were better paid than women workers and children who were employed extensively in the textile factories and other trades. In terms of income and status, therefore, there was a wide gulf between the artisans and the unskilled, a factor that was a major obstacle to any prospect of common action by the working classes.

Occupations. There was also an enormous diversity of occupations. The experience of working in a cotton factory with its long hours and rigid discipline was very different from the experience of the more traditional handcraft trades such as handloom weaving or the knitting of stockings on a handframe, which was usually based in the worker's own home. Coal mining was an extremely dangerous and dirty occupation and miners tended, partly because mines were located in remote rural districts, to be set apart from workers in other industries. Birmingham contained a large number of small workshops engaged in various branches of the metal-working trades. London was home to traditional craftsmen, many possessing old craft skills that were still in demand in the luxury trades. This diversity was another factor that made class-wide action by working people unlikely.

Standard of living. There has been a continuing debate between economic and social historians for more than 40 years over whether the industrial revolution, in its early stages, led to an improvement or a decline in the standard of living of the working classes. The details of this debate

The aristocracy of labour
This term has been used by historians and sociologists to describe the skilled artisans who commanded the highest wages and enjoyed a higher status than the majority of working people. Workers in the luxury trades, such as coachbuilding, bookbinding or clockmaking, could normally expect to earn wages of over 30 shillings per week and sometimes as high as £2 per week. Printers, carpenters, bricklayers, wheelwrights, shipwrights and tailors could earn 30 shillings per week during periods of good trade.

are beyond the scope of this book but students interested in the reform movements of this period need to be aware of it. The statistical evidence on wage rates and price movements shows a long-term improvement in the real wages of the majority of working-class people during the early nineteenth century. Within this overall picture of an improving standard of living, however, there were significant exceptions. Many working people suffered severe distress from a variety of causes. Long hours of work were common to both factory and workshop-based industries. Periodic trade depressions resulted in high unemployment or short-time working. The introduction of new machinery could make old craft skills redundant. Bad harvests led to increases in bread prices. All of these factors added to the insecurity of working-class lives.

Collective action. That there was discontent and a desire for change among different groups at different times is clear from the evidence available. The growth of trade unions towards the end of the eighteenth century, the outbreaks of machine-breaking by the **Luddites** in the years 1811–13, and the growing involvement of working people in political protests, all point to an underlying discontent and a determination to act collectively. Different forms of protest, however, suited different groups. Craftsmen within a particular trade and a particular district could see some benefit from organising collectively into a trade union; cotton spinners in the large factories were also among the earliest groups to form trade unions. This form of collective action, however, was not relevant to handloom weavers who, as domestic outworkers, were widely scattered through the rural areas. Political action, to secure legal protection for their trade, had more relevance for weavers and other craftsmen whose skills were becoming redundant. The Luddite disturbances, on the other hand, were a more direct form of action, intended to prevent the introduction of the new machinery which was the immediate cause of their troubles.

The growth of the labouring classes, who by the 1830s made up about four-fifths of the population, fundamentally altered the traditional social structure. The traditional sources of influence and authority, the Church

Luddites were groups of working people who attacked the new machines which, they believed, were putting them out of work. Their name was taken from the mythical leader of the movement, Ned Ludd. Luddite machine-breaking was particularly prevalent in the textile districts of South Lancashire and the hosiery trade of the East Midlands.

of England and the local landowners, had little influence in the growing industrial towns. In some industrial areas, such as Birmingham, co-operation between the middle classes and the labouring classes was possible because masters and employees still worked side by side in small workshops. In the factory districts, however, the growing separation between masters and workmen led working people to begin to act independently. Either way, the working classes were beginning to make their presence felt on the political system in the early nineteenth century.

The growth of nonconformity in religion

The end of the eighteenth century and the beginning of the nineteenth saw a remarkable increase in the membership and influence of nonconformist religious groups. Nonconformity (dissent from the established church) in religion had been tolerated in Britain since 1689. There were long-established congregations of Baptists, Congregationalists, Quakers and Presbyterians, which had grown up alongside the established church but differed from it in their form of worship and services. Members of these 'Old Dissenting' groups came mainly from the middle classes and were concentrated in London and the South of England, particularly in the small towns and larger villages.

The remarkable growth of nonconformity at the end of the eighteenth century, however, was sparked off by the emergence of a new group, the Wesleyan Methodists. Beginning as a movement within the Church of England, the Methodists had by 1795 developed into an independent sect with their own organisation and chapels. Between 1780 and 1815 the membership of **Methodism** increased fourfold and by 1820 had reached 200,000. The growth of Methodism stimulated the older dissenting groups and both the Congregationalists and the Baptists also grew considerably in this period. In 1811, a survey carried out by the Church of England revealed that in the larger parishes the number of dissenting chapels outnumbered the Anglican places of worship by a ratio of seven to five.

KEY TERMS

Old Dissenters The Baptists, Congregationalists and Presbyterians were all religious sects that grew out of Puritanism in the 17th century. They were different from the Church of England in many ways, but in particular because their churches were self-governing rather than being part of a hierarchical organisation controlled by bishops and archbishops.

Methodism grew out of the Church of England in the 18th century. The emphasis in Methodism was on preaching and hearing the word of God; services were often held out of doors, and were conducted in a revivalist spirit, very different from the rather staid and restrained atmosphere in an Anglican Church service. The name came from the highly structured devotional life that Wesley and his followers adopted.

Methodism. Methodism was particularly successful in attracting converts from the working classes. Through the missionary work of **John Wesley** himself, **George Whitefield** and hundreds of Methodist itinerant preachers, the movement flourished in the north of England's industrial areas, Staffordshire and the North Midlands, and among the tin miners of Cornwall. By 1830, almost two-thirds of the membership were from the skilled working classes. An offshoot of the Wesleyans, known as the Primitive Methodists, attracted people from lower down the social scale.

Impact of Methodism. Nonconformity had always been viewed as a threat to the authority of the established church but the growth of Methodism caused particular alarm. Itinerant preachers 'invaded' the parishes of Anglican clergy, implicitly challenging the traditional authority of the parson within his own community. The fact that many preachers were lay members of the church was another affront to the hierarchy of the church, as were the setting up of class meetings which allowed adherents to engage in discussion about the gospels. Although Wesley himself was a Tory, and historians like E. P. Thompson have argued that the influence of Methodism was a very conservative one, there were close links between the rise of nonconformity and the development of political radicalism. Both involved criticism of the existing system in which there were strong links between church and state; both encouraged people from the lower classes to act and think independently. Methodist lay preachers gained experience in organisation and in public speaking, skills that could be transferred to a political context. Methodist organisation, with its mass meetings, weekly classes, penny-a-week contributions and a central conference, was copied by radical political organisations like the Hampden Clubs.

John Wesley (1703–91) was the son of an Anglican clergyman. He was educated at Oxford and whilst a student founded a 'Methodist Society' devoted to forms of worship which followed a systematic method. In 1738 he underwent a personal religious conversion which led him to preach a brand of religion based on a strong sense of sin and a need for complete faith in Jesus. The appeal to the emotions of his congregations led to him being banned from many churches and he was forced to preach at large open-air gatherings. Wesley himself remained a member of the Church of England, but by the time of his death Methodism was beginning to separate from the established church.

George Whitefield (1714–1770) was one of the leading Methodist travelling preachers who was particularly associated with the 'revivalist enthusiasm' of Methodism. (Revivalism involved the public confessions of sins often with much emotion – crying, groaning and tears of repentance.)

HEINEMANN ADVANCED HISTORY

SUMMARY QUESTIONS

1 Summarise the hierarchical structure of traditional rural society. Explain the connections between the different social groups in terms of their economic relationships and of their social obligations.

2 Why was membership of a common church considered to be so important to maintaining the stability of this society?

3 Summarise the main changes in society brought about by the industrial revolution.

4 Which groups gained and which groups suffered as a result of industrialisation?

5 How did the rise of nonconformity in religion affect society?

CHAPTER 2

How was Britain governed?

BRITAIN IN 1815

In June 1815 the Duke of Wellington led the British army to victory over Napoleon Bonaparte's French army at Waterloo. This brought to an end a war that had lasted, save for one short period of peace, for 22 years. The government of the day, led by the Prime Minister Lord Liverpool, could feel some satisfaction in having steered the country to victory and having preserved a stable political system. But in the years immediately following Waterloo, that political system came under severe strain as economic discontent fuelled demands for reform. Between 1815 and 1820 **radical** demands for reform of the political system gained popular support and led to outbreaks of disorder at Spa Fields in London in 1816, in Derbyshire and Nottinghamshire in 1817 and at St Peter's Fields in Manchester in 1819. The determination of the government and local authorities to resist the demands for reform and to deal firmly with the protesters, was demonstrated by the actions of the magistrates who were in attendance at St Peter's Fields. Faced with a crowd of, by their own estimate, 60,000 orderly demonstrators who had gathered to listen to political speeches by the leading radical orators of the day, they panicked and sent in a unit of local militia to arrest the main speaker, Henry Hunt. In the confusion that followed 11 people were killed and over 400 wounded. The event became known, in an ironic comment on the prowess of the British army, as the massacre of 'Peterloo'.

Demands for reform of the political system had been voiced before, towards the end of the eighteenth century, and would be raised again in the years following Peterloo. In order to understand why demands for reform became such a feature of these years we must first examine the workings of the political system.

The political system

Contemporary supporters of the British political system praised the 'balance' of the constitution. Power was shared between the monarch and Parliament, made up of the House of Lords and House of Commons, under an arrangement which had been laid down in 1688. Since then the system had evolved – for example, the power of the monarch had gradually declined during the eighteenth century – but there had been no fundamental changes in the constitution by legislation. This 'balanced constitution' had the following features:

- The **monarch** held sovereign power. The monarch was not involved in the day-to-day business of governing the country but the government was conducted in his or her name. He or she was responsible for appointing and dismissing ministers and for summoning Parliaments to meet. Ministers who lost the monarch's confidence could expect to be dismissed. The monarch could also influence the results of elections for the House of Commons through 'influence' – many voters would normally support candidates who expressed loyalty to the monarch's ministers – and through 'patronage'. No government that had the support of the ruling monarch ever lost an election in the eighteenth century or early nineteenth century.
- The **House of Commons** had, by the beginning of the nineteenth century, become the most important element in the political system. Elections were held every seven years or on the death of a monarch. The most significant power in the hands of the Commons was its control over the government's finances since all taxation had to be approved annually. Ministers, although appointed by the Crown, had to have the support of a majority of MPs. Those who lost the confidence of the Commons through pursuing unpopular policies or through their own incompetence could not be kept in office by the Crown. All legislation had to pass through the House of Commons and be approved by MPs.
- The **House of Lords** still retained considerable power and influence within the constitution. Composed entirely of hereditary peers and the senior bishops and archbishops in the Church of England, the House of

Lords had the power to amend or reject (veto) legislation passed by the House of Commons. Aristocrats dominated the governments of the time – nine out of 13 ministers in Lord Liverpool's government were members of the House of Lords – and through their own use of patronage they were able to exert some influence over the House of Commons as well.

Checks and balances. This was a political system in which there were inbuilt checks and balances. Government was carried on in the monarch's name and the monarch had the right to choose ministers and influence the policies they adopted. But Parliament had control over taxation and thus could control the means of carrying out those policies. The monarch's ministers, therefore, had to have the support of Parliament, and particularly of the House of Commons which had exclusive powers over taxation. The House of Commons had thus become more important than the House of Lords; but the Lords' power of veto over legislation passed in the Commons was a significant check on the power of the elected House.

It is important to note that this was a system of government that was praised by many contemporaries as being enlightened and balanced and conducive to efficient administration. The role of government at the beginning of the nineteenth century was very much more limited than today. Governments concentrated on maintaining law and order, collecting taxes, conducting foreign policy and defending the country. It was not the function of government to educate the people, relieve their poverty or promote their health. Economic policy was limited to the regulation of trade between Britain and other countries. For most ordinary people the only contact with central government was the payment of taxes; local government made more impact on their lives. The primary unit of local government was the parish, which was responsible for the relief of the poor, the maintenance of the roads and the appointment of constables. Central government was remote from the lives and experience of most people and, in the early nineteenth century, few were prepared to argue that the role of government should be enlarged.

KEY QUOTE

From Lord Braxfield in 1793: 'Two things must be attended to which require no proof. First, that the British constitution is the best that ever was since the creation of the world; and, it is not possible to make it better.'

Demands for reform of the system were, however, increasingly being voiced in the years after Waterloo. The main focus of the reformers' criticism was the way in which the House of Commons was elected. This was attacked as being corrupt, outdated and biased in favour of the aristocracy and the Crown, resulting in a House of Commons which was unrepresentative of the nation as a whole. Reformers also argued that the influence of the Crown over elections to the House of Commons had distorted the balance of the constitution. As society was changing, so radicals demanded that Parliament had to be reformed in order to reflect those changes.

The electoral system

The distribution of seats. The way in which the House of Commons was elected had evolved over many centuries. MPs represented constituencies which had been viable communities in the Middle Ages but which did not necessarily reflect the social changes that had been set in motion by the industrial revolution. There were 658 Members of Parliament in 1815; 122 of them represented county seats and the rest represented **parliamentary boroughs**. This distribution of seats had been created centuries earlier when the bulk of the population lived in rural areas and when the south and east of the country were the most heavily populated areas. The industrial revolution, however, led to the growth of large towns in the Midlands and north of England, and a gradual shift in the distribution of the population. Large and growing industrial cities such as Manchester, Birmingham, Leeds and Sheffield had no representation in Parliament other than the MPs who represented the counties in which they were situated. Small and declining boroughs in the south of England, on the other hand, were still able to send two MPs each to Parliament on the strength of royal charters granted to them in the Middle Ages. There were also the **University seats**. The most glaring anomalies in the system, which were frequently quoted to illustrate its inequalities, were the boroughs of Old Sarum in Wiltshire, Gatton in Surrey and Dunwich in Suffolk. All had declined in population to such an extent that Old Sarum had a mere seven voters, Gatton only six, whilst Dunwich,

KEY TERMS

Parliamentary borough
These were towns which had been invited to send two representatives to the parliaments called by medieval monarchs. As the calling of parliaments became a more regular occurrence, the towns that were invited to send representatives became established as 'parliamentary boroughs'. There had been virtually no change in the distribution of seats to the boroughs since the 17th century.

University seats The Universities of Oxford and Cambridge were also represented in Parliament by 2 members each. The franchise in university elections was restricted to graduates of the universities.

a once thriving port on the east coast, was mainly submerged under the sea. By 1830 only 43 of the 202 parliamentary boroughs in England had a population of over 1000, whereas Manchester with a population of 144,000 and Birmingham with 182,000 were allowed no representation in their own right.

The basic imbalance between population distribution and the distribution of parliamentary seats was already evident by the middle of the eighteenth century; it became more marked as social and economic change accelerated in the early decades of the nineteenth century. The south of England was heavily over-represented. The ten counties

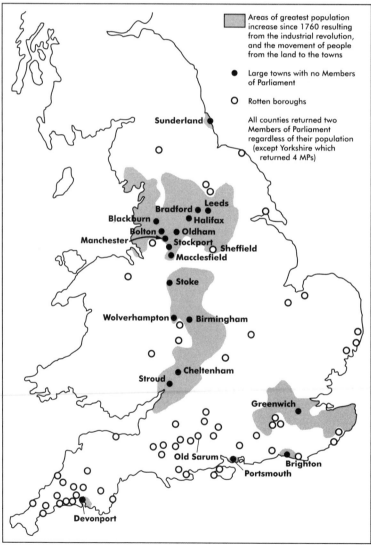

Parliamentary representation before the Great Reform Act 1832.

south of a line between Bristol and London elected about 40 per cent of all MPs. Cornwall, with a population of 300,000 in 1831, sent 42 MPs to Parliament whereas Lancashire, which was at the leading edge of the industrial revolution and had a population of 1,300,000, returned only 14. Thus, one of the main criticisms of the electoral system was that it produced a House of Commons whose members were increasingly remote from the realities of life in large parts of the country.

The electorate. Because there was no requirement for voters to be registered before 1832, historians cannot give accurate figures for the size of the electorate, but there is no dispute about the fact that only a minority of the adult population qualified for the right to vote. Recent estimates give a figure for 1831 of about half a million people who could vote out of a total population in the United Kingdom of 24 million. This figure represented about 3 per cent of the adult male population.

The franchise qualification varied according to the type of constituency. In the counties the right to vote was conferred on men who owned freehold land or property worth at least 40 shillings a year. This limited the electorate in county seats to landowners or others who earned relatively substantial incomes. In the boroughs the situation was more varied and more complex. There were five main types of franchise qualifications in parliamentary boroughs:

- In **burgage boroughs** the right to vote was held by the owners of certain plots of land (burgages). There were 37 such boroughs, including Old Sarum. In such boroughs all of the burgages could be bought up by one man who would then have the right to nominate the two MPs.
- In **corporation boroughs** the franchise was restricted to the mayor and members of the town corporation, a group who were chosen by nomination rather than election. Bodmin, Bath and Bury St Edmunds came into this category.
- In **freeman boroughs** the right to vote was conferred on those who had been granted the freedom of the

borough. This honour could be obtained by inheritance, marriage, nomination or purchase. In some boroughs this could result in a relatively large electorate but it was a system which was open to abuse. As freeman status could be granted by the town corporation, it was possible for the party which controlled that body to confer the freedom of the borough onto its own supporters, even when they did not reside in the town, in order to fix the result of parliamentary elections. In Carlisle, the Earl of Lonsdale secured freeman status for 14,000 coal miners employed by him so that they could vote for his candidates in the election.

- In **potwalloper boroughs** the franchise was open to all male householders who had a fireplace on which they could boil a pot. This often resulted in larger electorates and relatively open elections.
- In **scot and lot boroughs** the vote could be exercised by all male householders who paid local rates and who did not receive poor relief. Northampton and Stockbridge were in this category. Like the potwalloper franchise, scot and lot also produced larger electorates and relatively open elections.

With such a wide range of voting qualifications it is difficult to generalise about the composition of the electorate. In many constituencies the right to vote was restricted to the wealthier and more privileged groups but in other constituencies, such as Westminster, Coventry and Preston, the franchise was relatively democratic and produced an electorate that was broader in its social composition than those who were allowed to vote after 1832. In such constituencies, voters exercised a greater degree of freedom of choice at election times and the representation of these boroughs in Parliament was less likely to fall under the control of a single powerful individual.

Elections. There was no secret ballot in parliamentary elections; voters had to declare their choice of candidate on the 'hustings' in full view of the crowds who attended these spectacles. Polling was also spread over a period of 15 days. In these circumstances electioneering could become more akin to a carnival than a serious political contest. Rival

An engraving by the eighteenth-century artist Hogarth, showing the corruption during an election campaign.

bands of supporters would parade through the streets with banners, hurl abuse and missiles at each other and indulge in violent brawls. Many voters were open to bribery; occasionally votes were bought and sold openly but there were also other inducements that could be used to secure votes. These included the supply of copious quantities of beer – a practice known as 'treating' – and the offers of jobs or contracts. Where bribery was unsuccessful, intimidation was an alternative practice. Cooping, which involved the kidnapping and forcible imprisonment of a rival candidate's supporters for the duration of the election, was one such practice.

Expense of elections. Elections under such circumstances were expensive affairs. The Yorkshire county election of 1807 is estimated to have cost the three candidates involved a combined total of nearly £125,000, and the election in Liverpool in 1830 cost over £100,000. Although the amount of bribery and corruption in elections at this time was exaggerated by reformers it was by no means unusual, and candidates could expect to have to find at least £20,000 to finance their campaigns. It is not surprising therefore that election contests were frequently avoided; in the elections held between 1815 and 1832 about two-thirds of the Members of Parliament were returned unopposed.

Uncontested elections were particularly common in the county seats. In the countryside, the great landowning families still held sway and the representation for the county in Parliament was usually settled by compromise between the leading families in the county. Only nine counties were contested in 1807 and two in 1812. The county elections in Northamptonshire were contested only four times in the 35 elections between 1708 and 1832. The influence of the leading landowning families in the counties was so strong that voters would not normally challenge their wishes. Tenant farmers, tradesmen, solicitors and doctors all depended on the goodwill of the landowners for a large part of their livelihoods and could be expected to show due deference.

Aristocratic patronage. Many boroughs also came under the direct influence of aristocratic landowners. In general, the smaller the number of voters in a constituency, the more likely it was to be under the direct influence of an aristocratic patron. Burgage boroughs were particularly likely to fall into this category but it was also possible for boroughs with a scot and lot franchise or even a freeman franchise to have their representation controlled in this way. As with county seats, influence and deference were powerful tools in the hands of the landowners. Where the majority of tradesmen depended on an aristocratic patron for a large part of their business or a large number of people were directly employed by him, they could be expected to cast their votes obediently for the patron's nominee. These boroughs, which were known as 'nomination' or 'pocket' boroughs, were very numerous. In 1827 the writer J. W. Croker estimated that 276 borough seats were filled by nomination. Not all of these, however, were controlled by aristocratic families as the government was able to control the representation of about 30 seats. These included royal dockyard towns such as Chatham and Portsmouth where the majority of voters would be employees of the Crown, but there were also boroughs where Treasury money was used to bribe voters. As Gash (1979) has pointed out, however, the ability of governments to influence elections and control Members of Parliament declined from the 1780s because of the impact of spending restrictions.

Members of Parliament

Most MPs were wealthy men and the system was designed to ensure that this remained the case. Members of Parliament were paid no salary and would therefore need other forms of income to support their political duties. There were also high property qualifications for MPs – an income of £300 a year from land for borough members and £600 for county members – which excluded people from the lower classes from membership of the House of Commons. In light of the way in which MPs were elected, and the restrictions on entry to the House of Commons, it is not surprising that a large number of members were from aristocratic families. Between 1780 and 1830 about one-fifth of MPs were the sons of peers. Through family connections and patronage, leading aristocratic families such as the Cecils, the Dukes of Newcastle and Devonshire, and Earl Fitzwilliam were able to exercise influence beyond their own preserve in the House of Lords.

Independent members. Not all MPs, however, were in the pockets of aristocratic patrons or of the government. Through the late eighteenth century and into the early years of the nineteenth about 200 MPs were country gentlemen who, being landowners in their own right, were independent of both aristocratic patrons and government alike. These members tended to distrust the professional politicians. They would normally, out of patriotism and respect for the Crown, support the king's ministers in parliamentary votes, but their allegiance could not be taken for granted. Ministers who proved themselves to be incompetent could expect to lose the support of the independent MPs.

Virtual representation. Despite its corruption and bias in favour of the landowning classes, the electoral system did not prevent men from other backgrounds from becoming MPs. Supporters of the system argued that it allowed other 'interests' to be represented in Parliament. 'Interest' in this context meant the ownership of property, and in the eighteenth century the prevailing assumption was that only those who held a stake in the country through the ownership of some form of property had a right to be represented. As long as Members of Parliament included men from backgrounds in the armed services, the law, industry, trade, shipping, banking, brewing and the colonies it could be argued that every major interest was represented. Those interests that were not directly represented – such as perhaps the shopkeepers and tenant farmers – were 'virtually' represented by the borough or county members who could speak on their behalf. The dominance of the landowners in Parliament could also be justified by virtue of the fact that agriculture was considered to be the most important interest in the nation and that landowners were the natural leaders of society.

Parties

Party labels – **Whig and Tory** – were part of the common currency of politics in the early nineteenth century, but political parties in the modern sense did not exist. Modern parties are organised on a national basis for the promotion of particular policies, and elections are a struggle for power between the major parties. The legacy of the eighteenth century, when Whig 'factions' engaged in a self-interested competition for power whilst the Tories were marginalised by their stubborn determination to support the discredited Stuart line of succession to the throne, had devalued the concept of party politics in the eyes of the more independent-minded MPs and voters. By the beginning of the nineteenth century, however, the idea of a two-party system began to take on a new shape. The king's ministers, supported by the independent backbench MPs, came to accept the label Tory as a badge of honour rather than a term of abuse. The Whigs, in perpetual opposition between 1808 and 1830, expressed pride in their name and its association with a tradition of opposition to the Crown stretching back to 1688.

By the 1820s it was possible to discern some clear lines of demarcation between the two parties on a range of issues:

- The Tories were the traditional defenders of the rights of the monarch and of the position of the Church of England. They were sometimes referred to as

Whig and Tory The party labels originated as terms of abuse during the political and religious controversies of the 1680s. The term 'Tory', an Irish word for bandit, was applied to the supporters of the Catholic king James II. The term 'Whig', a Scottish word meaning horse-thief, was applied to those who removed James II from the throne in 1688 and invited his son-in-law, the Protestant Prince William of Orange, to become king.

'Church and King' Tories. They resisted any further reduction in the powers of the Crown and any concessions to nonconformists or Roman Catholics.

- The Tories regarded themselves as staunch defenders of law and order. In the face of protests and demonstrations in the years 1815-20 the Tories supported the government's repressive approach.
- The Tories believed that reform of Parliament would be a dangerous precedent that could open the way to ever-increasing demands for radical change. They believed that the landowners were the class who were best fitted to rule the country and that democracy would be tantamount to mob rule. The violent excesses of the French Revolution were, for them, a warning of what could happen when a governing class lost its nerve and conceded the case for changes in the political system. Popular movements for reform were regarded as the work of dangerous agitators who wished to subvert the political system.
- The Whigs believed in reducing the powers of the monarch and asserting the primacy of the House of Commons within the constitutional framework.
- The Whigs supported the demands of the nonconformists and Catholics for greater religious and civil equality and the removal of discrimination against them.
- The Whigs believed they were more in touch with public opinion. They were less alarmed than the Tories by agitation for reform and less inclined to support repressive measures against reform movements.
- The Whigs took up the cause of reform of Parliament. This was not because they were any less determined to preserve the position of the landowning classes than the Tories, nor because they were any less concerned about the possibility of a revolution occurring in Britain. The Whigs differed from the Tories on this issue for tactical reasons. They believed that the best way to preserve the position of the landowning classes was to make concessions to other interests, particularly middle-class property owners, by giving them a greater share of representation in Parliament. In that way Parliament would genuinely represent all of the main interests in

society while the property-less lower classes would still be excluded from participation in politics.

SUMMARY QUESTIONS

1 What was meant by the term 'a balanced constitution'?

2 By what means could the aristocracy and the Crown influence elections for the House of Commons?

3 How representative of British society was the House of Commons in the early nineteenth century?

4 What were the similarities and the differences between the Tory and Whig parties?

CHAPTER 3

Why did pressure for parliamentary reform increase after 1815?

INTRODUCTION

In the years between the end of the war against France in 1815 and the accession of the new king, George IV, in 1820, Britain experienced an upsurge of radical agitation in support of demands for parliamentary reform on an unprecedented scale. Radical clubs and societies sprang up in London and many provincial cities. Radical newspapers, which challenged the laws against seditious and blasphemous libel, were widely read. Such newspapers defied the imposition of a stamp duty that was designed to make newspapers too expensive for the lower classes to buy. Large public meetings and demonstrations were held and petitions sent to Parliament with large numbers of signatures. In this phase of the movement for reform of Parliament, five events in particular stand out:

- In December 1816 a reform meeting held at **Spa Fields** in London ended in violence when part of the crowd looted shops and used firearms.
- In March 1817 a group of handloom weavers from the Manchester area attempted to march to London to present a petition to Parliament. This **March of the Blanketeers** (so-called because each man was to carry a blanket) was broken up by troops on the orders of magistrates, and several men were arrested.
- In June 1817 in Derbyshire some 300 unemployed framework knitters marched on Nottingham Castle as part of what they believed was a general uprising against the government. This **Pentridge Rising**, led by **Jeremiah Brandreth**, was also broken up by the authorities and many arrests were made. Four men, including Brandreth, were executed for their part in this conspiracy.

KEY PERSON

Jeremiah Brandreth (d.1817) was known as the 'Nottingham Captain' for his role in the Pentridge Rising. A stockinger by trade, he may have been involved in the earlier Luddite disturbances. Brandreth was executed for his part in the rising.

- In August 1819 at St Peter's Fields in Manchester, a large crowd of over 60,000 people gathered to listen to the leading radical orator, **Henry Hunt**, speak on the need for reform. The crowd was orderly and peaceful but nevertheless the magistrates feared a threat to law and order. They ordered the local militia at the meeting to arrest Hunt and disperse the crowd. In the ensuing confusion and mêlée the cavalry used their sabres against the crowd and 11 people were killed, with another 400 injured. In an ironic reference to the Battle of Waterloo this event became known as the **massacre of Peterloo**.
- In 1820 a small band of men, led by **Arthur Thistlewood**, plotted to kill the entire cabinet, seize the Bank of England and establish a revolutionary provisional government. After being betrayed by an informer among their number they were arrested in Cato Street. This **Cato Street Conspiracy** resulted in the execution of Thistlewood and four other conspirators and the transportation of another five.

These events disturbed the government but did not threaten its position or the stability of the political system. Lord Liverpool's Tory government held the line against the calls for reform and there were few in Parliament who were prepared to give support or encouragement to the radicals outside. The Whigs were ambivalent in their attitude to reform, with only a minority among the parliamentary Whigs prepared at this time to openly voice support for parliamentary reform. The majority of the middle classes were unwilling to give the radical movement their backing because of its association with violence and threats to property. Nevertheless, the post-war radical agitation was a significant stage in the development of the parliamentary reform movement that led to the passing of the First Reform Act in 1832. Thompson (1968) has argued that the events of 1819 were a dress rehearsal for 1832. It is therefore useful to look more closely at the post-war radical movement, and at its origins, in order to help us make sense of the agitation for reform that reached its height in 1831–2.

Henry Hunt (1773–1835)
A gentleman-farmer from Wiltshire, 'Orator' Hunt had built a reputation as a skilful speaker and had previously spoken at the Spa Fields meeting in London in 1816. His quarrelsome nature led to frequent disputes with other radical leaders.

Arthur Thistlewood (1770–1820) A leading member of the Spencean Society (see p. 53), who believed in an armed seizure of power and the establishment of a republic. Thistlewood was a former army officer and a gentleman-farmer who may have fought with the French revolutionary army in the 1790s.

WHAT WERE THE ORIGINS OF THE REFORM MOVEMENT?

Sporadic outbreaks of rioting were a feature of life in eighteenth-century Britain. Food riots occurred during periods of shortages and high prices. In 1727, for example, the miners of Kingswood boarded ships in Bristol docks to prevent the export of grain at a time when bread prices were high. Attacks on turnpike gates and toll-houses which had been built to collect tolls from road users were another example of direct action. In the Bristol area it was the coal miners of Kingswood who were again to the fore in this kind of protest. In the countryside, farm labourers also rioted at times of severe hardship and this tradition continued into the early nineteenth century. The years 1816–17 saw outbreaks of rick-burning, cattle maiming and the burning of farm buildings in East Anglia, as labourers vented their anger against farmers who were regarded as profiting at their expense. Such outbreaks were often difficult to control and severely tested the forces at the authorities' disposal; but at no time did food riots or acts of arson in rural areas threaten the stability of the political system. The rioters acted from economic motives – food rioters, for example, wished to preserve a controlled market in grain which gave them some protection from price rises – and their targets were merchants, farmers or members of **Turnpike Trusts** rather than the political system. Popular action in support of political demands and directed against the government or the political system was unknown before the late eighteenth century.

Demands for parliamentary reform had been made by various groups since the late 1760s. In the late eighteenth and early nineteenth centuries, various groups had begun to challenge the existing political system and to demand changes in the way Parliament was elected. The details of these early attempts at reform can best be summarised in the form of a table.

Early attempts at reform

Date	Event	Details and significance
1760s and 1770s	**John Wilkes** led an agitation against the abuse of royal power	Wilkes published a newspaper, *The North Briton*, in which he made attacks on George III. He was found guilty of publishing 'libels' and prevented from taking the seat in Parliament that he had won in the Middlesex constituency in 1768. Wilkes presented his personal struggle with the government as part of a wider battle against the abuse of royal power and he successfully enlisted the support of London artisans and small shopkeepers to stage street protests. The late 1760s were a time of growing economic distress and the Wilkite agitation was able to combine a revolt against economic hardship with political agitation for parliamentary reform. Although Wilkes himself withdrew from the agitation after 1774 to pursue his own career, he had helped to create a new radical tradition in which the economic discontent of working people was linked to dissatisfaction with the political system.
1780s	The Whigs in Parliament took up the cause of parliamentary reform	In 1783 a coalition government led by Lord North and **Charles James Fox** was dismissed by George III, despite having majority support in the House of Commons. For the Whigs this struck at the heart of the balanced constitution since royal power had been used to override a parliamentary majority. Fox therefore took up the cause of parliamentary reform as an essential step towards creating a more 'independent' House of Commons and thus restoring the balance of the constitution. The Whigs' proposals, however, were limited to the redistribution of some seats and a modest extension of the franchise. As an aristocratic parliamentary group, the Whigs made no attempt to link with reform groups outside Parliament.

John Wilkes (1727–97)
The son of a distiller, Wilkes led a dissolute life and incurred gambling debts. His entry into Parliament in 1757 was probably motivated by his desire to escape the debtors' prison, since MPs enjoyed immunity from prosecution. Wilkes's 'libels' against the king and his ministers were published in his newspaper, *The North Briton*.

Charles James Fox (1749–1806) was a brilliant but flawed politician. He ran up huge gambling debts and often attended parliamentary debates whilst drunk, but he was a skilled debater and strong supporter of reform. He believed that the role of the Whigs was to defend liberties and promote necessary reforms, but his concept of liberty was limited to restricting the power of the Crown. His supporters were the most aristocratic group in Parliament and he had no sympathy for popular radicalism.

KEY TERM

Democratic system
Demands to make the parliamentary system more democratic had first been put forward by Major Cartwright (see p. 46) in 1776. His list of six demands became the focus for radical political programmes in Britain until the 1850s:

universal suffrage, i.e. one man, one vote;

annual parliaments, i.e. a general election every year;

secret ballot;

payment of MPs;

equal electoral districts, i.e. based on the number of voters;

abolition of the property qualification for MPs.

KEY PERSON

Tom Paine (1737–1809)
Born in Thetford, Norfolk, the son of a stay-maker, Paine emigrated to America in 1774 and his writings had an important impact on the American Revolutionary War against British rule after 1776. Returning to Europe in 1787, he went to France where he became involved with the Revolution there after 1789. He returned to Britain in the early 1790s and his ideas made a great impact on the developing radical movement. Government repression, however, forced him to flee back to France.

| 1790s | Impact of the French Revolution | The French Revolution, beginning in 1789, gave a boost to the campaign for reform in Britain. The fact that the French revolutionaries were fighting against excessive royal power and aristocratic privilege struck a chord with British reformers. The ideals of a **democratic system** of government based on a popular assembly elected by universal suffrage and legal guarantees of the rights of the individual, which were expressed through the French Declaration of the Rights of Man in 1790, were popularised in Britain by the writings of **Tom Paine**. His main work, *The Rights of Man*, sold over 200,000 copies in its pamphlet form. |

Inspired by the ideals of the French Revolution, a London Corresponding Society was founded in 1792. The LCS campaigned for democratic reform and attracted support from artisans and small tradesmen. Similar organisations were set up in provincial cities. The government was seriously alarmed by the emergence of an English 'Jacobin' movement and began to introduce repressive measures. The leaders of the LCS were arrested, booksellers were fined or imprisoned, meetings were banned and there was strict enforcement of the laws of libel to prevent criticism of the monarchy. By 1797 the reform movement was in decline.

| 1807 | Westminster election | Two radical candidates, **Sir Francis Burdett** and **Lord Cochrane**, were elected for the constituency of Westminster. The election of two radical MPs did not alter the fact that the vast majority of MPs were opposed to parliamentary reform, but the manner of their election was significant. A new type of political organisation was formed to organise the election campaign. Known as the Westminster Committee, it relied for its success on the voluntary efforts of |

its committed supporters, rather than on the money of a wealthy patron. It made a virtue of its independence from bribery, patronage and wealth. The committee appealed for the support of the artisans and small tradesmen who formed the bulk of the electorate in Westminster. In other words, the election showed that popular radical politics were beginning to revive. Moreover, the men who took a prominent role in the Committee were to become the backbone of the radical political movement in the post-war agitation. They included **Francis Place**, **William Cobbett** and **Major John Cartwright**.

Conclusion

By the time peace came in 1815 the issue of parliamentary reform had been placed on the political agenda and a reform movement had begun to take shape. This movement had three distinct strands:

- Support from within Parliament from the descendants of the Foxite Whigs. This group was very small and their support for the parliamentary reform cause was often little more than lip-service. Moreover, the Whigs were weak and divided and had very little prospect of forming a government.
- A moderate reform movement associated with middle-class radicals such as Francis Place. Moderate reformers favoured an extension of the franchise to all householders and were afraid that universal suffrage would place too much power in the hands of the uneducated working classes. Even a moderate reform of the electoral system, however, was considered too dangerous by the bulk of the middle classes at a time when memories of the excesses of the French Revolution were still very recent.
- A more radical reform movement which was based on the democratic ideas of Paine and which had support from among artisans, small shopkeepers and master craftsmen in London. Supporters of this brand of

A very serious man, he was self-taught, energetic, and a skilled organiser. He was a follower of Jeremy Bentham and believed that working men could not achieve reform on their own. His strategy was to form links between popular radical movements and middle-class and aristocratic reformers in Parliament.

William Cobbett (1763–1835) was the foremost radical leader of the post-war years. A farm boy from Surrey, he was self-taught but became a formidable journalist and writer. His newspaper, *The Political Register*, was the most influential radical journal of these years and reached a wide audience among working men because Cobbett defied the tax on newspapers (stamp duty) and issued a cheap, unstamped edition. Cobbett wanted radical political reform to rid the country of corrupt, aristocratic misgovernment but he was essentially backward-looking. His ideal was to recreate a mythical harmonious and prosperous rural society. Cobbett's great strength was his ability to link the economic discontents of working people with the need for parliamentary reform. His clear and frequently repeated message was that the discontents of the people resulted from misgovernment by the corrupt, aristocratic elite who controlled Parliament – whom he referred to as 'Old Corruption'.

political radicalism believed that the hardships of ordinary people were caused by misgovernment, and that the solution was a reform of the parliamentary system on democratic principles, including the extension of the franchise to all adult males. Although there had been some stirrings of interest in such ideas among provincial working men in the 1790s, the vast majority of working people had not yet been involved in political agitation. This situation was to change in the post-war years. Artisan radicals had a respect for the constitution and were determined to stay within the law. Pressure for change had to come from 'the people' but their methods needed to be kept within the bounds of the law.

WHY DID THE MOVEMENT FOR REFORM REVIVE AFTER 1815?

During the Napoleonic wars the government had been able to rely on appeals to patriotism to isolate the radicals. Agitation for reform was tainted by association with the ideas and symbols of the French Revolution and was regarded by the great bulk of the population as treasonable at a time when Britain was at war with France. After the defeat of France the climate of opinion was able to develop in a less fevered atmosphere. There were also three major factors that led to the growth of radical agitation:

- Serious economic discontent arising from the disruption caused by the end of the war and a trade depression.
- The policies and actions of the government.
- The actions of the radical leaders themselves.

Economic discontent
The end of the war brought serious economic dislocation. The end of government contracts for armaments and uniforms caused a severe drop in demand for the iron and textile industries. European markets took time to readjust to peacetime conditions. This meant that unemployment was already rising when about 300,000 soldiers and sailors were demobilised from the forces and returned home in search of work. The competition for employment drove down wages at a time when a particularly bad harvest, in

the summer of 1816, resulted in a crippling rise in bread prices. The trade slumps were particularly bad in 1816–17 and in 1819, which were also the years when radical agitation and political disturbances were at their height. The areas which were most affected were the textile districts of Lancashire, where the handloom weavers experienced a dramatic slump in their wages, the East Midlands, where the framework knitters were experiencing distress, and London.

Government policies

The government of Lord Liverpool believed themselves to be helpless in the face of the serious economic problems facing the country. They did introduce a Poor Employment Act in 1817, which provided government loans for public works schemes to give employment to some of the unemployed, but this was inadequate. For the most part Liverpool, a competent if unimaginative Prime Minister, believed that the government would have to ride out the storm, and petitions to Parliament from the distressed areas for relief were ignored. Two of the measures introduced by the government, however, were widely regarded as making the situation worse.

Corn Law. The first of these was the introduction of a Corn Law in 1815. Under this law the import of foreign-grown corn was prohibited until the price of home-grown corn reached 80 shillings per **quarter**. The intention behind this measure was to protect British farmers from foreign competition and falling prices. In trying to maintain higher prices for corn, however, the government was seen to be giving priority to the interests of farmers and landowners at the expense of consumers. The poor would suffer from higher bread prices at a time when bread was their main source of nutrition. Moreover, employers of labour would have to pay higher wages to compensate. The Corn Law was therefore widely regarded, both by middle-class manufacturers and by working people, as a blatant example of class legislation. Radical politicians and journalists were quick to seize on the Corn Law as an example of the way an unreformed Parliament, which was unrepresentative of the nation as a whole, was legislating in the interests of one class at the expense of the rest. The

KEY PERSON

Major John Cartwright (1740–1824) came from a landed family and had served in both the navy and the militia. His involvement in radical politics, particularly as a writer, dated back to the 1770s. In his pamphlet, *Take Your Choice*, written in 1776, he had outlined the key demands for radical political change. He had been active in the London Corresponding Society in the 1790s and founded the Hampden Clubs (named after a leading parliamentarian and opponent of the Crown from the 17th century) in 1812–13. Like Cobbett he campaigned for democratic reforms but was essentially backward-looking; he harked back to a mythical Anglo-Saxon past when Englishmen, he believed, still had their liberty.

KEY TERM

A **quarter** was an old imperial measurement of volume equal to eight bushels. Corn was sold in sacks which held one bushel. One quarter in imperial measurement is equivalent to 2.9 hectolitres in metric.

inequality of treatment between landowners and manufacturers was emphasised even more by the government's decision to retain the duties on imported raw wool and cotton, a measure which was opposed by the manufacturers because it increased their costs.

Abolition of income tax. The second measure introduced by Liverpool's government was the abolition of income tax. The burden of this tax, which had been imposed as a temporary wartime measure by William Pitt, fell mainly on the middle classes, and its abolition once the war was over was the subject of a flood of petitions. The landowners in Parliament were equally keen to abolish the tax. Its abolition left the government short of revenue, however, and other high wartime taxes, which fell most heavily on the poor, had to be retained. Once again the radicals had a ready target for their attacks. The burden of taxation on the poor at a time of serious distress was blamed on a corrupt political system which impoverished the working man in order to finance the profligate expenditure of the **Prince Regent** and the 'stock-jobbers', who received interest on the money they had lent to the government during the war. In a speech by Henry Hunt in 1816, which is typical of the tone of these radical attacks, he blamed 'a boroughmongering faction who think of nothing but oppressing the people and subsisting on the plunder wrung from their miseries'.

Radical movement

The radical movement which led the campaign for reform in the post-war years was more widely supported than the Wilkite campaign of the 1760s or the 'Jacobin' movement of the 1790s. Although the extent of this support should not be exaggerated, since there were large areas of the country and many groups of people who were untouched by the agitation, it is also important to acknowledge that there was an emerging national movement in favour of reform. London radicalism was still, as in the late eighteenth century, a vital part of the movement but petitions for reform also flowed in from the provinces, especially from the industrial areas of the north and the Midlands, and provincial radicals helped to set the tone of the movement.

Three radical leaders deserve particular attention for the contributions which each made to the development of the movement:

- **Major John Cartwright** was an old and experienced radical campaigner who had founded the Hampden Club in 1811. Through this organisation, which was initially based solely in London, he carried on his campaign for universal suffrage, annual parliaments and a secret ballot. Cartwright's most important contribution was to go on speaking tours around the country, especially in 1812, 1813 and 1815 when he visited the **Luddite counties**. In 1812 Cartwright visited Leicester, Loughborough, Manchester, Sheffield, Halifax, Liverpool and Nottingham and in his wake there sprang up local Hampden Clubs. Although he did not set out to create a working-class radical movement his evangelising tours of the distressed industrial areas led to a remarkable growth of pro-reform sentiment among handloom weavers and other displaced craftsmen. By March 1817 there were 40 Hampden Clubs in the Lancashire cotton district.

- **William Cobbett** was the most influential radical journalist of the time. He had published a weekly *Political Register* since 1802 but its circulation had been restricted by the stamp duty which increased its price to more than a shilling. In 1816 Cobbett exploited a loophole in the stamp laws to reduce the price to 2d (the Twopenny Trash) and the circulation of *The Political Register* soared. The first edition sold over 200,000 copies in two months. *The Political Register* fulfilled a vital function within the radical movement because it provided a link between the far-flung groups of supporters and a largely London-based leadership. Samuel Bamford, a weaver who was prominent in the radical movement in Lancashire, recounted how the arrival of a new edition of *The Political Register* was eagerly awaited. Through its pages Cobbett set the tone and style of the radical movement and identified the targets for the anger of distressed working people. His attacks on 'Old Corruption' and the wrong-doers who profited from the system, such as royal dukes, profiteering contractors, bankers and stock-traders, together with his advocacy of parliamentary reform, provided a focus which helped to bring disparate groups together and create a radical consensus.

- **Henry Hunt** was the foremost public orator of his time. He was the main speaker at the Spa Fields meeting in London in 1816 and at Peterloo in 1819. With his great booming voice and passionate rhetoric he voiced the emotions of the movement, although he could be accused of saying whatever would provoke the loudest cheer.

The leadership provided by Cartwright, Cobbett and Hunt was not entirely coherent, nor were they able to work together in a common cause, but their influence on the development of a movement which was still in its infancy was nonetheless considerable. Equally significant, especially for the long-term development of a radical political movement, were the creation of new organisations and the establishment of a radical press.

- **New organisations.** The radical movement had learned lessons from its experiences in the 1790s and in the 1807 Westminster election. Cobbett opposed the creation of political societies of any kind, believing that only open general meetings were capable of giving voice to the true feelings of the people. But the experience of the Westminster Committee, which depended for its success on the voluntary efforts of its supporters rather than on money from wealthy backers, provided a prototype for radical organisations. The provincial Hampden Clubs that were established in 1816–17 took this development a stage further for they were almost entirely working class in their composition and thoroughly democratic in tone. The ability of working men to organise independently was not entirely new since the participants in the Hampden Clubs drew on their experiences in trade unions, friendly societies and dissenting chapels. In 1818–19 the Hampden Clubs were superseded by new political unions which sprang up in northern industrial towns. These were well-organised groups of working men who wished to campaign for the right to vote and to extend the political education of those working men who would benefit from it. They were based on the model of the Methodist class meeting and some of their local leaders were ministers or lay preachers. Thus the radical movement in the north grew out of a working-class culture which proved to be an important source of strength.

- **Radical press.** The press had a vital role to play in political education and in challenging the culture of deference. Cobbett's *Political Register* was the most successful and influential of the radical newspapers at this time but there were many others which flouted the laws of libel and challenged the stamp laws. **William Hone's** *Reformist's Register* and **Jonathan Wooler's** *Black Dwarf* were followed by many others, initially in London but later spreading to the provinces. These were writers who were prepared freely to criticise the monarchy, the government and the church in language more extreme than Cobbett's. One of the most extreme was **Richard Carlile** who published *The Republican* from Dorchester gaol, whence he had been sent after publishing an account of the Peterloo massacre in 1819. The campaign for a free press, unhampered by libel laws and the stamp duty, went hand in hand with the struggle for parliamentary reform as both were expressions of a desire for greater freedom and democracy.

WHY WAS THE POST-WAR REFORM MOVEMENT UNSUCCESSFUL?

By 1820 the radical movement was in decline without having achieved any of its objectives. Circulation of the radical newspapers dropped, demonstrations could no longer attract the large crowds, and reform petitions to Parliament dried up. In 1824, when Wooler ceased publication of *Black Dwarf*, he complained that there was 'no public devotedly attached to the cause of parliamentary reform'. 'Where hundreds and thousands once clamoured for reform,' he wrote, 'they now only clamour for bread.' The decline of the movement was due to four main factors:

- the improvement in trade;

- the actions of the government;
- the failure of the radical movement to attract broadly-based and consistent support;
- the weaknesses of the radical movement itself.

The improvement in trade

Trade improved after 1820 and with this came lower unemployment and growing prosperity. The reform movement had depended very largely on the distress of groups such as the handloom weavers and framework knitters for its mass support. The onset of better times caused this support to wither away. Cobbett himself summed up the situation facing the radical movement after 1820. 'I defy you,' he said, 'to agitate a man on a full stomach.'

Government actions

The government of **Lord Liverpool**, in office since 1812, was determined to deal with the reform movement with the utmost severity. Believing in the fundamental virtues of the existing political system they could see no motive other than mischief-making for the actions of the radical leaders. They believed that the independence of Parliament had to be protected against undue pressure from outside and that repressive measures were necessary to contain and control the protests. Fear of revolution, even though the French Revolution had happened a quarter of a century before, was still very much in the minds of men like **Viscount Sidmouth**, the Home Secretary, and **Viscount Castlereagh**, the Foreign Secretary, and led them to oppose any concessions on the parliamentary reform question. Sidmouth urged magistrates, who had the prime responsibility for maintaining law and order in their districts, to suppress disorder with severity and reminded them that they had the right to arrest anyone caught selling blasphemous or seditious literature. Sidmouth also introduced a number of repressive measures, of which Parliament approved:

- In 1817 Habeas Corpus was suspended. This was a law which protected people from being arrested and held in custody without trial. Its suspension gave the authorities

KEY PEOPLE

Tory ministers

Lord Liverpool (1770–1828) was Prime Minister from 1812–1827. He had a reputation for firmness and common sense. He was the longest serving Prime Minister of the 19th century.

Viscount Sidmouth (1757–1844) was Home Secretary in Liverpool's government until 1822. He had previously been Prime Minister in 1802–04. He was a good administrator but rather bureaucratic in outlook and lacked imagination. He was notorious for his extensive use of spies to report on the activities of the radical movement.

Viscount Castlereagh (1769–1822) was Foreign Secretary, in which capacity he showed great creativity and skill. He was, however, indifferent to public opinion and showed hostility towards popular radicalism; he was one of the foremost supporters of repressive legislation in Liverpool's government. He committed suicide in 1822.

much greater powers to arrest and detain those whom they considered to be dangerous agitators.

- In 1817 a **Seditious Meetings Act** was passed which introduced severe restrictions on the holding of public meetings. When it was enforced it had the effect of suppressing most of the Hampden Clubs which had been created in the provinces, and driving the movement underground.
- In 1819, after Peterloo, the **Six Acts** were passed. These included a law to prohibit the possession or carrying of arms, another to restrict even further the right to attend a public meeting, and two laws to impose more severe restrictions on the freedom of the press.

Armed with these powers, the authorities were able to press down hard on the radical movement and its supporters. In 1817 Cobbett fled to America to escape arrest, most of the Hampden Clubs closed down and the movement was forced into more secret, conspiratorial channels. In such an atmosphere one of the other weapons in the government's armoury, the use of spies, was much more effective. Sidmouth employed a network of spies who infiltrated radical groups and sent regular reports back to the Home Office. The most notorious of these spies was Oliver, who acted not merely as a spy but also as an **agent provocateur** and was deeply involved in the plotting which led to the failed Pentridge Rising of 1817. The executions which followed the suppression of the Pentridge Rising also contributed to the decline of the movement in 1818. However, when the movement revived in 1819 and preparations were made for the meeting at St Peter's Fields in Manchester, important lessons had been learned. Conspiratorial methods were rejected and the political unions that emerged in 1818 and 1819 made a virtue out of operating as openly as possible.

Support for government policies. It is worth noting that the government was urged by many of the country gentlemen who served as MPs on the backbenches to adopt even more severe measures against the radicals. It is also important to note that the government had the overwhelming support, not only of the landowning classes but also of the middle classes for its actions. The fact that

KEY TERM

Agent provocateur Spies such as Oliver had a vested interest in having something dramatic to report to their political masters and were therefore involved in not merely infiltrating radical movements but also in encouraging their members to believe that they were part of a wider revolutionary movement. Oliver was almost certainly involved in helping to plan the Pentridge Rising and then passing on information about it to the authorities.

Lord Liverpool was able to forge an alliance of the property-owning classes against the reform movement was perhaps more important in bringing about the defeat of that movement than any specific repressive measures. Even in an age when the franchise was restricted and the middle class did not yet possess political power, the weight of public opinion was a significant factor in determining the success or failure of government policies.

Support for the radical movement

The reform movement which emerged after 1815 was the largest mass movement seen in Britain up to that time. As with the late eighteenth-century radical movements, strong support for its aims came from artisans and small traders in London – the groups which had traditionally made up the London crowd. The fact that reform petitions also came in from the provinces, where Hampden Clubs were flourishing and reform meetings were attracting large crowds, testifies to the fact that this movement was more broadly based than any of its predecessors. Within this picture of a broadly-based mass movement, however, we need to recognise some of the limits to this support:

- The majority of the middle classes were hostile to popular radicalism, particularly after the violence of the meeting at Spa Fields in London. As property owners they were as concerned about the apparent threat to order and their property as were the landowners. It is worth noting that many of the yeomanry cavalry who attacked the crowd at Peterloo were middle-class manufacturers, merchants, publicans and shopkeepers.
- The movement cannot accurately be described as a working-class movement because its support among the various groups that made up the working classes at that time was very variable. Support was strongest among such people as handloom weavers in the small towns and villages of Lancashire and the framework knitters in the East Midlands. Their livelihoods were much more vulnerable to the swings of the trade cycle at a time when their security was being undermined by the introduction of new machinery. Having had their petitions to Parliament for legal protection for their trades turned down, it was a logical next step for them

to turn to demands for a reform of Parliament. The workers in the new cotton factories, however, showed much less interest in political agitation as a remedy for their troubles. Although subject to bouts of short-time working and unemployment due to trade depressions, the main channel for factory workers to air their grievances was through trade unions rather than political clubs. Subject also to more rigid discipline within the factories than the independent 'outworkers', they had less time and opportunity for involvement in political activity.

Weaknesses in the radical movement

Although the post-war radical movement made more impact than any previous agitation, there were serious weaknesses which undoubtedly limited its effectiveness.

- In many ways the leaders, with their different strengths, complemented each other but there were also serious disagreements and personality clashes between them. Cobbett has been described as vain and too inclined to personalise the political struggles he was involved in. He was also almost impossible to work with. It was said of him that he was unhappy in any movement which was 'not subdued to his influence'. Francis Place described Cobbett as an 'unprincipled, cowardly bully' and Henry Hunt as 'impudent and vulgar'. With such deep personal antagonisms between the leaders, unity was impossible.
- Although the Hampden Clubs did provide a link between London radicalism and the provinces, there was no national organisation to provide a lead on policy or strategy and hence no discipline. The movement generated a great deal of energy but their efforts were uncoordinated and ineffective.
- There were disagreements over the aims of the movement. The key question for radicals was whether the franchise should be limited in any way or whether there should be universal suffrage. Place and the **Benthamites** (see page 84) were in tune with middle-class opinion when they advocated no more than a householder franchise. This would limit the right to vote to men who could exercise independent political judgement because they had some measure of economic

security. Both Cobbett and Cartwright were intially in favour of a householder franchise but as the movement began to attract support from the working classes they became convinced of the need for 'one man, one vote'. Cobbett was particularly influenced by the case in favour of universal suffrage put forward by **Samuel Bamford**. There was general agreement on the need for reform, on opposition to the government's repressive measures and on contempt for the weakness of the Whigs, but common aims were impossible to achieve in a movement which contained many diverse strands.

- Finally, there were differences of opinion over tactics, particularly over the use of force to achieve their ends. Place and the Benthamites were firmly on the side of constitutional methods of protest. Place described the Spa Fields rioters as a 'contemptible set of fools and miscreants'. On the other hand, there was a tradition in London and in parts of the north, born out of repression, of a conspiratorial underground movement. In London this was based on the taverns where radicals usually met. Thompson (1968) has written that there was probably 'a physical force conspiracy' in 1817 which formed part of the backdrop to the Pentridge Rising of that year. There were also the **Spenceans** who were involved in the Spa Fields riot in 1816 and in the Cato Street Conspiracy of 1820. Cobbett, Cartwright and Hunt were more ambivalent on the use of force. Cobbett opposed clubs and secrecy as playing into the government's hands since they could be presented as evidence of a plot. But he and Cartwright supported the right to resist oppression by force, and Cartwright was a staunch supporter of the citizen's right to carry arms. The later **Chartist** slogan, 'Peaceably if we may, forcibly if we must', perhaps best expresses the prevailing attitude of the radical movement to the use of force.

Without a common ideology to unite them, radical politics were highly personalised. Differences between the leaders were a serious handicap even though their individual energies and popular appeal were assets to the movement. Meetings were held to attempt to achieve more cohesion, such as a Hampden Club convention in January 1817, but such meetings did more to expose the divisions within the movement than to promote greater unity. After the Hampden Club convention, the radical movement fragmented, even before the government increased the pressure through suspending Habeas Corpus and introducing the Seditious Meetings Act. In 1819, when the movement revived, the new political unions were firmly constitutionalist in character but there was still no national organisation to link these groups together. Thus, although the economic situation and the government's repressive policies were major factors in the failure of the radical movement to achieve its aims at this time, we must also acknowledge the serious internal weaknesses within the movement which militated against success.

WHAT DID THE POST-WAR RADICAL MOVEMENT ACHIEVE?

Although the radical movement did not achieve any of its objectives in terms of parliamentary reform, there were some positive outcomes of the agitation which were of great significance when the movement for parliamentary reform revived in 1830.

- The campaign for a free press went hand in hand with the campaign for parliamentary reform and was ultimately successful. After Peterloo and the passing of the Six Acts the authorities increased the pressure on the publishers and sellers of the '**unstamped' press** with a wave of prosecutions. They were supported in this by **The Society for the Suppression of Vice** and **The Constitutional Association** which initiated many prosecutions against booksellers. Richard Carlile, publisher of *The Republican*, was in prison from 1819 until 1825 but his newspaper was kept alive by members of his family and by relays of volunteers from all over the country. By 1825 the government realised that repression was counter-productive and that the radical journalists and their supporters could not be repressed. The prosecutions were ended and those in gaol were released. No laws had been changed and the stamp duty remained in force but the right of the press freely to criticise the government and the church had been successfully asserted. The existence of a free press was of incalculable value to the campaign for parliamentary reform when it re-emerged in 1830.

- Despite its weaknesses in organisation in the post-war years, the radical movement had learned some important lessons from its experiences. The emergence of political unions in 1819 was of special significance since they were a model for the political unions which led the campaign for reform after 1830. The unions were open in character, constitutionalist in their methods and stressed the need for order and discipline at their demonstrations. The existence of a working-class membership of these unions was evidence of the growing realisation that only through organisation could they transform themselves from a 'mob' into an effective political force.
- Peterloo evoked widespread sympathy for its victims. The Whigs who, at best, had been equivocal on the issue of reform during the post-war years, were galvanised into declaring more open support for the cause after Peterloo. Although deploring radical violence, the Whigs also opposed repressive measures by the government. They were concerned that the nation seemed to be more divided and that revolution might result. Their prescription to prevent revolution was parliamentary reform. In Parliament, the Whigs criticised the actions of the Manchester magistrates and the government's repressive policies. Outside Parliament they organised several county meetings in protest. Thus the Whigs had found an issue on which they could rally public opinion against the government. They became a more effective opposition in Parliament and also in attempting to steer the reform movement into more constitutional channels they were helping to make it more respectable and more acceptable to the middle classes.

CONCLUSION

The reform movement had placed the issue of parliamentary reform at the forefront of political debate in the post-war years but had not achieved any of its central objectives. By the mid-1820s the movement had declined both inside and outside Parliament as its support had evaporated. The Tory government of Lord Liverpool, who had been in office since 1812, was as firmly established as ever and, as long as Liverpool remained Prime Minister, parliamentary reform was impossible. Liverpool shared the feelings of the conservative country gentlemen, on whom he relied for his parliamentary majority, that despite its imperfections the electoral system was fundamentally sound because it allowed all of the important interests in the country to be represented in Parliament. To concede an extension of the franchise and a redistribution of seats would set a dangerous precedent since it would be a concession to agitation from outside Parliament.

Liverpool's government appeared to be built on solid foundations. The support of the king and of the country gentlemen in Parliament assured him of a parliamentary majority. A combination of sound administration and cautious reform in economic and social affairs were qualities that won the admiration of the middle classes. Liverpool himself, although not an outstanding or charismatic leader, was very effective in managing a cabinet full of powerful personalities and maintaining both unity and a sense of direction. The Whig opposition in Parliament was still unable to offer a serious challenge. With an anti-reform government so firmly entrenched in power, parliamentary reformers had no realistic chance of success.

SUMMARY QUESTIONS

1 Which were the main groups who supported the reform of Parliament, and why?

2 What were the connections between economic distress and support for reform?

3 Explain the roles of Cobbett, Cartwright and Hunt in the reform movement.

4 What were the main factors that led to the upsurge in support for radical reform after 1815?

5 Was the failure of this movement mainly due to government action or to the weaknesses in the reform movement itself?

6 Did the post-war reform movement achieve anything of lasting value?

CHAPTER 4

Why did Parliament vote to reform itself?

WHY DID THE TORIES LOSE POWER IN 1830?

In February 1827 the Prime Minister, Lord Liverpool, suffered a stroke and was unable to continue in office. The removal of a central pillar in the structure of the Tory government had far-reaching consequences. Liverpool had been able to hold together a cabinet made up of representatives from both the '**Liberal**' and '**Ultra**' wings of the Tory Party. Without his steadying influence, the splits within the party became more open and more damaging. Over the next three years the unity of the party disintegrated, policy direction was lost, and the way was left open for a Whig administration to take office.

- In April 1827 Liverpool was replaced by **George Canning**, who had previously held the post of Foreign Secretary. Because of their deep personal distrust of Canning, several leading figures within the Tory Party, including the Duke of Wellington, **Sir Robert Peel** and Lord Eldon, refused to serve in his cabinet. Canning could only form a government by inviting some Whigs to join him.
- After Canning's death in August 1827, a new government was formed by **Viscount Goderich**. The new Prime Minister was even more disastrous than his predecessor, being temperamentally unsuitable for the task of leading a divided cabinet. In January 1828 the king was forced to accept that his choice of Prime Minister had been a mistake and persuaded Goderich to stand down.
- This led to the appointment of the Duke of Wellington as the next Prime Minister. As the architect of the victory over Napoleon at Waterloo, Wellington enjoyed an immense prestige in the country. He was known as a strong leader, a good administrator and a courageous

reputation derived from his keenness to cultivate public opinion and from his apparent support for revolutionary movements in other countries. In domestic policy, he supported Catholic emancipation but opposed all other reform movements.

Viscount Goderich (1782–1859) was Chancellor of the Exchequer. Along with the President of the Board of Trade, William Huskisson (1770–1830), he helped to begin the process of reducing duties on imports and exports.

Although these so-called Liberal Tories made a number of reforms, they were all still opposed to a reform of Parliament.

politician. He was identified, however, with the staunchly anti-Catholic wing of the party and, as such, was not equipped to heal the rifts that had begun to open up. Wellington was also overbearing, indifferent to the need to build a consensus and rather remote from the intrigues and jealousies of party politics. He was committed to the maintenance of the fundamental institutions of the state and resistant to the demands for reform from radicals, but his misjudgements over the two years in which he served as Prime Minister led to the appointment of a Whig government and the passing of a Reform Bill.

The crisis over Catholic emancipation

In 1828 Wellington's government was thrown into crisis by events in Ireland. Since the Act of Union with Ireland in 1801 the issue of **Catholic emancipation** had become one of the defining issues in British politics. It not only divided politicians on party lines – the Whigs favoured allowing Catholics to become MPs – but it also divided the various factions within the Tory Party. The Canningites supported Catholic emancipation whereas the 'Ultra Tories' were adamantly opposed. The cause of Catholic emancipation was given fresh impetus after 1823 when Daniel O'Connell, an Irish Catholic lawyer, founded the Catholic Association. Membership grew rapidly and the British government became alarmed at the prospect of widespread demonstrations and a breakdown of law and order in Ireland.

County Clare by-election. In 1828 events were brought to a climax when O'Connell stood for election to Parliament in the County Clare by-election. Although the law prohibited Catholics from becoming MPs it did not prevent O'Connell from standing as a candidate. He won the election by a huge majority but the law prevented him from taking his seat. Wellington's government now faced a serious dilemma. If the law was not changed to allow O'Connell and other Catholics to sit in Parliament, there was a very real prospect of civil war in Ireland. As a soldier, Wellington knew that even a very large English force could not maintain control of Ireland in the face of a hostile population. If, however, Wellington bowed to the inevitable, and introduced a change in the law, he would alienate the anti-Catholic 'Ultra' wing of his own party and, possibly, lose his majority in Parliament.

Split in the Tory Party. In 1829 Wellington, and his Home Secretary Sir Robert Peel, decided to concede Catholic emancipation rather than risk civil war in Ireland. With Whig support, the bill to allow Catholics to be MPs was passed. Its passing, however, had very significant consequences for the parliamentary reform movement:

- The Catholic Relief Act, allowing Catholics to become MPs, had been introduced by a government in order to avert the threat of civil war. This threat had been made more credible by the disciplined way that the Catholic Association had organised its campaign. The parliamentary reform movement was taught a lesson in how to apply pressure through an extra-parliamentary campaign.
- The Tory Party was split over the issue of Catholic emancipation. Wellington and Peel were accused of betrayal by the 'Ultras' who took their revenge on the Prime Minister by voting against him on another issue. Wellington's government was brought down by this split and, in November 1830, a Whig government led by Lord Grey took office. The Whigs, in power for the first time since 1806, saw their first priority as being the introduction of a parliamentary reform measure.

The revival of the reform movement

The campaign for parliamentary reform in the country had begun to revive even before the Whigs took office in 1830. As before in 1815, the trigger for this revival was the return of economic distress. A bad harvest in 1829 had led to increased bread prices; a trade depression brought unemployment and wage cuts in the industrial districts. These were the conditions in which the oratory of Hunt and the words of Cobbett could find a receptive audience. The radical leaders began to show renewed energy in their quest to convince the people that their distress was due to government mismanagement, which could only be remedied by a reform of Parliament.

Birmingham Political Union. The first signs of this revival appeared in Birmingham and London. In Birmingham a

Thomas Attwood (1783–1856) was a banker from Birmingham. He had started his involvement in radical politics in 1812 and became a key figure in the reform campaign of 1831–2. After the Reform Act was passed he was elected MP for Birmingham. His interest in parliamentary reform stemmed from his belief that it was an essential first step towards his ultimate goal, currency reform. He advocated the printing of more paper money and the greater availability of credit as a means of stimulating the economy.

The **Rotunda** was a lecture hall and meeting place in Blackfriars, London, so-called because of the circular arrangement of its seating. It became one of the main meeting places for London radicals in the early 1830s.

William Lovett (1800–1877) was a cabinet-maker by trade. He was born in Cornwall. After moving to London he became involved in trade unionism and then radical politics. Proud, dedicated and class conscious, he was one of the foremost advocates of the use of 'moral force', i.e. peaceful persuasion, rather than violence to achieve their aims. After 1836 he was prominent in the Chartist movement.

local banker, **Thomas Attwood**, founded the Birmingham Political Union in January 1830. The strength of the BPU lay in the fact that it had the support of both the middle classes and working classes of the town. This gave it a unique position within the reform movement. The form of organisation adopted by the BPU was copied by similar political unions in other cities, but the element of class co-operation was not so well suited to the conditions of northern industrial cities such as Manchester or Leeds. In Leeds, for example, there were three separate organisations; one for the middle classes, one for the working classes and one which attempted, with little success, to bring the classes together. The other strength of the BPU lay in Attwood's insistence that it conduct a peaceful and disciplined campaign. In this way it was able to appeal to both moderate reformers and radicals, and attracted enormous crowds to its meetings.

London radicalism. The reform movement in London was more fragmented. Radicals such as Carlile used the **Rotunda** to preach a doctrine of class conflict and to demand full democratic rights for the working classes. More moderate men like Francis Place kept their distance from the 'Rotundists' and tried to limit their influence. The result was that, in London, two rival organisations emerged during the reform crisis of 1830–2. The radicals channelled their energies through the National Union of the Working Classes which was set up in April 1831 and led by **William Lovett** and **Henry Hetherington**. They agitated for universal male suffrage. The moderate, middle-class reformers, on the other hand, established the National Political Union to campaign for a householder franchise. Between the two organisations, therefore, there was often bitter rivalry which diminished the effectiveness of the reform movement in London.

Cobbett and Hunt, two of the most prominent leaders of the post-war reform agitation, were also active in the years 1830–2. Hunt was elected MP for the borough of Preston in 1830 and so was able to use his powers of oratory on the parliamentary stage. Cobbett displayed his customary vigour in taking the campaign beyond London into the industrial districts and agricultural areas. In 1830 he undertook speaking tours through Yorkshire and Nottinghamshire, East Anglia and the Midlands and finally a tour of Yorkshire, Lancashire and the north of England.

By the time the Whigs took office in November 1830 the reform agitation in the country was already underway. Agricultural distress had led to outbreaks of machine-breaking and arson across the southern and eastern counties. Reform demonstrations in the large towns and cities were often larger than the Peterloo meeting of 1819. Especially significant for the government was the growing support for reform from the middle classes. MPs of all parties could not fail to be aware of the strength of feeling for reform 'out of doors'. Despite Wellington's pronouncement in November 1830 that there was no need for parliamentary reform, the pressure for reform was becoming irresistible.

WHAT WAS THE WHIG APPROACH TO REFORM?

The government that took office in November 1830 was led by Lord Grey, who had long been in favour of parliamentary reform. His ministers were far from united on the subject although there was general agreement that some measure of reform was necessary and unavoidable. Grey himself did not take office with a blueprint for a Reform Bill already prepared. He was in favour of an increase in the representation of the counties, since county members tended to be more independent of the executive; he accepted the need for the growing industrial towns to be granted representation in Parliament at the expense of the 'rotten' boroughs; and he was in favour of a uniform franchise qualification for borough seats to replace the chaotic diversity of borough franchises. The precise details of the Reform Bill, however, were left to a small committee of ministers to consider.

Reform in order to preserve

The Whigs were a thoroughly aristocratic party and no less committed to maintaining the power of the landed aristocracy than were the Tory opponents of reform. **Lord Grey** and his **Whig ministers** had no sympathy for the

KEY PERSON

Henry Hetherington (1792–1849) was a printing worker, a member of the Freethinking Christians sect, and a founder member of the London Mechanics Institute (a body which enabled working men to gain an education in their spare time). He was the publisher of *The Poor Man's Guardian*, 1831–5, a newspaper which was the mouthpiece of the National Union of the Working Classes. Since this was an unstamped newspaper, Hetherington was arrested and imprisoned many times.

KEY QUOTE

Lord Grey, writing to the king in 1830 on the subject of reform:
'With the universal feeling that prevails on this subject, it is impossible to avoid doing something; and not to do enough to satisfy rational expectation (I mean the satisfaction of the rational public) would be worse than to do nothing.'

KEY PEOPLE

The Whig ministers

Lord Grey (1764–1845) the Prime Minister, was a long-standing supporter of parliamentary reform, having proposed a measure for reform in 1797. He had been associated with Charles James Fox in the late 18th century.

**Lord John Russell
(1792–1878)** was the third son of the Duke of Bedford. Russell was the major tactician of the Whigs during the 1820s when the party's fortunes were beginning to revive, and he was responsible for steering the Reform Bill through the House of Commons. He went on to have a long political career, serving as Prime Minister on two occasions.

**Viscount Melbourne
(1779–1848)** was Home Secretary in Grey's government. Although a Whig, he was intensely conservative in his attitude to popular radicalism and was much less enthusiastic about reform than Grey or Russell. In 1836 he said that 'The duty of government is not to pass legislation but to rule'. He was Prime Minister in 1834 and again from 1835–41.

radical demands emanating from the popular reform movements and they approved wholeheartedly of the severe sentences passed on the **'Swing' rioters**. The Whig ministers were, however, acutely conscious of the state of public opinion in favour of reform, especially the growing support for reform among the middle classes. Traditionally the Whigs had supported the principles of government by consent and resistance to oppression. Unless aristocratic government could count on the support of 'respectable' public opinion – which was equated with the middle classes – its power would become increasingly ineffective and dependent on coercion. The prospect that alarmed all members of the landed classes was an upsurge of revolutionary activity that would destroy the hierarchical political system and lead to wholesale confiscation of their property. That danger would be much greater if the middle classes allied with the 'lower orders' in an effort to force changes on an unyielding aristocracy. Whigs such as Grey and Macaulay, another leading advocate of reform, believed that the threat of revolution could only be averted if the aristocracy were prepared to make concessions to the rising middle classes. Otherwise, as Macaulay warned, there was a danger that the aristocracy might 'push over to the side of revolution those whom we shut out from power'. By making concessions to the middle classes, on the other hand, the aristocracy could strengthen the constitution and protect their own position since a reformed Parliament would be more genuinely representative of all of the important interests in the nation. 'Reform that you may preserve' was the basis of the Whig approach to parliamentary reform.

The Reform Bill

Grey's instructions to the committee of ministers who drafted the Reform Bill were to prepare a measure 'large enough to satisfy public opinion and afford sure ground of resistance to further innovation'. The Bill was presented to the House of Commons in March 1831. In accordance with Grey's instructions, the terms of the Bill were a mixture of concessions to the middle classes together with other measures to strengthen the existing constitution.

For the middle classes there were the following proposed changes:

- Many small, so-called 'rotten', boroughs were to lose their representation in Parliament, and some of the seats thus gained were to be redistributed to the growing industrial towns. Thus Manchester, Birmingham, Leeds, Bradford, Halifax and Oldham would be among 22 towns to gain two seats each in Parliament.
- The franchise qualification in borough elections was to be made uniform. Those who owned or occupied a building with a rental value of £10 a year – **the £10 householders** – would have the right to vote. This line was drawn very carefully to ensure that only the 'respectable' middle classes would be allowed to vote in the boroughs.

The interests of the aristocracy, however, were to be protected by the following:

- Many seats gained from disenfranchising small boroughs were redistributed to the counties, thereby increasing the representation in Parliament of the landed interest.
- The county franchise was to remain with the 40-shilling freeholders, thereby limiting the electorate in rural areas to owners of land.
- Voters in the new boroughs, such as Birmingham and Manchester, were to be disqualified from voting in county elections. This would protect the power of landowners in county constituencies which were close to the industrial areas.
- Not all of the 'nomination' boroughs were to lose their representation. Some were retained in a conscious move to preserve some safe seats for government ministers.
- There would be no secret ballot. The committee considered this proposal and rejected it on the grounds that voting by ballot would be furtive and 'un-English'.

HOW DID THE BILL PROGRESS THROUGH PARLIAMENT, 1831–2?

The Reform Bill was presented to Parliament by Lord John Russell in March 1831. It passed its second reading in the

House of Commons by one vote but its Tory opponents then succeeded in amending the Bill at the committee stage. Grey refused to accept this amendment and persuaded the king to dissolve Parliament and call a general election. The result was a decisive majority for the government and the reformers. In the boroughs which had a relatively 'open' franchise, and in the counties, the election revealed an overwhelming public opinion in favour of reform. The Tory opponents of reform suffered heavy losses; those who remained in Parliament after the election were mostly returned by the very 'nomination' boroughs which the Bill proposed to abolish.

A second Reform Bill was introduced into the next Parliament and once again the Tories tried to amend it in the committee stage. One amendment, the so-called 'Chandos clause', by which the right to vote in county seats would be extended to tenant farmers, was accepted by the government. By the end of September 1831 the Bill had passed through all its stages in the House of Commons and was sent on to the House of Lords.

Resistance in the Lords
The House of Lords, composed entirely of hereditary peers and the senior bishops and archbishops in the Church of England, was far more 'Tory' in its sympathies than the elected House of Commons. The Bill was rejected by the Lords, which still had the power of veto over legislation. This provoked a storm of protest in the country. Mass demonstrations were organised by the political unions; numerous petitions were sent to Parliament; the radical press was particularly critical of the bishops, some 21 of whom had voted against the Reform Bill. More seriously, there were riots in Nottingham, Derby and Bristol. The worst of these were in Bristol where the disturbances continued for three days before order was restored by the military. During the riots the crowd had destroyed the Bishop's Palace, the Mansion House and the Customs House and had released prisoners from three of the local gaols. Estimates of the number of deaths varied from 12 to 120. Lord Melbourne, the Home Secretary, was said to have been 'frightened to death' by the Bristol riots.

Cavalry cutting down rioters during the Bristol riots of October 1831.

The government had no alternative but to continue the struggle to get the Reform Bill through both houses of Parliament. The Bill was revised to meet some of the objections of its opponents and a third version of the Bill was presented to the Commons in December. By March 1832 the Bill had been approved by the Commons and was introduced to the Lords. Once again the opponents of reform attempted to delay the measure by proposing an amendment. Grey had reached the end of his patience towards the opposition's attempts to dictate the terms of reform to the government. He asked the king to create 50 new Whig peers in order to overcome the Tory majority in the Lords. When King William IV refused, Grey resigned and the king invited the Duke of Wellington to form a new government.

'To stop the Duke, go for gold'

The radical movement now played a crucial part in the proceedings. Once again the political unions organised mass meetings and petitions in support of reform. There was talk of plans for an armed uprising, starting in Birmingham. Place and Attwood appeared willing to support the use of force and urged members of the political unions to arm themselves. They also urged the middle classes to refuse to pay their taxes and to withdraw their funds from the banks. 'To stop the Duke, go for gold' was a cry that was intended to precipitate a financial crisis and thereby apply indirect pressure on Wellington's attempt to form a government.

Wellington admitted defeat in his enterprise when Peel refused to join him. The king had no choice but to recall Grey and give him the necessary promise to create Whig peers, should the need arise. At this point, the opposition to reform in Parliament collapsed and the Whig peers were not needed. The Reform Bill was duly passed by the House of Lords in June 1832 and was then given the royal assent. The Reform Act of 1832 had become law.

HOW IMPORTANT WAS PRESSURE FROM OUTSIDE PARLIAMENT IN THE PASSING OF THE REFORM BILL?

The long struggle in Parliament to pass the Reform Bill took place against a backdrop of meetings, petitions, demonstrations and occasional riots in the country. The Whig ministers did not refer directly to the agitation outside Parliament during the debates on the Bill; to do so would have laid them open to the charge that they were giving in to unconstitutional pressures. But the existence of the reform campaign was a vital element in the Whig strategy for passing the Reform Bill through the two Houses of Parliament in the face of determined opposition. The Whig case was that a reform of Parliament was needed to avoid revolution. That argument was made credible by the agitation outside Parliament and the apparent willingness of the radical leaders to countenance violence. The Tory opposition to reform complained that Grey was inflaming public opinion and using the agitation to force the Bill through Parliament. They were alarmed that the aristocracy was being overborne by physical force and that this would encourage radical forces to use the same tactics to extort further concessions in the future.

Whig attitudes

The relationship between the pro-reform Whigs in Parliament and the extra-parliamentary reform movement was a complex one. Grey took office in 1830 committed to reform and this was a view shared by other leading Whigs such as Russell, **Durham**, **Brougham** and **Hobhouse**. The exact extent of the reform they would propose, however, was by no means fixed in their minds. When Grey set up a committee to draw up detailed proposals for a Reform Bill, the secret ballot and a reduction in the duration of parliaments were not ruled out. These changes would have meant a much more radical bill than the one which was actually put forward. Equally, there were members of the Whig government who were much less enthusiastic about reform than Grey or Durham and who would have preferred a much less sweeping reform, one which would have made fewer changes to the distribution of seats and a more modest extension of the franchise. The Reform Bill that Grey's government introduced had to be radical enough to secure middle-class support but not so radical that it would enfranchise the working classes and thereby alienate both the aristocracy and the middle classes.

Whigs and reformers

There were links between the Whig ministers and some of the leaders of the moderate reform movement. The Home Secretary, Lord Melbourne, regarded Francis Place as a reliable source of information on the state of public opinion. Hobhouse and Brougham had close links with leading radicals such as **James Mill**. When the £10 householder franchise qualification was being considered, Russell commissioned **Edward Baines** to carry out a survey in Leeds to check whether this would be an effective device for excluding working-class males from the franchise. These links were important to both sides during the struggle to pass the Bill, but the Whigs were not being manipulated by the radical movement. The agitation did play a vital role, however, at particular stages of the crisis.

In October 1831 and in May 1832, when the progress of the Bill had been effectively blocked in Parliament, extra-parliamentary agitation strengthened the hands of the Whig ministers in Parliament, and of Grey in his dealings with the king. The 'Days of May' were of major importance in preventing the Duke of Wellington from forming a government, and in thus leaving the king with no alternative but to agree to Grey's request for additional Whig peers. It is also likely that the apparent threat of revolution strengthened Grey's resolve in persisting with the Bill in the face of opposition in Parliament. Once he

KEY PEOPLE

James Mill (1773–1836) was a Scottish writer and philosopher and a close friend of Jeremy Bentham. In 1821 he wrote *Elements of Political Economy* which became one of the leading textbooks for the new science of economics. He was a supporter of the extension of the franchise to the middle classes. He was the father of John Stuart Mill who, in the late 1860s, was one of the early advocates of women's suffrage.

Edward Baines (1774–1848) was a teetotal, nonconformist, middle-class radical who owned the leading provincial newspaper, the *Leeds Mercury*. Through his newspaper he attacked aristocratic privilege, campaigned for free trade and the repeal of the Corn Laws, and opposed the factory reform movement. He supported a taxpayer franchise but was strongly opposed to universal suffrage, believing that it would be damaging to middle-class interests if working men gained the right to vote.

had started on the road to reform he calculated that there was more danger of revolution if he turned back than if he continued.

HOW REALISTIC WAS THE THREAT OF A REVOLUTION DURING THE REFORM BILL CRISIS OF 1831–2?

Historians have been divided in their judgements on this question. Thompson (1968) has written that in the autumn of 1831 and in the 'Days of May' Britain was 'within an ace of revolution'. Gash (1979) and Evans (1996) do not subscribe to this view. Wright (1970) points out that during these years many of the ingredients of a revolutionary situation were present. These were:

- Widespread economic distress caused by poor harvests and unemployment.
- A deep division within the ruling classes. Not only were the Whigs and Tories in disagreement over reform, but the Tories themselves were deeply divided.
- A well-organised radical movement with widespread support among both the middle and working classes.
- Outbreaks of rioting in several places.
- The arming of members of the political unions.
- The call for a run on the banks and the non-payment of taxes.
- The influence of a successful revolution in Paris in July 1830.

All of these factors seem to indicate that there was at least the potential for a revolution at some point during 1831–2. There were, however, many factors that made a revolution unlikely:

- The radical movement itself was deeply divided. Birmingham was unusual in having a reform movement that united middle- and working-class radicals. Elsewhere there were class antagonisms that divided the movement. This was particularly true in the northern industrial cities of Manchester and Leeds but was also apparent in London. In the capital, two rival organisations vied for support. The moderate National Political Union, led by Francis Place, kept its distance from the more radical National Union of the Working Classes (NUWC), led by Hetherington and Lovett. They were divided also in their attitude to the Whig Reform Bill. Middle-class radicals were naturally in favour of a Bill which extended the franchise to middle-class property owners. Working-class radicals, favouring universal manhood suffrage and other democratic reforms, were placed in a quandary. The NUWC rejected the Bill as a betrayal and a trap, a reform which offered nothing to the working classes. Cobbett, however, was prepared to support the Whig measure on the grounds that 'half a loaf' would be better than none.

- Moderate radical leaders such as Attwood and Place had no intention of leading a revolution. Their middle-class supporters were just as alarmed by the outbreaks of violence and apparent threats to property as were aristocratic landowners. They were committed to achieving change by peaceful means, but on the other hand the existence of an apparent revolutionary threat was their main argument for extracting concessions from the aristocracy. They therefore had an interest in playing up the strength of the agitation and raising the temperature. They took a calculated risk in urging the members of the political unions to arm themselves. This could lead to the situation spiralling out of control but, on the other hand, their apparent willingness to support the use of force prevented the more radical leaders from gaining control of the movement. Moreover, if popular violence did break out, armed middle-class property owners would be in a stronger position to defend themselves.

- The government kept its nerve during the crisis. Apart from their treatment of the Swing rioters, the government did not use severe repression to quell the reform movement. The forces at the government's disposal would have been severely stretched if the popular unrest had been more widespread and more sustained. There was a lack of professional police forces outside London; there was also a shortage of regular troops and in critical situations such as the riots of October 1831 the government was forced to rely on semi-trained yeomanry and untrained special constables. The violence certainly alarmed the authorities but the government never lost complete control of the situation. Indeed, the very fact that the government was engaged in a major reform and did not allow parliamentary opposition to deflect it from its objective enabled ministers to retain control over events.

Whether or not a revolution was possible in the Reform Bill crisis was ultimately, as Evans (1996) has pointed out, not important. 'What mattered', Evans has written, 'was that enough MPs and Peers believed that it was, and acted accordingly.' The passing of the Reform Act of 1832 cannot be explained other than as the result of a combination of factors. The Whigs intended to introduce parliamentary reform, but their ability to pass such a measure through an unreformed House of Commons and a Tory-dominated House of Lords depended on the perception that there was an overwhelming weight of public opinion in favour of reform and a danger of revolution if that reform was not carried.

SUMMARY QUESTIONS

1 Why did the Tories lose power in 1830? Why was this change in government so significant in the context of the parliamentary reform movement?

2 What other factors led to the revival of the reform movement in 1830?

3 Summarise the main aims of the Whigs in introducing a Reform Bill.

4 Which was more important in the passing of the Reform Bill through an unreformed Parliament – the actions of the Whig government, or the pressure for reform from outside Parliament?

CHAPTER 5

What was the impact of the Great Reform Act?

HOW WAS THE POLITICAL SYSTEM CHANGED?

The Whig strategy had been to 'reform in order to preserve'. Their objectives were to give the vote to new interest groups, to purge the system of some of its worst abuses, such as the notorious 'rotten boroughs', and to give extra representation to the counties in order to strengthen the independence of the House of Commons against the Crown. These were not radical objectives and the Act itself did not make fundamental changes to the political system. The political system after 1832 contained many features that had long been the subject of criticism in the pre-reformed Parliament. This has led historians such as Gash (1979) to downplay the significance of the Act. 'The Reform Act', wrote Gash, 'represented no more than a clumsy but vigorous hacking at the old structure to make it a roughly more acceptable shape.' More recently, Evans (1996) has argued that the Reform Act was 'legislation of prime importance' since it redrew the political map of England. Moreover, the reformed Parliament had a wider base of support that gave it the confidence to embark in the 1830s and 1840s on wide-ranging schemes of reform of the church, of local government and of social policy. 'The Reform Act', says Evans, 'had dynamic as well as conservative implications.' These implications are the theme of this chapter.

What was changed by the Reform Act?
Voters. The number of adult males who were entitled to vote increased from around 478,000 to over 800,000. Although this represented a near doubling of the electorate, the total who qualified for the franchise after 1832 still represented only 8 per cent of the total population. In the boroughs it was largely the middle classes who had gained the vote under the £10-householder franchise, although this varied from one town to another. In the counties, the

40-shilling freeholders were joined as voters by the tenant farmers.

Constituencies. Many new parliamentary boroughs were created. Twenty-two new boroughs had two seats in Parliament, of which the majority were the new industrial towns, and there were 20 new parliamentary boroughs which returned one member to Parliament. Among the new constituencies were **watering places**, such as Brighton and Cheltenham, and older industrial towns such as Stroud and Frome. The Whigs were seeking to enfranchise 'interests' rather than numbers and this included interests other than manufacturing. Fifty-six of the smallest boroughs lost both of their seats in Parliament while 30 small boroughs lost one of their members. County representation in Parliament was increased.

KEY TERM

Watering places In the late 18th and early 19th centuries, towns such as Cheltenham and Brighton benefited from the increasing popularity of drinking spa waters (Cheltenham) and sea-bathing (Brighton) among the aristocracy. Such towns became known as 'watering places'.

Elections. The Act made few changes to electoral procedure but the reform did have one very significant effect on elections after 1832; there were more of them. The percentage of contested elections never rose above 38 per cent in the years 1806–32, and was normally below 30 per cent. In the first election held after the Reform Act was passed, there were contests in 74 per cent of seats and, in the period 1832–65, the average percentage of contested elections was 59 per cent. Not only could more people vote after 1832, but also more of them were given the opportunity to exercise that right.

What was not changed by the Reform Act?
Voters. The majority of working-class people were not allowed to vote. In London some of the better-off artisans qualified under the £10-householder franchise but this line had been deliberately drawn to exclude the working classes. Indeed, because of the abolition of the 'potwalloper' and 'scot and lot' franchises, there were fewer working-class men eligible to vote *after* 1832 than there had been before.

Constituencies. Even after the withdrawal of representation from the most notorious of the 'rotten boroughs', there were still many small towns which retained their representation in Parliament. After 1832 over 60 constituencies had fewer than 300 voters, while larger

towns with populations in excess of 10,000, such as
Doncaster and Loughborough, continued to have no
representation in Parliament. The **University seats** also
remained. There was some redistribution of seats to reflect
the changing demography of industrial Britain but the
industrial areas and London were still underrepresented in
the new Parliament. So too were the counties. The English
and Welsh counties had nearly 57 per cent of the
population but only 32 per cent of the seats in Parliament.

KEY FACT

University seats Oxford
and Cambridge Universities
retained their representation
in the reformed parliament.
Indeed, they did not lose
their parliamentary seats until
1950.

A typical example of a poster appearing during an election campaign.

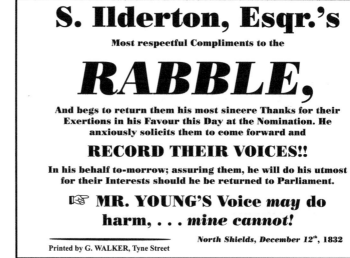

S. Ilderton, Esqr.'s

Most respectful Compliments to the

RABBLE,

And begs to return them his most sincere Thanks for their Exertions in his Favour this Day at the Nomination. He anxiously solicits them to come forward and

RECORD THEIR VOICES!!

In his behalf to-morrow; assuring them, he will do his utmost for their Interests should he be returned to Parliament.

☞ MR. YOUNG'S Voice *may* do harm, . . . *mine cannot!*

North Shields, December 12ᵗʰ, 1832

Printed by G. WALKER, Tyne Street

Elections. The Whigs rejected demands for a secret ballot and elections continued to be open as before. Bribery and corruption at elections not only continued but also became more visible and, probably, more prevalent. There was no effective limit on election expenses for candidates and the new voters were every bit as corrupt as their predecessors. At the 1841 election, votes were sold for £4 at Penryn, £7 at Sudbury and £15 at Ipswich. Contested elections cost candidates large sums of money; at Nottingham in 1841 the unsuccessful candidates spent £17,000.

There were other forms of influence which were still brought to bear. The new voters among tenant farmers were vulnerable to eviction by their landlords unless they voted according to their wishes. Aristocratic patrons could still influence the 'shopocrat' voters by the simple device of threatening to withdraw their custom. Violence and intimidation were still common in post-1832 elections. The result was that patronage survived. Gash (1979) has calculated that some 60 or more parliamentary seats were still controlled by 42 aristocratic patrons. Family boroughs still existed. Sir Robert Peel, for example, represented the borough of Tamworth, a seat that was in the 'pocket' of his father. Despite the efforts of the radicals to discredit such a system, much contemporary opinion considered the exercise of influence in this way to be quite legitimate and, as a result, patrons could usually rely on their own status and the deferential attitudes of the voters rather than resort to threats and inducements.

WHO EXERCISED POLITICAL POWER IN THE POST-REFORM ERA?

Social composition of Parliament

Parliament still consisted mainly of aristocrats and country gentlemen. Aydelotte (1954) has calculated that the election of 1841 returned 342 members who were closely related to peers and 240 who were country gentlemen. This represented 71 per cent of the total. He also calculated that no more than 22 per cent of MPs were middle-class businessmen. This was not a significant increase on the number of MPs from middle-class backgrounds in the pre-reformed Parliament. Members from working-class backgrounds were conspicuous by their absence and there were barely any more nonconformists among the post-1832 batch of MPs than there had been before.

There were a number of reasons why the composition of Parliament was so slow to change, despite the 1832 Reform Act:

- Members of the landed classes still had greater experience of political life and government than the middle classes. There was still a tendency for the middle classes to defer to their social superiors.
- The landed classes had time to attend parliamentary debates because of their more leisured lifestyle. Most middle-class businessmen had to devote most of their time to the running of their businesses.
- Until 1858, county members had to possess land to the value of £600; borough members had to have a £300 estate.
- MPs were not paid a salary. Members of Parliament, therefore, needed a substantial private income to be able to perform their duties.

Aristocratic domination

Not only did Parliament remain dominated by the landed classes, government was also virtually an aristocratic preserve. Of the eight prime ministers who led administrations in the period 1832–65, only Sir Robert Peel came from a non-aristocratic background and even he had had the same upbringing and education as his aristocratic colleagues. During that same period, every foreign secretary and most other senior members of the various Whig, Tory and Liberal governments were men who came from the landed classes. Given also their powerful position in the House of Lords, the aristocracy retained control over most of the levers of power. This was exactly what the Whigs had intended; Grey said as much when he called the Reform Bill 'the most aristocratic measure that ever was proposed in Parliament'.

HOW WERE POLITICAL PARTIES CHANGED BY THE REFORM ACT?

Gash (1979) has described the Reform Act of 1832 as 'the point of departure for a new party system'. This was not something which had been in the minds of the Whigs when they framed the Reform Bill. Once the Act was passed a new political landscape began to take shape in which political parties were seen to be much more important than in the pre-reform era. Eighteenth-century political parties were very different from their modern counterparts. 'Whig' and 'Tory' were labels attached to loose groupings of politicians which formed around powerful aristocratic patrons and which were primarily concerned with levering themselves into office. There were differences between Whigs and Tories on some issues but common policies were not the main factor that united them. Indeed, party unity and party discipline were very loose and parties lacked any formal organisation, either in Parliament or outside.

Decline of patronage

Patronage was at the heart of eighteenth-century politics. Party groupings were held together by the patronage of powerful aristocrats; governments were guaranteed a majority in the House of Commons through the exercise of royal patronage. By the 1830s, neither of these methods were as effective as they had been in the 1780s. Royal patronage had been steadily reduced by a programme of '**Economical Reform**' and aristocratic patronage suffered a severe blow from the abolition of many 'rotten boroughs' in the Reform Act. The old methods of ensuring that governments which had been appointed by the Crown had a majority in the House of Commons were no longer effective. Party organisation therefore became more important to governments than patronage.

Party organisation

The Reform Act also gave a powerful stimulus to the development of party organisation. Voters now had to be registered and it was therefore to the advantage of the parties to ensure that their known supporters were placed on the electoral register. This led to the establishment of local political associations and registration committees and also of local party agents, all of whom attempted to get their own voters onto the register and remove their opponents' voters. Parallel to this development came the establishment of party organisation at Westminster. The Tories established their **Carlton Club** in 1832 and the Whigs founded their **Reform Club** in 1836. Links between the central organisations and the local committees were, however, very loose, as was party discipline in general.

Conservative Party

Both existing parties had to attempt to broaden the basis of their support in order to survive in the post-reform era. Ironically it was the Tories, now under the leadership of Peel, who were the first to declare their hand. The granting of votes to the middle classes and the representation of the growing industrial towns in Parliament were, despite the opposition of the Tories, part of the new reality. If the Tories remained a party exclusively of Anglican landowners, they would not survive. So-called 'Tory Radicals' such as Richard Oastler favoured an alliance with the working classes on such issues as factory reform; this was unlikely to solve the Tories' problem since the working classes did not have the right to vote. Peel recognised the need to appeal to the newly enfranchised middle classes

Economical Reform This was a process, begun in the 1780s, whereby the spending of the monarch on patronage was reduced, partly to save money but mainly to curb the Crown's influence in Parliament. Many 'sinecure' posts, i.e. jobs in the Crown's service that carried large salaries but few responsibilities, were abolished.

The **Carlton Club** and the **Reform Club** were both similar to the many other 'gentlemen's clubs' which existed in London but they took on the role of being the unofficial headquarters of their respective parties. They had no formal role within the party organisations but membership of these clubs was essential to any politician wishing to advance his career. Discussions about party tactics and policies would take place within the informal club atmosphere.

Sir Robert Peel, writing in 1839, on the subject of party organisation:
'[There is] a perfectly new element in political power – namely the registration of the voters . . . That party is the strongest in point of fact which has the existing registration in its favour.'

who would be looking for other reforms in the wake of the Reform Act. He stated his position in the Tamworth Manifesto of 1834. In this he declared his acceptance of the Reform Act as 'a final and irrevocable settlement of a great Constitutional question' and went on to say that, in the 'spirit of the Reform Bill', he was prepared to consider 'the correction of proved abuses and the redress of real grievances'. He also, however, restated the Tory conviction that government must be based on 'the respect for ancient rights and the deference to prescriptive authority'. In this document, therefore, Peel was setting out the guiding principles for a new Conservative Party. It would be a party which would continue to resist wholesale changes to the established institutions such as the church and the monarchy but which would be prepared to consider cautious, limited changes where necessary.

Liberal Party

The Whigs also attempted to establish a new identity. The presence in Parliament of Irish Catholic MPs after 1829 and a sprinkling of radical MPs after 1832, combined with a large number of reform-minded Whig members, helped to create a political situation which Grey had difficulty in controlling. The resulting division led to the king dismissing the Whig ministers in 1834 and inviting Peel to form a government. Through tactical necessity the Whigs, now under the leadership of Lord Melbourne, made an alliance with the Irish and the radicals to get rid of Peel's new Conservative government. This alliance, formalised in the **Lichfield House Compact**, was only intended to be a temporary expedient but in fact became the basis for the Victorian Liberal Party.

'Within ten years of the Reform Act', wrote Gash, 'politics was dominated by two major parties to an extent previously unknown in British history.' By 1841 it was common for newspapers to report election results in terms of Liberal and Conservative gains or losses. The modern political system was beginning to take shape, and the rise of these political parties had serious implications for other elements in the constitution.

KEY TERM

Lichfield House Compact
This was the name given to an agreement between the Whigs, Irish and radicals, meeting at Lichfield House in February 1835, to combine together against Peel's minority Conservative government.

HOW DID THE REFORM ACT CHANGE THE BALANCE OF THE CONSTITUTION?

The Whigs believed that the balance of the constitution had been upset in the eighteenth century by the increasing use of royal patronage to guarantee the Crown's ministers a majority in the Commons. The Reform Act, together with economical reform, was intended to restore the independence of the House of Commons and thus restore the balance of the constitution. The Tories, on the other hand, warned that by exposing Parliament to a 'perpetual vortex of agitation' the Whigs were destroying the balance of the constitution and undermining stable government.

Role of the monarch

Undoubtedly the Reform Act did alter the balance of the constitution. Eighteenth-century monarchs had the power to appoint and dismiss ministers. This was a power exercised by George III in 1783 when he dismissed the Fox–North coalition government and appointed William Pitt to be Prime Minister. When William IV dismissed the Whig ministry in 1834, however, circumstances had changed. The King chose Peel as his Prime Minister but Peel was unable to form a stable government in the face of a hostile parliamentary majority. After 100 days he was forced to admit defeat; the King had no alternative but to invite the Whig leader, Lord Melbourne, to form a government. No longer could the monarch sustain ministers in office through patronage, nor could the monarch ensure that his or her government won a general election. Public opinion and party were increasingly what mattered after 1832 and the monarch was obliged to withdraw from active involvement in the choice of ministers.

Powers of the House of Lords

Although the Reform Act did not change the powers or the composition of the House of Lords, the way in which the Act was passed had profound implications for the Upper House. When Grey secured the king's agreement to create enough Whig peers to overturn the Tory majority in the

Lords, he was taking a stand on the supremacy of the elected House of Commons over the unelected House of Lords. When the Lords backed down in the face of Grey's threat, there was a tacit acceptance of this principle and of its corollary, the principle that the electorate were the final arbiter in any constitutional dispute. Although the Lords retained their power of veto into the twentieth century and the Tory majority in the Lords continued to use the veto to frustrate the wishes of Whig and Liberal governments, the way in which the Reform Act had been passed had established an important precedent.

SUMMARY QUESTIONS

1 Summarise, in the form of a table, those features of the political system that were changed by the Reform Act and those features that were not.

2 Did the Reform Act give power to the middle classes?

3 How did the Reform Act affect the development of political parties?

4 How did the Reform Act affect the role of the monarchy?

CHAPTER 6

Did the Reform Act lead to further reforms?

INTRODUCTION

In the years after 1832 the Whigs introduced a number of reforms affecting many institutions and aspects of social and economic life:

- Slavery was abolished in the British Empire in 1833.
- The first government grant to church schools was made in 1833.
- A Factory Act in 1833 limited the hours of work of women and children in textile factories.
- The Poor Law was reformed in 1834.
- A Municipal Corporations Act reformed local government in the towns in 1835.
- There were also reforms of the legal system and of the system of paying tithes to the church.

This was the most extensive and concentrated burst of reforming legislation that had ever been introduced by a British government. The fact that such legislation came so quickly after the Reform Act suggests that there was a direct connection between them. The exact nature of this link, however, is neither simple nor direct.

WAS FURTHER REFORM INEVITABLE?

The Whigs

In the House of Commons elected in December 1832, after the Reform Act was passed, there was a clear majority for the Whigs. It has been estimated that the Whigs won 320 seats to the Tories' 120. The Whigs under Grey, however, did not resume the business of government with any predetermined plan for extensive reform. They were still an aristocratic party and were committed to maintaining aristocratic rule. Just as they had introduced parliamentary reform in order to prevent a revolution, many Whig leaders believed that it was essential to bring in further reforms to complete that task. Lord Althorp warned Grey in January 1833 that, without 'popular measures', the 'Reform [Act] will lead to revolution'. Thus with a pro-reform majority in the House of Commons and a Whig government that recognised the strength of public opinion in favour of reform, further legislation was inevitable. The precise nature of this legislation, however, was still to be determined.

Radicals

There were also, in the new House of Commons, a significant number of radical MPs. Estimates of their number vary from 20 to 50. They were a highly diverse group, spanning the whole spectrum of radical politics from Cobbett to Attwood and, as such, they could not operate as a distinctive 'Radical Party'. The radical MPs were individuals who spoke either for themselves or for narrow sectional interests. Most were in Parliament to champion their own particular causes: nonconformists pressed for full civil and religious equality; Attwood wanted currency reform; some regarded the repeal of the Corn Laws as the main priority whilst others championed educational reform or factory reform. Outside Parliament the political unions were still active and there was a flood of petitions to Parliament in 1832 and 1833 calling for further reforms. There was, therefore, strong pressure both within Parliament and from outside for action from the government but this pressure was very diffuse and often contradictory.

Public opinion

Differences between classes and differences within classes meant that it was difficult to get an accurate idea of public opinion in the 1830s. It is more accurate to use the terms working classes and middle classes rather than to speak in terms of the working class and the middle class. It was the middle classes who had been enfranchised by the Reform Act and it was their opinions and interests which the Whigs now had to consider. There was, however, no single middle-class view on almost any of the main issues of the day. Local issues often took precedence over national issues in elections. Parties were not yet sufficiently developed to act as channels for public opinion. Newspapers were beginning to inform and shape public opinion, particularly in the larger provincial towns which had a vigorous local press. Thus although Parliament in the post-reform era was bound to be more responsive to public opinion, there was not a clearly defined or organised public opinion which could shape policy in any meaningful way. Organised pressure groups, however, were a way of rallying support behind a particular cause and maximising the impact of public opinion.

The Benthamites

There was, however, a group of radical thinkers who did exercise an influence over policy which was out of all proportion to their numerical strength. The Benthamites had been active in the campaign for parliamentary reform and they were to continue to influence the Whig reforms. James Mill, Francis Place, **Edwin Chadwick**, **Thomas Southwood Smith**, **James Kay-Shuttleworth** and **John Roebuck** were among the more prominent of **Jeremy Bentham**'s followers. The Benthamites provided the Whigs with a set of principles which they could apply to the task of shaping policy. The first step was to ascertain the facts through a commission of inquiry; this was to be followed by the drafting of legislation based on the findings of the commission's report and, finally, there was the drafting of regulations to enforce the new law. The Benthamites were not an organised group but they did have important links with Whig ministers. Henry Brougham, Lord Chancellor from 1830 to 1834, based his legal reforms on Benthamite principles. Lord Althorp, Chancellor of the Exchequer from 1830 to 1834, was a member of James Mill's Political Economy Club. It is perhaps no accident, therefore, that leading Benthamites such as Chadwick had a major role in important reforms such as the Poor Law Amendment Act of 1834.

Conclusion

It is clear that there was a general public mood in favour of further reform after the Reform Act of 1832. Most of those who demanded parliamentary reform saw it as a means to

The Benthamites

Jeremy Bentham (1748–1832) was the founder of a school of thought known as Utilitarianism or Philosophic Radicalism. Bentham himself had been a child prodigy who had gone to Oxford University at the age of 13 and read law. Instead of entering the legal profession he spent his life formulating his ideas and attempting to influence others to implement them. His basic premise was that every law and institution should be subject to a 'utilitarian test', i.e. what use does it serve? His method for determining the utility of a law or institution was to ask, 'Does it promote the greatest happiness of the greatest number?' Laws and institutions that served only minority interests should be abolished and replaced by those that served the interests of the majority. He taught his followers to ascertain the facts about their particular concerns through detailed and thorough research and then to formulate practical and detailed proposals for reform. Bentham and his followers believed in reforming legislation as the key to achieving social and political progress.

Edwin Chadwick (1800–90) was a barrister and journalist. His quick grasp of a situation and his clear sense of what needed to be done won him the respect of politicians and civil servants and he was asked to serve on a number of Royal Commissions. In particular he was involved in the investigation into the Poor Law and played the leading role in the investigation into public health. His overbearing manner, however, made him many enemies.

Thomas Southwood Smith (1788–1861) was a doctor and a Unitarian by religion. He played an important role in public health reform.

James Kay-Shuttleworth (1804–77) was a doctor whose work among the poor in Manchester led him to conclude that there was a connection between dirt and disease. He was an Assistant Poor Law Commissioner and later became involved in the administration of government grants for education.

John Roebuck (1801–79) was a radical MP (for Bath) and a campaigner for a national system of education.

an end, not an end in itself. It is also clear that the Whig government after the election of December 1832 knew that further reform was essential if they were to be able to manage the House of Commons with its strong pro-reform majority. The Whigs were thus carried forward by pressures that they could not control, except through making concessions. The reforms were shaped by those pressures, particularly from groups like the Benthamites, rather than by any preconceived programme of reform.

WHAT REFORMS WERE ACHIEVED?

The abolition of slavery, 1833

In 1833 slavery was abolished throughout the British Empire. This was the culmination of a long campaign led by nonconformists and Anglican **Evangelicals**, among whom **William Wilberforce** was particularly prominent. The first fruits of the campaigner's efforts had been the abolition of the slave trade in 1807. Further campaigning had stirred public feeling in favour of abolition, and slavery had been an issue in the election of 1830. Abolition had been vigorously opposed, however, by the powerful West Indian plantation owners and shipping interests. The so-called 'West Indian interest' had held a number of rotten boroughs in pre-reform parliaments and was therefore able to mount a strong defence. In 1833, with support from key figures in the government such as Brougham, the abolitionists succeeded in their campaign, but the generous compensation given to former slave owners – £20 million – showed that the 'West Indian interest' still retained some influence in Parliament.

The Factory Act, 1833

Reformers. Attempts to regulate the long hours and dangerous working conditions for children employed in the textile factories had been made before. The Factory Acts of 1802 and 1819 had been narrow in their scope – the first applied only to parish apprentices, the second to all children in the cotton trade – and unenforceable in practice. It was left to local magistrates to enforce the law and prosecutions were rare because inspections were not carried out and magistrates generally tended to favour the employers. By the early 1830s, however, the movement for factory reform had become much more effective through an alliance between Tory **paternalists**, humanitarian Evangelicals and the cotton spinners' trade union. **Richard Oastler**, a land agent and Tory paternalist, launched the campaign with his open letter, published in the *Leeds Mercury* in 1830, entitled 'Yorkshire Slavery'. The cause was supported in Parliament by **Michael Sadler** and **Lord Ashley**, both Tories and Evangelicals. Outside Parliament, the campaign was led by the Short-Time Committees, which were linked to the unions and were aiming to persuade Parliament to legislate for a ten-hour day for workers of all ages. There was also support from some of the landed gentry in the north, motivated by contempt for the middle-class manufacturers.

Manufacturers. Opposition to regulation of hours and working conditions came, unsurprisingly, from manufacturers. The Association of Master Manufacturers argued that shorter hours would undermine competitiveness and interfere with the free market in labour. Their views were championed by Edward Baines and his *Leeds Mercury*, that was becoming one of the leading radical provincial newspapers. They had support also from Lord John Russell and Sir James Graham, two leading members of the government. Not all manufacturers, however, opposed legislation. Owners of large and successful factories such as John Wood of Bradford, John Fielden of Todmorden, John Marshall of Leeds and John Hornby of Blackburn lent their support to the campaign. To a certain extent manufacturers divided in their attitudes to reform according to the size of their enterprises. It was the smaller manufacturers, especially those in rural areas, who were most obdurate in their opposition to shorter hours legislation. Larger, more successful manufacturers had often already implemented shorter hours and better working conditions. The extension of these rules to the smaller firms would reduce their ability to undercut prices by working their employees harder.

Sadler's parliamentary campaign, backed by the agitation from the Short-Time Committees, convinced the Whigs banker from Leeds by profession. A Tory, he sat in the House of Commons until 1832.

Lord Ashley (1801–85) was an Evangelical Christian and Tory. He came from a wealthy aristocratic family and eventually succeeded to the family title, the Earl of Shaftesbury. Apart from factory reform, he was involved in a number of campaigns on behalf of the poor and disadvantaged, including taking up the cause of the climbing boys employed by chimney sweeps.

that factory reform was inevitable, but with so many conflicting pressures, the extent and precise nature of that reform was not fixed. The Whigs turned to the Benthamites, in the form of Edwin Chadwick and Thomas Southwood Smith, who led a Royal Commission which was set up to investigate the factory reform question. Their report supported the manufacturers' contention that a ten-hour day for adults would ruin many firms but they also accepted the reformers' case that children in the factories needed protection from employers who overworked them.

The resulting Factory Act of 1833 prohibited the employment of children below the age of nine in all textile factories. Children between the ages of 9 and 13 were limited to eight hours' employment a day, and young people up to the age of 18 were not to work more than twelve hours a day. Most important, however, was the provision of a new system of professional factory inspectors who would visit factories, prosecute employers and make recommendations for further regulations. Although there were still problems with enforcement after the establishment of the factory inspectorate, a significant start had been made in curbing the worst abuses of the factory system.

Education Grant, 1833

Before 1833 there was no state involvement in the provision of education in Britain. Schooling of children was generally considered to be the responsibility of parents. The middle and upper classes were able to ensure that their children received an education at the fee-paying public schools or grammar schools. For the working classes there was a variety of different types of schools but the main providers of education for the children of the poor were the churches. The nonconformist British and Foreign Society and the Anglican National Society had developed in competition with one another but, with the greater resources at its disposal, the National Society had opened the larger number of schools. It claimed, in 1831, to be educating half a million children. The quality of the education provided in these schools was highly variable and there were enormous gaps in provision. The length of time spent in school by working-class children in the

1830s was rarely more than three and a half years and often less than two. The result was that the majority of working-class children were growing up with only minimal education.

Benthamites. Pressure for a national system of education came from many quarters but especially from the Benthamites. J. A. Roebuck had been trying since the 1820s, with the support of Brougham, to persuade Parliament to establish a national system of education under which all children between the ages of 7 and 14 would attend schools which were locally managed. With the Whigs in power Roebuck tried again but his efforts resulted in only a small grant, of £20,000, being made available to the existing church societies to support the building of schools.

Influence of the Anglican Church. That Roebuck did not achieve more was due to the influence of the Anglican Church, which jealously guarded its position in the educational field. The grant money was distributed to the church societies in proportion to their own efforts, with the result that the Anglican National Society received four-fifths of the total amount since it was the organisation with access to greater private donations. Roebuck's further efforts to extend state involvement in schools were also thwarted by the Church of England. In 1839 a proposal to set up state-run training colleges for teachers and a system of inspection for state-aided schools was defeated by the supporters of church education. The money for the training colleges was transferred to the churches to enable them to set up their own colleges, and the Church of England bishops were given control over the appointment of school inspectors.

The establishment of a national system of education was delayed. Even in the post-reform Parliament, the power of old established interests like the Church of England had been clearly demonstrated.

The Poor Law Amendment Act, 1834

Reform of the system of poor relief had been on the government's agenda even before the Reform Act had been passed. Complaints from farmers and landowners about the growing burden of paying the local poor rates had been increasing. The 'Swing' riots of 1830 had alarmed the government and led to further calls for a reform of the system and, in 1832, a Royal Commission was established to enquire into the workings of the old Poor Law and suggest changes.

The old Poor Law. The existing system of poor relief was based on a law passed during the reign of Elizabeth I in 1601. This law made each parish responsible for the relief of the poor within the parish. A special poor rate, levied on landowners and farmers, would cover the cost of poor relief. Each parish was to appoint an Overseer of the Poor, whose job it was to collect the rates and distribute relief. The Justices of the Peace supervised the system and set the rates of poor relief. The system was thus local and amateur, since none of the officials were paid.

Speenhamland System. In the south of England the system of poor relief had been modified at the end of the eighteenth century in response to the widespread distress in the countryside. In 1795 the JPs of Berkshire, meeting in the village of Speenhamland, decided to give allowances of money to poor families based on the number of children and on the price of bread. This 'allowance' system could be used to make up the wages of employed men at times when wages were low. In the conditions of wartime, when bread prices were unusually high, and in the immediate post-war years, the system spread rapidly across the agricultural districts of southern and eastern England. By 1818 the cost of poor relief had soared to £8 million; expenditure declined during the 1820s but, when another economic crisis occurred in 1829–30, the costs rose again to £7 million.

Criticism of this system came not only from the farmers and landowners who claimed the rates had become an intolerable burden. Malthus and his followers denounced the allowance system for encouraging farm labourers to have larger families, thus increasing the dangers of overpopulation. Political economists believed that the old Poor Law, under which a person could only claim relief in the parish of his or her birth, was an obstacle to the development of a free market in labour. The Benthamites were offended by the ad hoc and amateurish way in which the law was administered; its very lack of a rational 'system' was its most damning characteristic in their eyes. All of these groups were represented on the Royal Commission. Among the more prominent members were **Nassau Senior**, Professor of Political Economy at Oxford, and Edwin Chadwick, a leading disciple of Bentham.

The Commissioners very assiduously collected evidence to show that the old Poor Law was inefficient and was actually responsible for creating more poverty than it relieved. Their recommendations were as follows; but not all of these were included in the Poor Law Amendment Act of 1834:

- The allowance system was to be abolished. Henceforth there was to be no payment of 'outdoor relief' (allowances) to the able-bodied poor.
- Applicants for poor relief were to be offered only 'indoor relief' within a workhouse.
- Conditions within the workhouses should be made 'less eligible' than those of the lowest-paid independent labourer in order to deter all but the most desperate from applying.
- Parishes were to be grouped together in 'Unions'. The administration of relief within each Union was to be the responsibility of a Board of Guardians, which was to be elected by the ratepayers of the district.
- A central Poor Law Commission would be established to oversee the administration of the new law and to draw up regulations for the local Unions.

Opposition to the new Poor Law. The Poor Law Amendment Act passed through Parliament with very little opposition and became law in 1834. Once the Commissioners tried to implement the law in practice, however, opposition began to grow. It came from several sources. Landed gentry resented the loss of their powers as JPs over the administration of poor relief. There was particular hostility to the centralisation of control and supervision in the hands of the Poor Law Commission, which was seen as alien to the British tradition of leaving

KEY PERSON

Nassau Senior (1790–1864) was a leading economist and became famous for arguing against the restriction of factory working hours on the grounds that profit was only made in the last hour of working.

local affairs in the hands of local, unpaid people. When the Commissioners attempted to implement the new law in the north of England, during the depression years after 1837, the opposition was altogether more widespread and more vigorous. The system of poor relief in northern industrial towns had never been based on the 'allowance' system; relief policy had to reflect industrial conditions in which boom years were followed by years of depression and high unemployment. Workhouses were inappropriate in the circumstances of mass unemployment which existed in Lancashire and Yorkshire between 1837 and 1842. Working-class resistance to the introduction of workhouses – labelled 'Poor Law Bastilles' to highlight their prison-like conditions – coincided with opposition from Tory paternalists such as Oastler and Fielden. The Anti-Poor Law Associations which sprang up in the north united working-class radicals with Tory paternalists, an alliance which had already borne fruit in the agitation for factory reform in the early 1830s. Large public meetings, riots and demonstrations forced the Commission in London to stage a tactical retreat. The payment of outdoor relief to the unemployed was allowed to continue in Lancashire and the West Riding of Yorkshire and no workhouses were built in the West Riding until the 1850s.

Significance of the new Poor Law. Two final points need to be made about the significance of the new Poor Law. Firstly, the creation of elected Boards of Guardians introduced the electoral principle into local government for the first time. Although in the rural areas the Boards of Guardians were dominated by the local landowners, in the towns the control of the Poor Law fell upon the shoulders of the professional middle classes and small shopkeepers. Having gained the right to vote in parliamentary elections in 1832, the middle classes now had a vital role in the exercise of one of the functions of local government. The right to vote in Boards of Guardians' elections was given to ratepayers and this included female ratepayers. From 1875 women could also be elected to Boards of Guardians. There was also, however, another new feature to the administrative framework of the new Poor Law – the establishment of a central supervising commission which could oversee the implementation of the law. This compromise between an elected local body and a central supervising board of control set the pattern for future reforms of local government.

Secondly, the interests of farm labourers and urban workers were overridden in the passing of the Poor Law Amendment Act. The commission that produced the report and the ministers who framed the legislation worked on the assumption that poverty among the able-bodied poor was almost entirely due to 'indigence' and 'vice'. The workhouse system was therefore designed to be punitive and a deterrent against idleness. Working-class reactions in the north were entirely predictable but, having been excluded from the franchise in 1832, their chances of influencing government policy were limited. However, through effective organisation and widespread direct action the opponents of the Act were at least able to delay and modify its application in the north of England.

The Municipal Corporations Act, 1835

Following the Reform Act the next target for middle-class reformers was the system of local government in the towns. Most towns were run by closed corporations; that is, they were small, self-elected bodies of men which were frequently corrupt and which carried out none of the functions of a modern local authority. They were accountable to nobody. Because nonconformists were unable to hold municipal office before 1828, the town corporations tended to be Tory-Anglican **oligarchies**. The pressing problems of the growing towns were dealt with, if at all, by ad hoc bodies separate from the corporations. For example, improvement commissioners could be set up by Act of Parliament to undertake the paving, lighting and drainage of the streets.

In 1835, following the report of a Royal Commission whose secretary was the Benthamite, **Joseph Parkes**, the Whigs steered the Municipal Corporations Act through Parliament. The closed corporations were abolished and replaced by elected councils. The right to vote in local elections was given to all male ratepayers. The councils were given powers over lighting and safeguarding the streets but they could also petition Parliament for

KEY TERM

Oligarchies An oligarchy is a governing body consisting of a small number of powerful people, usually self-appointed. Most towns in the 18th century were controlled by small groups of Tory-Anglican landowners and merchants who were determined to keep power in their own hands.

KEY PERSON

Joseph Parkes (1796–1865) was a Birmingham lawyer who acted as the Liberal Party agent in the 1830s.

additional powers. Over the course of the next 20 years many town councils began providing museums, libraries, baths and wash-houses, and some began to involve themselves in the provision of gas and water.

Significance of the Municipal Corporations Act. The Municipal Corporations Act marked an important step in the direction of local democracy. The ratepayer franchise in council elections was far broader than the franchise in parliamentary elections. Moreover, the fact that one-third of councillors had to retire each year meant that there were annual elections for local government. The main beneficiaries of the Act in political terms were the Whig-Liberals. The Tory oligarchies were abolished and in the large industrial towns of Manchester, Leeds, Birmingham and Sheffield, Liberal majorities controlled the new town councils. Established local businessmen often predominated in local government although, from the 1840s and 1850s, increasing numbers of shopkeepers and professional people became involved.

Local government in the countryside, however, was left largely untouched in the post-reform era. County government was left firmly in the hands of the Justices of the Peace until elected county councils were established in 1888. The control of rural areas by the landed classes, therefore, survived largely unscathed.

Conclusion

After 1835 the Whigs lost much of the reforming impetus that they had shown in the previous five years. Although Melbourne, who succeeded Grey, was in office until 1841, his government lacked direction and confidence. Their parliamentary position was weak, as they depended on the Irish and the radicals for their majority, and their legislation was weakened by uncertainty and compromise. The main reform measures were:

- The establishment of civil registration of births, deaths and marriages in 1837.
- A Tithe Commutation Act for England and Wales, passed in 1836. This allowed tithe payers (mainly farmers) to pay tithes in money rather than in kind.

- A Tithes Act for Ireland, in 1838. This extended the changes in the method of tithe payment adopted for England and Wales to Ireland.
- Nonconformists were allowed to use their chapels for marriage services, rather than have to be married in the parish church.

These reforms only partly satisfied the demands of the English and Welsh nonconformists and of the Irish Catholics for the removal of any obligation which they owed to the Anglican Church. On many issues, therefore, the groups that had campaigned for reform in 1832, in the hope that it would lead to further, far-reaching reforms, were disappointed. The nonconformists felt let down on the issue of education and on their failure to secure full civil equality with the Anglicans. Working-class radicals had been excluded from the franchise in 1832, they had failed to secure the ten-hour day in factories and they had had the hated Poor Law imposed on them. Factory owners and businessmen were disappointed that the Whigs had not taken up the cause of free trade. Powerful established vested interests such as the church could still force compromises onto the Whigs on education and church reform. Despite their weakness after 1835, however, the Whigs did achieve much. An aristocratic party had recognised that the rising middle classes could not be denied a place in the constitution and they had set out on a course of further reform to accommodate the demands of a variety of groups. If their reforms were pragmatic compromises, this was no more than could be expected given the realities of the political situation at that time.

WHAT REFORMS WERE INTRODUCED BY THE MINISTRY OF SIR ROBERT PEEL, 1841–6?

The Whigs lost the general election in 1841 and the Conservatives, led by Sir Robert Peel, took office. As Home Secretary in the 1820s Peel had introduced reforms of the penal code, the prisons and of the Metropolitan Police. In his Tamworth Manifesto of 1834 he had outlined a cautious, pragmatic approach to reform, based on a recognition that the Reform Act had inaugurated a new political era in which middle-class interests would have to be accommodated within the constitution. As Prime Minister, therefore, Peel was prepared to be pragmatic in his approach to demands for reform but, as leader of the Conservative Party, he also had to take care not to alienate the party's traditional constituencies, the Anglicans and the landowners.

During the years 1841–6, a number of reforms were introduced by Peel's government.

- In 1842, a Mines Act prohibited the employment of women and children under the age of ten in the mines. Mines inspectors were appointed to check that the law was being applied.
- In 1844, a Factory Act set a maximum working day of twelve hours for women in textile factories. An attempt to include a stipulation that all children employed in factories should receive three hours' schooling per day had to be withdrawn after the nonconformists objected that the factory schools would be under the control of the Anglicans. Peel's government also rejected the demand for a ten-hour day.
- In 1844, a Bank Charter Act began the process of creating a more stable banking system whereby the Bank of England would have a monopoly over the issue of bank notes.
- In the budgets of 1842 and 1845 Peel took major steps towards free trade. In his 1842 budget he lowered tariffs generally and reintroduced income tax to make good the deficit in government revenue which would result. The 1845 budget went even further. Export duties on British goods were abolished. Import duties on most raw materials, including cotton, were also abolished and other duties were reduced.

These reforms generally won favour with the middle classes but Peel's pragmatic approach was causing increasing nervousness and unease among traditional Tories. Anglicans were alarmed in 1845 when Peel made the first annual state grant to a Catholic college at Maynooth in Ireland. Landowners and farmers grew increasingly concerned that the logic of his free trade policies was leading to the repeal of the Corn Laws, a form of agricultural protection that landowners and farmers considered to be vital to their interests.

Repeal of the Corn Laws

By 1845, Peel had indeed become convinced in his own mind that the Corn Laws would have to be repealed. Given the strength of opposition from within his own party to what many regarded as an act of betrayal, he preferred to wait until the next general election before he announced his change of policy. The onset of a serious famine in Ireland in 1845, caused by the failure of the potato crop, led Peel to bring forward his proposal to repeal the Corn Laws. The repeal of the Corn Laws was carried in 1846 by a parliamentary majority made up of Peel's supporters within the Conservative Party, the Whigs, radicals and Irish. Within his own party, however, a majority of MPs supported the charge made by Benjamin Disraeli that Peel had betrayed his party and the traditional interests which it represented. Barely more than 30 per cent of Conservative MPs supported Peel; the cost of the repeal of the Corn Laws was a damaging and permanent split in the Conservative Party. Peel was defeated on another issue – an Irish Coercion Bill – a few weeks after Corn Law repeal was carried and was forced to resign.

The Anti-Corn Law League. Opponents of the Corn Laws had been campaigning for repeal since the 1830s. In 1839 various local Anti-Corn Law Associations, particularly the ones centred on Manchester and Leeds, had merged to form a national Anti-Corn Law League. The League became a highly effective pressure group. It represented the views of the majority of the manufacturers and merchants of the northern industrial towns. It was well financed; in **Richard Cobden** and **John Bright** it had effective leadership and its objective was limited to one single change in the law.

Tactics of the League. The League adopted the standard methods of pressure-group politics. Itinerant lecturers went on speaking tours, public meetings were held, petitions were presented to Parliament and sympathetic articles were published in newspapers. Apart from a brief flirtation in

KEY PEOPLE

Richard Cobden (1804–65) was a journalist. He was elected MP for Stockport in 1841. **John Bright (1811–89)** was a manufacturer from Rochdale and a Quaker. He was elected MP for Durham in 1843. Together these two men became leading parliamentary spokesmen for the 'Manchester School' of radical opinion, supporting free trade and laissez-faire policies during the 1850s and 1860s.

1842 by some League members with the idea of a tax strike and a shutdown of factories, the League studiously avoided any unconstitutional methods. Violence was out of the question. The League was overwhelmingly middle class in its composition; although it made some efforts to win working-class support, the League was treated with suspicion by most working-class radicals of the time since it was believed that the cheaper food which it was claimed would follow repeal would lead to a lowering of wages.

Initially the League made little headway in persuading Parliament to consider its arguments. In 1841, however, Cobden adopted a new tactic. By putting up candidates in elections the League hoped to demonstrate the extent of support for the cause of repeal and, when some of these candidates were elected, the League was able to take the debate into the House of Commons itself. In the election of 1841, League candidates were returned from Stockport and the two Manchester seats. Using the provisions of the 1832 Reform Act, the League followed political parties in working to ensure that its own supporters were placed on electoral registers. The League also encouraged its supporters to buy property in county constituencies so that they could qualify to vote as 40-shilling freeholders. In this way the League was also able to win some county seats.

The 'Anti-League'. The growing impact of the League's campaign prompted landowners and farmers to organise themselves in defence of the Corn Laws. Agricultural Protection Societies, which sprang up in various parts of the country in the early 1840s, were linked together in a Central Agricultural Protection Society in 1843. Supported by country gentlemen and tenant farmers, with aristocratic leadership, the 'Anti-League' as it came to be known, did not have the intellectual clout of the League. In rural areas, however, the Anti-League demonstrated the continuing solidity of the traditional conservative forces – the landowners, supported by Anglican clergymen.

Significance of the League. 'The Anti-Corn Law League carried organised pressure to levels of sophistication not yet seen in British political life' (Evans, 1996). The methods used by radicals since the late eighteenth century were adopted and refined by the League, which also took advantage of the opportunities for extra-parliamentary pressure created by the 1832 Reform Act. By so doing the League kept the issue of Corn Law repeal in the public mind through the entire lifetime of Peel's ministry. Ultimately, however, the decision to repeal the Corn Laws was made by Peel, not because he was subjected to pressure from the League, but because he considered that repeal was of greater long-term benefit to the landowners than retention. Like the Whigs in 1832, Peel was making a timely concession to middle-class opinion in order to forge an alliance between landed property and commercial and industrial property. This alliance could then be a defence against demands for further erosion of the landowners' power and influence.

SUMMARY QUESTIONS

1 Why did the Reform Act lead to a series of further reforms?

2 What were the main influences that shaped the reform legislation of the 1830s?

3 Summarise the significance of each of the main reforms introduced during this period.

4 To what extent did Peel's reforms continue the work started by the Whigs and to what extent did his reforms break new ground?

5 Why did Peel encounter problems with his own party over the repeal of the Corn Laws?

6 How did the Anti-Corn Law League exploit opportunities created by the Reform Act?

7 Summarise the reasons why the League's campaign was effective.

CHAPTER 7

What was the Chartist movement?

INTRODUCTION

In 1838 a group of radicals from the London Working Men's Association (LWMA), together with six radical MPs, drew up a 'People's Charter' which aimed to establish a democratic electoral system. The Charter had six points:

- The right to vote for every man over the age of 21, providing he was of sound mind and not undergoing punishment for crime.
- A secret ballot.
- The abolition of the property qualification for MPs.
- The payment of salaries to MPs.
- Constituencies to be of equal size, based on the number of voters.
- Parliamentary elections to be held annually.

These six points were not new. They had been part of the radical stock-in-trade since the late eighteenth century and had been popularised by leaders such as Cobbett and Hunt. The men who drew up the 'Charter' were aiming to draw up a draft parliamentary bill, incorporating the six points, and present it to Parliament accompanied by pressure from outside in the form of demonstrations and petitions. The successes of O'Connell's Catholic Association and Attwood's Birmingham Political Union in mobilising public opinion and bringing pressure to bear on Parliament were the models for this new campaign for the 'People's Charter'. Attwood himself was one of the radical MPs who drew up the Charter and helped to plan the pressure-group strategy. By 1839–40, however, the phenomenon of 'Chartism' had grown into the largest mobilisation of public opinion ever seen in Britain. It had outgrown the LWMA and the political unions and thrown up new organisations with a new generation of leaders.

WHY DID THE CHARTIST MOVEMENT APPEAR AT THIS TIME?

The Chartist movement grew out of disappointment with the Reform Act of 1832 and the failure of the reformed Parliament to improve the conditions of the working classes. The Whigs' strategy in 1832 had been to enfranchise the middle classes but to exclude working people from any participation in the political process. The political unions had mobilised popular support in favour of the bill and this pressure had been instrumental in getting the bill passed. Once the Reform Act became law and both parties declared themselves to be opposed to any further extensions of the franchise, those working people who had supported the Reform campaign felt betrayed. There were also other reasons why disillusionment with the reformed Parliament and the Whig government should have been so strong by the late 1830s:

- The Factory Act of 1833 favoured the manufacturers by not enforcing a ten-hour day and not regulating the hours of work of adult male workers.
- The Poor Law Amendment Act, which introduced workhouses based on the principle of 'less eligibility', was regarded as oppressive and punitive towards the poor. It is significant that the upsurge of Chartist activity in the north of England coincided with the start of the Poor Law Commissioners' attempts to apply the Act there.
- A severe trade depression began in 1837 and lasted until 1842. The same ingredients of social distress caused by high bread prices, unemployment and short-time working, which were important factors in the radical campaigns of 1816–19 and 1831–2, were also present in the Chartist years. The laissez-faire standpoint on economic policy, to which the Whigs largely subscribed, offered the unemployed no comfort that their distress could be relieved by government action.

There were therefore many reasons why working people should have been suffering distress at the end of the 1830s and why they should have felt disillusionment and frustration – with the Whig government in particular and the political system in general. Chartism drew all of these strands together and channelled the discontents into a campaign for the 'People's Charter'.

Chartism was not, however, simply a reflex response to the difficulties being experienced by working people at the end of the 1830s. It was the culmination of a long tradition of radical activity in London and the provinces which began with the London Corresponding Society in the late eighteenth century, continued through the post-war Hampden Clubs and political unions, and led on to the Reform Bill agitation of 1831–2. Even after the Reform Act was passed and most of the political unions faded into the background, radical political activity continued through the campaign for a cheap, unstamped, free press. Chartism, therefore, grew out of a radical tradition that had been challenging authority and campaigning for democracy over a period of 40 years. By the late 1830s there existed, in London and in the main industrial centres, a large core of politically-aware working men who formed the nucleus of the radical organisations that merged into the campaign for the People's Charter.

HOW DID THE CHARTIST MOVEMENT TRY TO ACHIEVE ITS AIMS?

Following the publication of the People's Charter, large meetings to promote it were held in many parts of the country. For example, there were large rallies in Glasgow, Birmingham, Manchester and Leeds in 1838. Work was begun on collecting signatures for a national petition and on organising a Chartist National Convention to put pressure on the government.

National Convention
The National Convention met in London in February 1839; but immediately splits began to appear over the issue of a 'moral force' (peaceful persuasion) versus 'physical force' (violence) strategy to achieve their ends. The Convention moved to Birmingham and began to draw up plans for a 'sacred month' (general strike) and a run on the banks. By the summer, the Chartist movement was facing

serious difficulties. Parliament rejected the petition by 235 votes to 46; arrests were made in Birmingham; the Convention broke up in confusion. There was talk of a national rebellion, but only in South Wales was there any serious attempt at an uprising. In November 1839 about 300 coal miners and ironworkers marched on Newport. In the violence that followed over 20 marchers were killed. Following this incident the government decided to suppress the movement and over 500 Chartists were arrested, including most of the movement's leaders.

National Charter Association

In 1840 a National Charter Association was formed, led by **Feargus O'Connor**. The NCA became the main organisational focus of the movement during the 1840s. At its height in 1842 the NCA claimed to have over 400 branches and 50,000 members. The revival of the movement in 1842 led to the calling of a second National Convention and the collection of signatures for a second petition. Once again Parliament rejected the petition, this time by 287 votes to 49. As in 1839, the failure of the constitutional approach to Parliament led to disturbances. Starting in Staffordshire and spreading to the industrial districts of the north of England and Scotland, there was a wave of strikes and industrial sabotage – in the so-called 'Plug Plot' the plugs of steam boilers in cotton mills were removed to stop them being used. Once again the authorities responded with a wave of arrests. By the end of 1842, with the economy reviving and the Chartist leadership collapsing in confusion, popular support for Chartism declined rapidly.

Revival in 1848

There was a further revival in 1848. Against a background of worsening trade and growing unemployment there were riots in Birmingham and Glasgow, and Chartist activity began to increase in the northern industrial districts. A third National Convention was summoned and a third petition was drawn up. This time the Chartists planned to accompany the petition to Parliament with a mass Chartist rally on Kennington Common in London. The authorities feared serious disorder would result from the rally and took extensive steps to contain the threat. In addition to the

Feargus O'Connor

HEINEMANN ADVANCED HISTORY

A contemporary engraving of the mass Chartist rally on Kennington Common in 1848.

large numbers of police and troops who were on duty in London on the day of the rally, over 10,000 middle-class recruits were enrolled as special constables. The procession to Parliament was banned. In the event, far fewer Chartist supporters than anticipated actually attended the rally, and O'Connor urged his supporters to disperse peacefully. Once again the petition was rejected by Parliament and Chartism had suffered a humiliating defeat. There was a further wave of arrests that removed most of the Chartist leaders from the scene, and the movement once again declined.

Although the NCA continued in existence until 1860, the movement never regained the mass support that it had attracted in its early years. By 1858 it was apparent that the campaign for the People's Charter was not going to achieve its objectives. The remaining Chartists decided to work with the parliamentary radicals for more moderate, limited reforms of the political system.

WHAT WAS THE NATURE OF THE CHARTIST MOVEMENT?

A national movement?

Chartism was a mass movement that had strong support in many different parts of the country; but support for the Charter was also very weak in other areas. The Charter was drawn up in London by radicals who belonged to a long tradition of popular radicalism in the capital. Men like

William Lovett had been involved in the Reform Bill campaign of 1831–2 and had links with earlier campaigns in the post-war years and in the 1790s. Attwood and the Birmingham Political Union were also involved in the early stages of the movement. Increasingly, however, the centre of gravity of the Chartist campaign moved to the industrial districts of the north of England – South Lancashire and the West Riding of Yorkshire. It was also strongly supported in the declining woollen towns of the west of England, in the framework-knitting towns of the East Midlands and in the industrial districts of Scotland. The Chartist appeal was strongest among the handloom weavers and framework knitters whose livelihoods were threatened not only by the short-term trade depression but also by the long-term displacement of their crafts by machinery. Support was weaker among the factory workers and almost non-existent among farm labourers.

The patchy nature of Chartist support has led some historians to conclude that it was not a national movement. Briggs (1959) stressed the local variations in the Chartist movement and began a move among historians to focus research on local studies. The works of historians such as Jones (1975) and Epstein and Thompson (1982), however, led to a re-evaluation of Chartism as a national movement. The Charter itself provided a common focus for the movement; work involved in collecting signatures for the Chartist National Petitions in 1839, 1842 and 1848, gave local groups a feeling of shared participation in a common national endeavour. After 1840 the National Charter Association, led by Feargus O'Connor, provided a co-ordination that had hitherto been lacking. Above all, **the *Northern Star*** and its proprietor, O'Connor, helped to 'nationalise the discontents'. The *Northern Star*, despite its name, was a national newspaper that, at its height in 1839 sold 36,000 copies per issue. Although O'Connor fell out with almost every other Chartist leader, he did provide an inspirational leadership which helped to sustain the movement through the 1840s.

Chartism, therefore, was a movement that had a national appeal. Although there were regional and local variations in

KEY FACT

The Northern Star The readership of the *Northern Star* was, of course, much higher than the bare circulation figures of 36,000 copies. Each copy would have been read aloud at meetings of local Chartist groups.

support for the Charter, the organisation provided by the NCA, the leadership of O'Connor and the support and encouragement of the *Northern Star* helped to build a national movement.

A political movement?

Support for Chartism grew out of economic and social discontent and mass support was at its greatest during times of severe economic depression – in 1838–9, in 1842 and in 1848. Chartism appealed most strongly to those groups who were suffering economic hardship, particularly the handloom weavers and framework knitters. The movement had little appeal in times of economic growth or to workers in industries that were booming, such as engineering. Many contemporaries and historians alike have therefore seen Chartism as essentially a social and economic movement rather than a genuinely political one.

Chartism was not, however, merely a reaction against bad times. Chartists made a connection between economic hardship and 'misgovernment' in the same way that earlier radical leaders such as William Cobbett had done. The Chartist case was that political reform in 1832 had not gone far enough in rooting out 'Old Corruption' and removing the oppressive weight of aristocratic government from the shoulders of the poor. They believed that a democratically-elected government would not tax the poor, would not govern in the interests of a narrow elite and would restore to the ordinary people their ancient liberties. Political reform was thus the essential prerequisite to economic advancement for the majority of the people. All of the demands of the Chartists were political; if implemented, the Six Points would have completely transformed the political system in the direction of a fully democratic system. Chartism was, first and foremost, a radical political movement.

A working-class movement?

The overwhelming majority of Chartists were working people but this does not necessarily mean that the movement was an outright expression of class politics. When the movement began in the late 1830s, it was a campaign of resistance to the policies of the Whig government and of protest against the severe distress that was sweeping through the industrial districts. As such, the campaign could attract support from sympathisers in the middle and landed classes. Attwood, the leader of the Birmingham Political Union, was closely involved in the drawing up of the Six Points. There were some middle-class representatives at the first Chartist Convention in 1839. After the failure of the convention and the violent turn of events that culminated in the Newport Rising, most middle-class supporters withdrew from Chartism. After 1840, the Chartist movement became more distinctively working-class in character.

Not all Chartists showed hostility to other classes, although there was a very strong element of class conflict in the language of some of the leaders and in some of the literature. The LWMA and William Lovett followed a strategy of class co-operation, similar to that adopted so successfully by the BPU in 1831–2. By contrast, the London Democratic Association, founded by **George Julian Harney** in 1838, adopted a strategy of class conflict. In the north of England, Chartists showed particular hostility to the Anti-Corn Law League, a middle-class organisation which they accused of campaigning for 'Cheap Bread' in order for manufacturers to reduce wages. In the factory districts, Chartists broke up League meetings. Much of the Chartist leadership believed Chartism to be a class movement, but among ordinary Chartist supporters there were variations in the degree of antagonism towards the middle classes. In Birmingham, for example, the class co-operation that had been evident in the campaign for the Reform Act was still a feature of the Chartist movement. **Joseph Sturge**'s Complete Suffrage Union, which was founded in Birmingham in 1842, was an attempt to build a united working- and middle-class campaign in support of both the Charter and the repeal of the Corn Laws.

Epstein and Thompson (1982) have shown how Chartism was 'informed by a strong sense of class identity, a strong defence of working-class institutions and customs and a pervasive belief in the importance and strength of the democratic process'. Chartism drew its support mainly from the industrial districts at a time when small,

KEY PEOPLE

George Julian Harney (1817–97) was a former shopboy who had worked for Hetherington. A Socialist in his politics, he became an ally of Karl Marx and Friedrich Engels. He had his own newspaper, *The Red Republican*.

Joseph Sturge (1793–1859) was a wealthy corn merchant from Birmingham. He was a Quaker by religion.

close-knit communities were still the norm. The shared experiences of early industrialisation for groups such as coal miners, handloom weavers, metal workers, framework knitters and factory workers bred a strong sense of community and a fierce independence. The Chartist movement continued a process of political education that had already begun in these communities in the years after the Napoleonic wars. The mass meeting, the collection of signatures for petitions, the lectures delivered by visiting lecturers and the reading aloud of radical newspapers were all part of this political culture. Chartism drew all of these strands together and gave local communities a sense that they were part of a wider national movement; but in the regions the movement reflected local conditions and developed distinctive local characteristics. It was this which gave the Chartist movement its vitality and its identity but, since the working-class communities varied considerably from place to place, a degree of fragmentation within the movement was inevitable. This factor alone made the Chartist achievement of building a national political movement with a common political programme all the more remarkable.

WAS CHARTISM A FAILURE?

By 1918 five of the Six Points of the Charter had been achieved, but none of the Chartist demands were met while the movement was in existence. In these terms, therefore, Chartism must be judged a failure. To conclude from this, however, that the Chartist movement achieved nothing would be a mistake. What, then, did it achieve?

- The movement developed a distinctive working-class political culture, particularly in the north of England. Through Chartism working people had learned how to organise protest movements; they had developed a healthy scepticism towards the state and they had learned the value of independent action. Later in the nineteenth century, former Chartists were key figures in movements as diverse as the campaigns for education reform and temperance reform, in trade unions and in the early socialist groups of the 1880s. Former Chartists also played a prominent role in the radical wing of the Liberal Party of the 1860s and 1870s.

- The Chartists kept alive the demand for a further extension of the franchise and other democratic reforms after both the Whigs and the Tories had declared that the Reform Act of 1832 was a 'final and irrevocable' settlement of the constitutional question. Although the next extension of the franchise in 1867 only happened after Chartist pressure had died down, the Chartist movement was a link between working-class support for the 1832 Reform Act and popular pressure for parliamentary reform in the 1860s.

WHY DID CHARTISM NOT ACHIEVE MORE?

In analysing the reasons why Chartism did not succeed in its central aims, historians have traditionally focused on divisions within the movement. There were two main divisions:

- **Disputes between the leaders.** O'Connor was the main inspiration behind the NCA and the *Northern Star* and dominated the movement in the 1840s. He denounced Lovett's moderation in 1839–40 and continued to attack his 'new move' from 1841 when Lovett concentrated more on education. O'Connor, in fact, alienated most of the other Chartist leaders at one time or another, but his force of personality, his powerful oratory and his clear-sighted view that only the NCA could provide the focus for Chartist unity, were vital to the Chartists' success in building a mass movement in the 1840s.
- **Divisions over tactics.** There was a basic division between those who advocated the use of peaceful persuasion (moral force) and those who were prepared to advocate an armed uprising (physical force). This argument caused the break-up of the first Chartist National Convention in 1839 and also lay behind the disputes between O'Connor and Lovett. The 'moral force' Chartists, who were drawn mainly from the skilled artisans, believed that the movement had to be careful not to alienate potential middle-class support and not to give the state an excuse to use the full force of repression

against them. 'Physical force' Chartists, on the other hand, believed that only the threat, or actual use, of armed force would win concessions from the state. These divisions were important in weakening the movement but the dividing line was not always clear-cut. Many 'moral force' Chartists were prepared to use violent language and supported the right of the citizen to bear arms; many 'physical force' Chartists talked the language of resistance but had no intention of leading an armed rebellion.

Disunity, therefore, can be exaggerated. Fragmentation was inevitable in a movement that brought together so many different strands. What was remarkable was the degree of cohesion that was actually achieved in such a disparate movement. Explanations for Chartist lack of success need to focus more on the role of the state, particularly in two respects:

- **Repression.** The Chartists came up against the power of the state at a time when that power was beginning to increase significantly. The government made full use of the powers of arrest to detain Chartists at critical times, such as 1839–40, 1842 and 1848. Chartist leaders were under almost constant risk of imprisonment. When mass demonstrations were held, the government could call on the regular army and the newly professionalised police forces. The new railways allowed troops to be moved rapidly to any trouble spots. When the Chartists attempted to overawe the government by sheer force of numbers in the Kennington Common demonstration of 1848, they were confronted by massive numbers of police, soldiers and special constables. The recruitment of special constables was especially significant. Most of those came from the middle classes; they enrolled in order to support the government's efforts to maintain law and order and protect property. The Whig strategy in the Reform Act of forging an alliance between aristocratic landowners and middle-class property owners so as to preserve the constitution, had succeeded.
- **Reform.** The Chartist message was that the cause of the people's troubles was misgovernment, stemming from a corrupt and unrepresentative political system. That

message was beginning to be undermined by the policies of Peel's government (1841–6) and the Whig government of Russell (1846–52). The Mines Act of 1842, the Factory Acts of 1844 and 1847 and the repeal of the Corn Laws in 1846 did seem to indicate that governments were beginning to rule in the interests of the people as a whole.

CONCLUSION

The experience of the Chartist movement showed how the political climate had been changed by the passing of the 1832 Reform Act. There were clear connections between the Reform Act and Chartism. Firstly, the campaign for the Charter was partly a reaction to the feelings of betrayal by working-class radicals, who were still denied the right to vote. Secondly, the success of popular pressure in forcing the Reform Act through, against the opposition of the House of Lords, encouraged radical politicians to believe that similar pressure, on an even greater scale, would force Parliament to grant further concessions. Ironically, the defences of the state against such pressure from the unenfranchised had been strengthened by the Reform Act. Aristocratic government now had the support of the middle classes in resisting any moves towards democracy; and the resources at the government's disposal had been strengthened by the era of reform which followed the passing of the Act.

SUMMARY QUESTIONS

1 Outline the main reasons why working people were feeling disillusioned and frustrated by the late 1830s.

2 To what extent was Chartism

   (a) a national movement?

   (b) a political movement?

   (c) a working-class movement?

3 What did Chartism achieve?

AS ASSESSMENT: PARLIAMENTARY REFORM, 1815–50

STRUCTURED, SOURCE-BASED QUESTIONS IN THE STYLE OF EDEXCEL

Study the source and then answer the questions which follow:

Source 1. *Lord Macaulay, speech in the House of Commons on parliamentary reform, 2 March 1831.*

> Unless this measure, or some similar measure, be speedily adopted, great and terrible calamities will befall us. I support this measure as a measure of Reform; but I support it still more as a measure of conservation. We say, and we say justly, that it is not by mere numbers, but by those with property and education that the nation ought to be governed. Yet we are excluding from all share in government vast numbers of property owners and also many who have good education.

1 What, according to Source 1, is Macaulay's attitude towards parliamentary reform? **(5)**

2 What arguments did those who opposed parliamentary reform use against it in the years 1830–2? **(7)**

3 What impact did the Reform Act of 1832 have on the political system in the period to 1850? **(18)**

Reading
Before answering these questions you should read Chapters 2, 3, 4 and 5 of this book.

Planning
Plan your answers before you begin. In your plans you need to identify the key points you wish to make and how they relate to the question. Each question contains key words which you need to identify and use as the focus for your answer. Use the mark allocation for each part of a structured question as a rough guide to the amount of time you should devote to it.

Writing

- Make sure your answers are focused directly on the questions. Key words are vital guides here.
- Your answers must have carefully selected quotes from the source(s) and/or factual examples drawn from your own knowledge. These are essential as supporting evidence to illustrate the points you are making.
- Your arguments must be coherent. They must follow logically from one point to another.
- Good grammar and spelling are important.

How to answer the questions

Question 1. This question is asking you to identify and explain Lord Macaulay's attitude to parliamentary reform. Use quotes from the source to show that Macaulay is clearly in favour of reform but that he wishes to restrict the franchise to those with property and education. A key phrase in the source is 'I support it . . . as a measure of conservation'. You need to highlight this phrase and explain, using your background knowledge, who Macaulay was and what he was trying to conserve.

Question 2. In this answer you need to use your background knowledge to identify those groups who opposed parliamentary reform and the reasons they gave for their opposition. Note that this question is specifically about the period 1830–2, by which time most of the middle classes had come round to support moderate parliamentary reform. Those who still opposed it during the reform crisis were the Tory Party and their supporters among the landowning aristocracy and gentry. Church of England bishops in the House of Lords joined the Tory peers in blocking the Reform Bill in 1831. Part of their opposition stemmed from their determination to protect their privileges and their vested interests in a governmental system based on patronage. An answer which focuses purely on these aspects, however, will not fully explain the reasons for their opposition. You should note that it was possible to oppose reform on grounds of principle as well as self-interest. Fear of revolution and a belief that only the aristocracy were capable of ruling in the interests of all were sincerely held beliefs. It would be useful to be able to quote from the speeches of Sir Robert Peel on the reform question.

Question 3. This question requires an essay-style answer in which you use your background knowledge to explain and analyse the consequences of the Reform Act. Note that the key words here are 'impact', 'political system' and 'period to 1850'. A brief summary of the main terms of the Act will be necessary before you go on to explain the consequences of the Act in terms of the following:

- Voters and constituencies, the distribution of seats.
- The conduct of elections.

- The influence of the aristocracy in the reformed system, including composition of the House of Commons.
- The impact of pressure from outside Parliament on government policies.
- Changes in political parties.
- Further reforms, e.g. the Municipal Corporations Act.

The better answers will be those in which candidates develop an argument about the extent of change which the Reform Act brought about. You may wish to agree with Gash's argument that the Reform Act actually changed very little, or with Evans who claims that the Reform Act did indeed have far-reaching consequences for the political system. Either approach is permissible; the key to a good answer is the way the argument is organised, whether it is sustained throughout the essay, and the quality of the supporting evidence which is used to illustrate the arguments.

A COURSE ESSAY QUESTION IN THE STYLE OF AQA

Question 1

'The Reform Bill is a trick to keep the aristocrats safe in their places.' Assess the validity of this criticism of the Reform Act of 1832.

Answering essay questions
To gain the highest marks in essay questions you will need to do the following:

Analyse throughout the essay. This can be done by making sure that you plan a line of argument before you start the writing. At the start of each paragraph you must make the next point of your argument, explain it and then use evidence to support your point. Always keep the question in mind, especially the key words. These will act as a reference point to help you keep the argument relevant.

To help you keep your analysis flowing, start each paragraph with words that lead into an argument. Some examples of these are:

The most important reason is . . .

Another key point is that . . .

In contrast with . . .

One of the most significant consequences was . . .

Support your argument with well-selected evidence. The factual examples you give must be accurate and relevant to the point you are trying to make. Give enough factual detail to make clear how the example relates to the point you are making but do not allow yourself to drift into irrelevant narrative. The lack of any factual examples will reduce your argument to the level of an 'unsupported assertion' which will earn very few marks at all.

Make a clear and consistent attempt to reach a judgement. In your essay you should argue throughout. You must reflect on the evidence you have given and make points which answer the question directly. Your conclusion must be consistent with the arguments you have developed through your essay.

Show evidence of independent thought. You do not have to be original. Independent thought means that you have reflected on what you have read in books and that you can explain the ideas you have encountered in your own words.

Refer to the works of historians you have read. You are expected to be familiar with the different interpretations put forward by historians and aware that many aspects of the subject are controversial. This should be reflected in your arguments.

Language skills are important. It is essential that you write in paragraphs and that your grammar is accurate. Learn the correct spellings of people and places.

How to answer this question

Reading. You will need to read Chapters 2, 4 and 5 in the AS part of this book.

Key words. In this question the key words are: 'Reform Bill', 'trick', 'keep aristocrats safe', 'assess the validity', 'criticism'.

Planning. At the outset, be clear in your mind what your main line of argument will be. This can be called the 'key theme' of your answer. In this case your key theme might be as follows:

> 'It was clear that the Whigs' strategy was to preserve the power of the aristocracy and to strengthen the political system against the demands for democracy. A comparison between the pre-reformed system and the system which emerged after 1832, however, shows that the system changed in ways that the Whigs had not predicted.'

Having outlined your key theme you can then begin to plan your paragraph structure. Bear in mind that this question requires a comparison between the pre-1832 and post-1832 systems of government. Comparisons work best if you use a point-by-point approach.

It will also be necessary for you to define terms such as 'aristocracy' and 'Reform Bill'. Although not made explicit in the quote, you would earn credit if you showed awareness that the quote was made by a radical critic of the Reform Bill.

Writing. In your answer you need to include the following:

- Analysis of the ways in which the pre-reformed system was dominated by the aristocracy.
- Acknowledgement of the fact that the pre-reformed system did allow other 'interests' to be represented in Parliament, either by direct election to Parliament of merchants etc., or through 'virtual representation'.
- Acknowledgement of the fact that the aristocracy was not a 'closed caste'. Successful middle-class businessmen could and did become landowners and gain acceptance among the landed classes.
- Analysis of the post-reform system of elections and of the composition of parliaments and governments. This should highlight those aspects which had not changed as well as those which had.
- Reference to the specific means by which the aristocracy were able to keep their influence over elections, e.g. the Chandos clause, the survival of pocket boroughs etc.
- An assessment of the extent to which the political system was changed by the Reform Act. This should be the main theme of your conclusion.

STRUCTURED, SOURCE-BASED QUESTIONS IN THE STYLE OF AQA

Study Sources A, B and C below and then answer the questions which follow:

Source A. *Resolutions of the Birmingham Political Union, January 1830.*

That Honourable House [of Commons], in its present state, is evidently too far removed in habits, wealth and station, from the wants and interests of the lower and middle classes of the people, to have any just views respecting them, or any close identity of feeling with them. The great aristocratical interests of all kinds are well represented there. The landed interest, the church, the law, the monied interest - all these have [taken over], as it were, the House of Commons into their own hands, the members of that honourable House being immediately and closely connected with those great interests. But the interests of Industry and Trade have scarcely any representation at all! These, the source of all its wealth and all its strength, are comparatively unrepresented.

Source B. *From a petition presented by Joseph Hume in favour of reform, 1830.*

[The petitioners] did not expect that any effectual remedies would be applied unless a thorough reform in Parliament should be accomplished, and the right of election given to every individual paying rates and taxes. But they conceived that no extension of the <u>elective franchise</u> would be beneficial, unless the mode of voting by ballot should be adopted.

Source C. *From a speech by Thomas Macaulay in defence of the Reform Bill, 1832.*

I hold it to be clearly [necessary] that, in a country like this, the right of suffrage should depend on a [financial] qualification. Every argument which would [persuade] me to oppose universal suffrage, [persuades] me to support the measure which is now before us. I oppose universal suffrage because I think it would produce a destructive revolution. I support this measure because I am sure that it is our best security against revolution.

(a) With reference to Source B and using your own knowledge, define the term 'elective franchise'. (3)

(b) Study Source A. What are the strengths and weaknesses of this source as evidence of the composition of the House of Commons before the 1832 Reform Act? (7)

(c) Study all the sources and use your own knowledge.
'An examination of the 1832 Reform Act shows that it was the views of Macaulay that prevailed, not those of the Birmingham Political Union and Hume.'
Do you agree with this point of view? Give reasons for your answer. (15)

Reading
In order to answer these questions you need to read Chapters 2, 4 and 5 of this book.

How to answer these questions
Question (a). Note that the question asks you to use the information in the source and your own knowledge. The question is worth three marks, so a long answer is not required.

From your reading of the source and your background knowledge you should know that the phrase 'elective franchise' means 'the right to vote' in parliamentary elections. Merely to state this in your answer, however, will not earn many marks. You need to demonstrate your knowledge and understanding by giving details of who could vote in elections before 1832 and pointing out that the actual numbers of voters represented a very small proportion of the adult population.

Question (b). This question is asking you to assess both how useful and how reliable this source is as evidence of the composition of the House of Commons before 1832. It is a question that can be answered on a number of levels.

At a basic level, it is clear that this source comes from one of the main organisations campaigning for reform in 1830–2 and that the people who drew up this resolution would presumably have been well informed about the situation in Parliament. Using your knowledge of the BPU and the debate over parliamentary reform, however, you should be able to recognise that the source comes from one side in that debate and that it will contain bias. In making the point about bias, however, you need to be able to quote selectively from the source to illustrate the point.

The best answers will place the source in its context and show that, although it gives a valuable insight into the minds of those who were campaigning for reform, it does not give a full and accurate picture of the composition of the unreformed House of Commons. You should point out that, although Parliament was undoubtedly dominated by the aristocracy, other interests were represented in Parliament and that the system allowed able men from non-aristocratic backgrounds, e.g. Sir Robert Peel, to rise to the top.

Question (c). In order to answer this question you first need to know who the authors of these sources were. The BPU, led by Attwood, was the most successful of the pro-reform groups outside Parliament, and attracted support from both middle-class and working-class reformers in Birmingham. It was in favour of parliamentary reform but not universal suffrage. Joseph Hume was a leading radical MP and campaigner for reform causes. He supported the extension of the franchise and the secret ballot, but not universal suffrage. Lord Macaulay was a leading spokesman for the Whigs in Parliament and advocated limited reform as a way of preserving the power of the aristocracy.

At first sight, the argument put forward in the quote seems to be correct. Note that Joseph Hume not only calls for a widening of the franchise but also 'voting by ballot'. You will know that the Whigs considered and then rejected a proposal to introduce a secret ballot in 1832. You will also know that the 'right of election' was not given 'to every individual paying rates and taxes' as Hume advocated. Simple agreement with the quote, however, will not be enough.

From your knowledge of the reform crisis and of the Reform Act that was eventually passed, you should be able to argue that reformers like Attwood and Hume were not campaigning for universal suffrage – the middle classes generally were just as afraid of enfranchising the working classes as were the Whigs – and that they were not entirely disappointed with the terms of the Reform Act. You should also note that many of the Whigs believed that the Reform Act had gone too far and were fearful of its consequences.

AS SECTION: VOTES FOR WOMEN, 1867–1928

INTRODUCTION

The story of the political struggle to win the vote for women begins in the 1860s, a time when the issue of extending the franchise for men had been put back onto the political agenda by organisations such as the Reform League. When a bill to enfranchise more men was put before Parliament in 1866–7, the Liberal MP **John Stuart Mill** put forward an amendment to give the vote to women on the same terms as men. Although the proposal was defeated, the issue of women's suffrage had taken a major step forward and was to be taken up by a growing number of women in the years that followed. As Parliament took tentative and cautious steps towards extending male suffrage – Reform Acts in 1867 and 1884 gave the vote to male householders and lodgers in the towns and then the countryside – the exclusion of women from the right to vote in parliamentary elections came to be seen as the most striking example of the civil inequality between men and women. There were many other ways in which women suffered inequality and discrimination, and the women who campaigned for female suffrage were also involved in other campaigns to gain greater equality and improve the opportunities for female advancement. As will be shown, these campaigns did achieve some success but progress was slow; increasingly, reformers came to the conclusion that further progress towards full equality for women would only be achieved when Parliament represented women as well as men.

International comparisons
The women's suffrage movement in Britain was not unique. Similar movements had emerged in other countries

in the second half of the nineteenth century, and in some countries progress had been more rapid. New Zealand was the first country to grant women the right to vote, in 1893, followed by Australia 1902, Finland 1906, Norway 1913 and Denmark 1915. There were many other countries, however, where a woman's right to vote was granted later than in Britain. Germany (1919) and the USA (1920) were behind Britain in this respect but ahead of Italy (1945) and France (1945).

Suffragists and suffragettes

The campaign for the female franchise which began in the late 1860s was overwhelmingly middle class in membership and used the classic tactics of peaceful persuasion used by pressure groups. These methods were successful in persuading Parliament to pass a number of reforms redressing some of the legal inequalities suffered by women and in converting a growing number of MPs to the merits of their case. Parliament debated Women's Suffrage bills every year between 1867 and 1884; by the late 1880s a majority of MPs had expressed their support but no Women's Suffrage Bill was passed. No government in this period would introduce its own Women's Suffrage Bill because to do so would reopen the whole debate about the male suffrage, and the main political parties were constrained by calculations as to how further reform would affect their fortunes. In 1903 a new, more militant women's suffrage organisation, the Women's Social and Political Union, was formed with the aim of forcing the issue of women's suffrage to the top of the political agenda. These 'suffragettes' captured the headlines during the period 1905–14 but it is debatable whether they advanced the cause of women's suffrage; much recent historical research has emphasised the continuing vitality of the non-militant 'suffragist' movement during these years and their contribution to the eventual success of their campaign.

The First World War

The war changed the climate in which the issue of votes for women was debated. The opportunities for women to take on work previously done only by men and their overall contribution to the war effort had a significant impact on attitudes. With the militant campaign suspended and increasing talk in the later years of the war of the need for post-war 'reconstruction', the debate over the issue was able to take place in a more positive atmosphere. When the government began to consider electoral reform in 1916, an opportunity presented itself for women's suffrage campaigners to press their case in a reasoned and calm manner. In 1918, before the war had ended, a Representation of the People Act was passed, giving some women the right to vote in parliamentary elections. That opposition to women's suffrage was not entirely dispelled by the war, however, is borne out by the fact that women were not granted the right to vote in 1918 on the same terms as men. The importance of the First World War in changing attitudes and creating opportunities is generally accepted by historians; but it is important not to lose sight of the fact that the movement for greater political equality for women reflected wider social and economic changes that had been gathering pace since the middle of the nineteenth century.

CHAPTER 8

What was the status of women in Victorian society?

'SEPARATE SPHERES'

A widely held view in the mid-nineteenth century – one held by many women as well as by men – was that men and women occupied 'separate spheres'. According to this view, men and women were fitted by nature to perform different roles. The man's world was that of work, politics and war. Women were best suited to the private, domestic sphere where they could raise children, act as moral guide and give support and comfort to their husbands. According to this view, which many held was part of God's design, women were the civilising element in society. Male and female opponents of female suffrage argued that to put women into politics would detract from their femininity.

The family

Victorian society cultivated a high ideal of the home and the family as being the basis of a stable social order. According to this ideal, morality and piety were first learned 'at the mother's knee' and, in the home, children learned the habits of obedience, loyalty, honesty and hard work. The conventional view of the family was that the wife's role was subordinate to that of the husband. This convention was backed by law. In law, every husband had the right of 'reasonable chastisement' of his wife. Wives did not have the *legal* right to leave an intolerable husband until 1852. Married women had no right to own property or keep an income independently of their husbands. In short, the law was based on the assumption that a woman, on marriage, forfeited the right to an independent existence. This model of family life mainly applied to middle-class families. In many working-class families the daily realities of the struggle to make ends meet necessitated the wife taking on paid employment, either outside the home or by taking in work, as well as having responsibility for the raising of children and domestic chores. Under such circumstances the ideal of the mother as 'the angel of the hearth' had little basis in reality.

Legal changes. The law, however, was beginning to be changed so that, by the 1880s, the legal position of married women was marginally improved.

- In 1839, a Custody of Infants Act allowed women who had separated from an intolerable husband the right to apply for the custody of children under the age of 7.
- In 1857, a Matrimonial Causes Act allowed for easier divorce. Before this change in the law, divorce was only available through a private Act of Parliament, a procedure which was far too expensive for all but the wealthiest. Under the new law, a Divorce Court was established and legal proceedings became cheaper, although divorce was still too expensive for working-class women. The terms on which divorce could be granted were also discriminatory. For a man to divorce his wife, he had only to prove that she had committed adultery. For a wife to divorce a husband, she had to prove that he had been cruel or that he had deserted her in addition to committing adultery.
- In 1870, a Married Women's Property Act allowed women to keep any property or income acquired after their marriage. This did not satisfy the demands of those women who had been campaigning for a change in the law. The original proposal to allow married women to keep all their property, irrespective of when it had been acquired, was defeated by opposition in the House of Lords, where it was viewed as an attack on the 'unity of the family, under the sovereignty of the husband'.
- In 1878, magistrates' courts were empowered to grant separation and maintenance orders to the wives of abusive husbands. This was a change that helped working-class women in particular, since proceedings in magistrates' courts were much cheaper than in the Divorce Court.
- In 1882, a second Married Women's Property Act allowed women to keep all property and income acquired independently of their husband, irrespective of when it had been acquired.

Middle-class women

Although employment opportunities for single women were improving by the latter part of the nineteenth century, the vast majority of women still sought marriage despite the loss of independence that this entailed. This was equally true for women from both the middle and the working classes although their experiences within marriage would be very different. Within the middle-class family, the wife's duties were the ordering of the home, the deployment of the servants and the rearing of children. Even if the wife had been employed before marriage she would be expected to give this up on marrying and devote herself to the home. For the majority of middle-class women marriage implied a life of 'genteel idleness', in which they would be deprived of a satisfying and influential role. Even child-rearing began to occupy less of their time as middle-class families began to have fewer children in the last quarter of the nineteenth century. Towards the end of the century, middle-class women typically married much later, thus restricting their opportunities for child-bearing. **Contraception**, although the methods were rather unreliable, became a more widely used and accepted part of middle-class marriage at this time. Smaller families gave middle-class women more time for activities outside of the home, but they still had to overcome many cultural barriers before their opportunities for greater fulfilment would improve.

Working-class women

Changes in the law were of little relevance to the majority of working-class women at this time. Marriage to a man who could hold on to regular employment and provide a settled and stable home was still the ambition of most working-class women. The reality was, of course, often very different. The insecurities of working-class employment, high mortality rates which made widows of many women, husbands who spent a large proportion of the weekly wage on alcohol or who abandoned their wives, all contributed to a situation where many working-class women had to cope with the effects of poverty. Large families and the experience of being pregnant on an almost annual basis were also a common experience for working-class women throughout this period.

EMPLOYMENT

The notion of 'separate spheres' ignored the fact that women constituted a significant group within the employed labour force. In 1871 nearly 32 per cent of the total British labour force was female. Single women were more likely to be employed than were married women; 55 per cent of single women worked outside the home compared with 10 per cent of married women. Working-class women were more likely to be employed than their middle-class counterparts but with many middle-class women remaining unwed, either through choice or through lack of opportunity, a growing number of single women had to strive to be economically independent. In employment, however, as in so many other fields, women suffered from a lack of opportunities and unequal pay.

Employment of women in England and Wales, 1851–81

	1851	1861	1871	1881
Total number employed (millions)	2.348	2.709	3.118	3.393
Percentage of female population	25.7	26.3	26.8	25.4

Domestic service

The most important paid occupation for women was domestic service. In rural areas, going into service represented almost the only opportunity for unmarried and widowed women to be self-supporting, especially as employment of women in agriculture was declining. Domestic servant numbers, on the other hand, were increasing. From a total of under 1 million in 1851, the number of servants had increased to over 1.5 million by 1881 and a growing proportion of these were women. Domestic service offered regular employment and improved marriage prospects but at the cost of very long hours for low pay and low status.

Textile workers

The next largest occupational group among women workers was employed in textile factories. Whereas the number of men employed in textile factories was declining in the years 1851–81, the number of women employed was increasing; adult female workers made up about half the total workforce of textile factories. Employers valued women for their special qualities – nimble fingers for tying together broken threads, their deftness of application and their endurance – but the value placed on these qualities was not reflected in the rewards paid to women workers. Women textile workers were paid between a third and a sixth of the wages paid to male workers. The better-paid jobs in the factories were barred to women who represented a reservoir of cheap labour for the employers.

KEY STATISTICS

Employment in textile factories (000s)

	Men	Women
1851	661	635
1861	612	676
1871	584	726
1881	554	745

Change and continuity in women's employment

There were changes in the pattern of employment for women from the mid-nineteenth century. Legislation in the 1840s had barred women from being employed in coal mines and their employment in other forms of rough manual labour such as brickmaking also declined. Growing employment opportunities began to become available in shops, especially with the development of new chain stores from the 1870s. The growth of clerical work in the civil service and in larger companies, particularly in jobs involving typing, became a largely female preserve.

'Pit-brow' lasses with spades and sieves. They had to sieve the coal by hand.

Artificial flower making was one of the 'sweated trades' in which women were engaged.

Although these were not highly paid jobs, their 'white-collar' nature represented an improvement in status and working conditions for young women whose mothers had been limited to domestic service, factory work or the **'sweated trades'**. Yet at the end of the century large numbers of women were still employed in the clothing workshops which, because of their long hours, low pay and appalling working conditions, had come to be known as 'sweatshops'. In whichever occupation women were employed they were often regarded with suspicion by male-dominated trade unions which feared that the position of male workers could be undermined by low-paid female workers. The result was that few women belonged to trade unions and their bargaining position in their dealings with employers was very weak.

Breaking the mould

Many middle-class women were beginning to challenge the preconceptions about female employment. The fact that a growing number of young middle-class women were delaying the age of their marriage until their late twenties or, in a small but significantly growing number of cases, choosing not to marry at all, meant that more women were seeking employment. Traditional opportunities for the unmarried to take up respectable employment had included work as governesses, but such posts were

notoriously underpaid and were also becoming less
available as the full-time education of girls became more
common. Teaching posts, however, particularly in
elementary schools, were increasing, and the vast majority
of elementary school teachers were women. Indeed, one
powerful impetus behind the early campaign for votes for
women was that, after 1867, women were teaching the
future voters but were denied the right to vote for
themselves. The work of **Florence Nightingale** in the years
after the Crimean War had done much to reform the
nursing profession and make it available to respectable
women. After the success of **Sophia Jex-Blake** and
Elizabeth Garrett Anderson in challenging the prejudices
of the medical profession and in forcing medical schools to
admit women, medicine also became a career open to
women. The number of women doctors increased from 20
in 1881 to 212 in 1901; by 1911 the number had reached
447 – statistically very small but symbolically very
important in breaking down a bastion of male exclusivity.

EDUCATION

Until the 1850s the opportunities for girls to be educated
outside the home were very limited. For working-class
children, church and charity schools existed to provide a
basic elementary education, but attendance was not
compulsory nor was it free. In many parts of the country
the provision of school places for working-class children
was simply inadequate. The result was that many working-
class children of both sexes, but particularly girls, received
little or no education. Among the middle and upper classes
the practice of employing governesses to educate daughters
at home was widespread. Boarding schools provided an
education for the sons of the upper classes while middle-
class boys could attend local grammar schools or one of the
growing number of boarding schools which were being
created to cater for the growing demand for a public school
education.

Elementary schools
The 1860s saw the beginnings of an expansion in schools
for all classes and for both sexes. Following inquiries into

the educational provision of church and charity schools that revealed serious gaps and failings, the state began to take a more direct responsibility for schools. The Education Act of 1870 established, for the first time, publicly owned and funded elementary schools as a first step to ensuring that all children between the ages of 5 and 11 should receive a basic education. Attendance at school for this age group was made compulsory after 1880 and free after 1891. Thus by the end of the century, boys and girls from working-class families were expected to be in regular attendance at school. The fruits of these reforms can be measured in the figures for literacy rates. Female literacy (as measured by the ability of women to sign a marriage register for themselves) increased from over 73 per cent in 1871 to almost 97 per cent in 1900.

Schools for girls

Pioneering work in the education of girls from middle- and upper-class families was undertaken by **Miss Buss** and **Miss Beale** in the 1850s. The foundation of the North London Collegiate School in 1850 and Cheltenham Ladies College in 1853 started a trend in girls' education which was taken up by the Girls' Public Day School Trust established in 1872. Between 1872 and 1894 the GPDST promoted the establishment of 36 new girls' schools which provided a classical, academic education similar to that which was on offer in the boys' public schools.

Grammar schools

By the time the state became involved in the provision of secondary education, after 1902, the case for providing girls with an education beyond the home had been well made. The 1902 Education Act opened the doors for a rapid expansion of secondary education through state grammar schools. The number of girls' grammar schools increased from 99 in 1904 to 349 in 1914. Such was the success of grammar school education for girls that by 1914 more girls than boys were remaining at school after the age of 16.

Universities

University education was also undergoing a general expansion with the creation of new universities in the larger provincial cities, all of which admitted women, as London University had done since the 1830s. Among the old established universities at Oxford and Cambridge, however, there was more resisitance to the admission of women, although the creation of Girton College in 1869 and of Somerville College and Lady Margaret Hall at Oxford in the 1870s began the process of breaking down the male exclusivity of these institutions.

CONCLUSION: THE 'NEW WOMAN'

By the beginning of the twentieth century there had been a number of small but significant changes in the status of women:

- Women were generally better educated than their mothers and grandmothers had been.
- The legal position of women had improved in several small but significant ways.
- There was a wider range of employment opportunities available to women.

Such was the impact of these changes that, in the early years of the new century, many contemporaries drew attention to the phenomenon of the 'new woman'. The 'new woman' came from the middle classes, was well educated, and did not place a good marriage as the height of her ambitions but instead sought to develop an independent career. Women were now working as doctors, dentists, pharmacists, factory inspectors, hospital almoners, and journalists. 'The new woman' was dressed in looser, more flowing and comfortable clothes than her mother had worn, reflecting the greater freedom in her lifestyle. If she married, she would bear fewer children than earlier generations of women and, with more labour-saving devices available to cut down on the drudgery of housework, she would feel less bound by the prison of domesticity.

Such an image of the emancipated woman did have some foundation in reality, but for the majority of women the picture was very different. The campaign for votes for women took place against a background of continuing inequality and lack of status.

SUMMARY QUESTIONS

1 Summarise the main inequalities faced by women in the mid-nineteenth century in

(a) the family situation;

(b) employment; and

(c) educational opportunities.

2 What were the main similarities and differences in the situations of working-class and middle-class women at this time?

3 To what extent had the position of women improved by the end of the nineteenth century?

CHAPTER 9

Why did the campaign for women's suffrage begin in the 1860s?

KEY PERSON

Mary Wollstonecraft (1759–97) led an unconventional lifestyle, living with another man before marrying William Godwin in 1797. She was described by Horace Walpole as a 'hyena in petticoats'. She died in childbirth. Her daughter Mary, who survived her, went on to become Mary Shelley, the writer and wife of the poet.

The issue of votes for women had been raised before the 1860s. In 1792 **Mary Wollstonecraft** had published *A Vindication of the Rights of Woman* in which she had asserted that women should have the same rights as those which Tom Paine had claimed for men. Women were involved in the post-1815 radical agitation for the right to vote and many women were present in the crowd at Peterloo in 1819. Henry Hunt had tried to amend the 1832 Reform Act to give women the vote on the same terms as men and there was extensive female involvement in the Chartist movement of the 1830s and 1840s. The radical campaigns for universal suffrage in the years 1815–50, however, tended to interpret the demand for universal suffrage as meaning 'manhood suffrage' and even when the issue of the female suffrage was raised, it was invariably seen as being subsidiary to the main aim of gaining full political rights for all adult men.

THE START OF THE CAMPAIGN

The first time a proposal to give the vote to women was put before Parliament was in 1867, during the debates that led to the passing of the Second Reform Act. Thereafter, between 1870 and 1884 when the Third Reform Act was passed, nine bills to enfranchise women were placed before Parliament by sympathetic backbench MPs. This effectively marked the start of the long campaign, both within and outside Parliament, to win the vote in parliamentary elections for women. The immediate origins of this campaign stemmed from a committee of women suffrage campaigners that had been established in 1866 to organise a petition to Parliament. This so-called 'Kensington Society' evolved into the London National Society for Women's Suffrage that was founded in 1867. Similar local societies were then founded in Manchester,

Edinburgh, Birmingham and Bristol; by 1872, the various groups had merged into the National Society for Women's Suffrage (NSWS). With a national organisation sending speakers to public meetings in many provincial towns, a journal dedicated to the cause of women's suffrage (*The Women's Suffrage Journal*) and energetic leadership at both national and local levels, the campaign for women's suffrage began to make an impact during the 1870s.

Manchester: a case study

A brief look at the story of the women's suffrage movement in Manchester will provide a useful case study. The first meeting of the Manchester National Society for Women's Suffrage was held in early 1867. Most of the early members were respectable middle-class women who had connections with the local Liberal Party and who belonged to the various nonconformist religious groups. The tradition of radical Liberalism in Manchester, associated with organisations such as the Anti-Corn Law League of the 1840s, was kept alive by leading local figures such as Jacob Bright, one of the local MPs, and Richard Pankhurst, an up-and-coming young barrister. There was a strong radical tradition for the women's suffrage campaign to draw upon, therefore, but the success of the Manchester NSWS in the late 1860s and 1870s was also largely due to the energy and organisational ability of its secretary, Lydia Becker. Born in 1827, Lydia Becker was a single woman of independent means who could devote her full-time efforts

A suffragist addressing a public meeting in 1870. Lydia Becker is seated at the table and Millicent Fawcett is on the left.

to the cause of women's suffrage. She adopted the methods of pressure groups such as the Anti-Corn Law League. Signatures were collected on petitions; meetings were held in drawing rooms; and large public meetings to demonstrate the strength of support for the cause were held in the Free Trade Hall. MPs were canvassed and sympathetic members were persuaded to introduce private members' bills into the House of Commons. Public speaking by women was considered shocking by many, but in most other respects the campaign was conducted in such a way as to demonstrate the respectability of those involved.

Such tactics succeeded in raising the issue of women's suffrage and getting it debated in Parliament. But the story of the Manchester NSWS also illustrates the limitations of the early suffrage campaign. Apart from a campaign on behalf of the '**pit-brow lasses**' whose jobs were threatened by trade union pressure, Lydia Becker and the NSWS did not attempt to enlist the support of working-class women for their cause. They were campaigning only for women householders to have the vote on the same terms as men, not for a more radical and general extension of the franchise. This emphasis narrowed the appeal of the Suffrage Society and by the 1880s it was beginning to lose momentum.

Why did the movement begin at this time?
There were a number of factors which led to the emergence of the suffrage movement at this time.

Education. The majority of those involved in the campaign were educated, middle-class women. The expansion of educational opportunities for middle-class girls was creating a new and growing group of women who felt increasingly frustrated by the obstacles placed in the way of the advancement of women and who had the time, the skills and the motivation to engage in political campaigning. One of the women who was prominent in the early women's suffrage movement in Bristol, for example, was Eliza Dunbar, the first woman doctor in the city.

KEY TERM

Pit-brow lasses Although women were banned from working underground in 1842, they continued to be employed on the surface (pit brow) of coal mines in sorting the coal sent up from the mines below. About 1000 women were employed in Lancashire coal mines in the early 20th century. There were repeated attempts in Parliament to ban women from doing this work and their cause was taken up by women's suffrage groups.

Radical politics. Many of the women involved came from nonconformist backgrounds, particularly Quakers and Unitarians. They had close links with the radical wing of the Liberal Party and some indeed were married to Liberal politicians. **Millicent Fawcett**, for example, was the wife of the Liberal minister, Henry Fawcett. In Bristol, Elizabeth Sturge was related to the Sturge family from Birmingham who were prominent Quakers and active in radical politics since the Chartist years.

Single-issue campaigns. Political activity among middle-class women began in the 1850s with a number of single-issue campaigns. The debate over changing the divorce law in 1857 stimulated a group of women to take up other causes. Members of this group, known as 'The Ladies of Langham Place', took up such causes as improving higher educational opportunities for women (**Emily Davies**), entry for women to the medical profession (Elizabeth Garrett Anderson) and the problem of violence against women within marriage (**Frances Power Cobbe**). This group were also involved in setting up the Society for Promoting the Employment of Women in 1859 and the *English Woman's Journal* in 1858.

Support from male politicians. While most male politicians in both major parties were opposed to women's suffrage, there was a small number of sympathetic MPs. John Stuart Mill, a leading Liberal intellectual, who was MP for Westminster from 1865–8, put forward the amendment to the Parliamentary Reform Bill in 1867 which would have granted the vote to women on the same terms as men. He also published *The Subjection of Women* in 1869 in which he argued that women could not rely on male voters to represent their interests – the doctrine of virtual representation – since the absence of a female voice in politics had led to the neglect of women's interests. Another prominent male supporter was **Jacob Bright**, Liberal MP for Manchester. Since women were not only denied the vote but also could not become MPs the only way that the issue of women's suffrage, or any other issue

KEY PEOPLE

Millicent Fawcett (1847–1929) was the sister of Elizabeth Garrett Anderson. She married the Liberal politician Henry Fawcett in 1867. One of the founding members of the women's suffrage campaign, she was a quiet, dignified leader whose strengths were in co-ordinating and conciliating rather than in public speaking.

Emily Davies (1830–1921) led the campaign to persuade the universities to open their doors to women. The first success of this campaign was the setting up of Girton College in 1869.

Frances Power Cobbe (1822–1904) was an Irish charity worker and writer who campaigned for women's rights. She was also a prominent anti-vivisectionist and a co-founder of 'ragged schools', i.e. schools for the poor.

Jacob Bright (1821–99) was the younger brother of John Bright, the leading radical and campaigner for free trade. Jacob became MP for Manchester and supported the campaign for women's suffrage in Parliament.

directly concerning women, could be raised in Parliament was through sympathetic male MPs.

The extension of the franchise to working-class men. The First Reform Act of 1832 had granted the right to vote to middle-class male property owners. Both the Whig Party, which had introduced the reform, and the Tory Party, which had reluctantly accepted it once it had been passed, had declared that this Reform Act was a 'final and irrevocable settlement' of the franchise question. During the years of the Chartist agitation, the bipartisan line of resistance to further extensions of the franchise had been maintained. By the mid-1860s, however, the political situation was changing. In 1866 **Gladstone** had introduced a bill to extend the franchise to a limited number of working-class men. His bill failed due to resistance from within his own party and from the Conservatives, but in 1867 a leading Conservative, **Benjamin Disraeli**, introduced his own measure to reform Parliament. The whole issue of who was fit to exercise the right to vote had been reopened.

The fact that Parliament was once again actively considering an extension of the franchise led to the first moves by women's suffrage campaigners to place their own demands for the right to vote into the parliamentary arena. When the Second Reform Act was passed the vote was given to adult male householders (and lodgers with one year's residence) in the towns. In effect this gave the vote to skilled male artisans. Although neither Gladstone nor Disraeli had any immediate plans for further extensions of the franchise, the fact that the principle of giving the vote to non-property owners had been conceded meant that Parliament had embarked on a step-by-step approach to the extension of the franchise. In 1884 this process was taken a stage further when male householders in the countryside were also granted the right to vote.

These extensions of the vote to working-class males were a major stimulus to the growing campaign by middle-class women for female suffrage. If male householders could vote, why not female householders – the spinsters and widows who ran their own households? If working-class

KEY PEOPLE

**William Gladstone
(1809–98)** was a leading politician in the Liberal Party in the 1860s and was Prime Minister on four occasions between 1868 and 1894. He was personally opposed to the enfranchisement of women.

**Benjamin Disraeli
(1804–81)** was a leading figure in the Conservative Party in the 1860s and became Prime Minister for a brief period in 1867. He was Prime Minister for a second time, 1874–80. He was personally in favour of giving women the vote on the same terms as men.

men could vote, why not the female teachers in the elementary schools who had taught them how to read and complete their ballot forms? If farm labourers, why not the female farming widows who were the employers of many male labourers? Also, many women were employed and paid taxes but had no representation of their own.

The moves by Parliament to extend the franchise to new groups of men alerted women to the fact that reforms of the franchise were once again on the political agenda. The enfranchisement of more men while women were still excluded created many anomalies which the suffrage campaigners could use as arguments in their favour. It is no accident, therefore, that the first wave of campaigning by the women's suffrage movement began in the years 1866–7 and intensified in the period 1867–84.

SUMMARY QUESTIONS

1 What were the main social and cultural factors that led to the emergence of the women's suffrage movement in the 1860s?

2 What were the main political factors that contributed to this development?

3 Explain the role played by key individuals in this story (e.g. Lydia Becker, Millicent Fawcett and John Stuart Mill).

CHAPTER 10

How successful was the early suffragist movement?

Viewed from one perspective, the early suffragist movement failed to achieve its central objective – the securing of the vote for women in parliamentary elections. Despite the fact that nine women's suffrage bills were placed before Parliament between 1870 and 1884, none of these bills made much progress. This judgement, however, is based on a far too narrow and unrealistic view of the movement's progress and achievements. As a result of the activities of the women's suffrage movement, significant progress was made in achieving greater political and legal equality for women and in challenging the stereotypes of women as being unsuited to public life.

POLITICAL RIGHTS FOR WOMEN

Between 1869 and 1907 a number of significant reforms were made which brought greater political equality for women and paved the way for their increased involvement in public life.

- In 1869, single female ratepayers were given the right to vote in municipal council elections. Thereafter, women comprised about 15 per cent of the total electorate.
- In 1870, when local School Boards were established, women ratepayers were allowed to vote and to stand as candidates in School Board elections. They were also allowed to vote and to stand as candidates in elections for Poor Law Boards of Guardians. By 1895, 128 women had been elected to School Boards and 893 as Poor Law Guardians.
- In 1888, elected county councils were established and female ratepayers qualified for the right to vote in these elections.
- In 1894, elected parish, rural district and urban district

councils were established and female ratepayers had the right to vote and to stand as candidates.

- In 1907, women were allowed to stand as candidates in county council elections.

Through various local government reforms, therefore, the principle of female suffrage had been conceded and women had established their right to a formal public role. By 1900 there were about 1 million women who could vote in local government elections. Moreover, women councillors, School Board members and Poor Law Guardians had made a distinctive impact on the policies of these bodies precisely because they were more aware than men of issues concerning poverty, the family and education. Female Poor Law Guardians, for example, encouraged the fostering of orphaned or abandoned children as an alternative to their long-term institutionalisation. On the London School Board, **Annie Besant** broke new ground by persuading the Board to introduce free school meals some years before Parliament legislated to extend this provision nationally.

There was still, however, considerable resistance to the enfranchisement of women in parliamentary elections. The main concerns of School Boards, Poor Law Guardians and local councils were with social and domestic matters – areas that were seen as being entirely appropriate for a woman's sphere of influence. Parliament, on the other hand, debated issues such as national defence and relations with other powers – matters that were regarded by many as being entirely outside a woman's competence. Thus, although women were entering into public life, the fact that women were only allowed a role in those areas of government that dealt with social policy showed that the doctrine of 'separate spheres' had merely been modified, not abandoned altogether.

IMPROVED LEGAL RIGHTS FOR WOMEN

Suffrage campaigners continued to be involved in campaigns to improve the legal position of women and some notable successes were achieved.

KEY PERSON

Annie Besant (1847–1933) was a leading socialist and radical campaigner. She worked as a journalist and achieved fame through her support for the women workers of Bryant and May's match factory in the East End of London when they joined a union and went on strike in 1888. She also gained notoriety when she and Charles Bradlaugh, another radical campaigner, were prosecuted for obscene libel in 1877 because they distributed a book on contraception.

- **Married Women's Property Acts** were passed in 1870 and 1882, allowing married women the right to retain ownership of any property or income gained independently of their husbands, either before or during marriage.
- The **Contagious Diseases Act** was finally repealed in 1886 after a long campaign. This Act, originally passed in 1864, was designed to protect soldiers and sailors from the dangers of catching sexually transmitted diseases. Under this legislation a woman could be declared a 'common prostitute' on the word of a police inspector or a doctor and forced to submit to a compulsory medical examination. If found to be infected with a sexually transmitted disease she could be immediately detained in a 'lock hospital' for up to three months. The Act also allowed the authorities in garrison and dockyard towns to license and control brothels. Led by **Josephine Butler**, the National Campaign against the Contagious Diseases Act was launched in 1869. Their case against the Act was that it violated a woman's civil rights, that men and women were treated differently under the law and that the licensing of brothels gave an official sanction to immorality. Using the standard pressure-group techniques of mobilising public opinion through mass meetings, pamphlets and the cultivation of sympathetic MPs, the campaign succeeded in persuading Parliament to repeal the law in 1886.

KEY PERSON

Josephine Butler (1828–1906) Born in Northumberland, she campaigned for women's education and in 1867 helped to found the North of England Council for the Higher Education of Women. While living in Liverpool she established homes for prostitutes and this led to her interest in the Contagious Diseases Act. She was involved in a number of campaigns, bringing a vigorous, crusading style to the task.

CHALLENGING THE DOCTRINE OF 'SEPARATE SPHERES'

When the first public meetings were held to promote the idea of women's suffrage in the late 1860s, the women who addressed the meetings were in a very real sense breaking the mould of Victorian society. It was thought to be unwomanly and sensational for a woman to address a public meeting, particularly one with men present. At one such meeting it was reported that a clergyman stood up and said that it was forbidden in Holy Scripture for women to speak or take part in public affairs. During the heated discussion which followed another man rose to say that his grandmother was a Quakeress and spoke regularly in Quaker meetings.

Women in political parties

At the start of the campaign for women's suffrage the main political parties largely ignored the interests of women and certainly did not allow them to be involved in any party political activity. By the 1880s, however, it was normal for women to be members of political parties and to play a key role in their work at constituency level. This was partly because the 1883 Corrupt Practices Act placed restrictions on the amount that candidates could spend on their election campaigns, with the result that parties came to rely more on voluntary helpers. Women, particularly from the middle classes, were more likely than men to have the time to be able to do this voluntary work. Such a change could only have come about, however, as the result of a marked change in male attitudes towards the participation of women in politics. Both the Conservative and Liberal parties took steps to formalise the involvement of women in their organisations.

- The Conservatives formed the **Primrose League** in 1883. The League recruited both men and women but at least half of its 1 million members in the early 1890s were women.
- The Liberals established the **Women's Liberal Federation** in 1887. Local Women's Liberal Associations had been created before this and, very much against the opposition of the Liberal leader William Gladstone, the national Federation was formed in 1887 to increase the involvement of women in the Liberal Party. By 1893, the WLF had about 43,000 members.
- **Women's Co-operative Guilds** were established in the main towns and cities from the mid-1880s. Led by **Margaret Llewellyn Davies**, the WCGs gave working-class women a vehicle for expressing their views on social policy. The WCG advocated maternity benefits, home helps, family allowances and school meals long before any of the main political parties gave any consideration to these matters.

Margaret Llewellyn Davies (1862–1944) Described as 'formidably energetic', Margaret Llewellyn Davies was General Secretary of the WCG from 1889. She was a niece of Emily Davies. She was the daughter of the Reverend Llewellyn Davies, a prominent Christian Socialist, and was educated at Girton College.

Parliamentary opinion

Within 20 years of the start of the suffrage campaign, therefore, the doctrine of 'separate spheres' was beginning to be successfully challenged and women had established a place in public life. Although the political parties viewed the role of women within their organisations as being essentially a supporting one, male politicians were beginning to give more sympathetic consideration to the case for women's suffrage. This shift in opinion was particularly striking in the Conservative Party. During the Parliamentary debates on women's suffrage between 1867 and 1884, the majority of Conservative MPs who voted were opposed to votes for women; in the period 1884–98, the majority who voted were in favour. As a result of the shift of parliamentary opinion in favour of votes for women, the two suffrage bills that were presented to Parliament in 1897 and 1908 achieved majorities. These facts have prompted Pugh (1980) to write that 'a suffragist majority had already been attained by the turn of the century under the steady influence of the non-militant campaign and the demonstration women had given of their political skills'.

WHY DID THE SUFFRAGIST MOVEMENT NOT ACHIEVE MORE?

Despite the genuine advances in the legal and political rights for women made as a result of the campaigning activities of the suffragist movement, at the turn of the century the vote for women in parliamentary elections had still not been won. There were a number of reasons why the movement did not achieve more.

The extent of its support. Anti-suffragists claimed that the movement represented a small, untypical minority of middle-class women. Evidence to support this claim came from the fact that there were large women's organisations, such as the Mothers' Union, that refused to back the demand for women's suffrage. Even the Women's Co-operative Guilds did not come out in favour of votes for women until 1900. The fact that many prominent individual women did not support the movement was also

Examples of anti-suffragist propaganda of the early 1900s.

damaging to its credibility. **Octavia Hill** and Florence Nightingale were opposed to the campaign whilst the leading socialist, **Beatrice Webb**, argued that women's suffrage, although right in principle, was less of a priority than dealing with the problem of poverty. More damaging was the fact that the most prominent woman of the period, Queen Victoria, was openly hostile to the cause of women's suffrage.

It is true that the suffrage movement did appeal mainly to middle-class women. It is also clear that, despite beginning as a small minority group, by the 1890s there were moves in some industrial areas to build a suffragist campaign that would have relevance to working women. The work of Liddington and Norris (1978) has revealed that the suffragists achieved some success in building a movement of working-class women in the Lancashire cotton towns. Suffragists in Bristol also attempted to link the trade union struggles of women workers in the years 1889–92 with the

KEY QUOTE

Queen Victoria, expressing her feelings on women's suffrage: 'this mad, wicked folly of "Women's Rights" with all its attendant horrors, on which her poor feeble sex is bent, forgetting every sense of womanly feelings and propriety.'

KEY PEOPLE

Octavia Hill (1838–1912) was a leading female philanthropist who involved herself in the improvement of housing conditions for the working classes in London.

wider campaign for women's suffrage. In Lancashire in the 1890s and early 1900s, a strong, locally-based movement of 'radical suffragists' was created which was linked to, but distinct from, the more middle-class suffragist societies. This development will be explored in more detail on pages 148–150.

Male attitudes. The unwillingness of men to abandon the notion of 'separate spheres' was evident among men of all classes and all political persuasions. It united the Liberal leader William Gladstone with the leading Tory imperialist, **Lord Curzon**. In response to the growing support within the Liberal Party for women's suffrage, Gladstone published a pamphlet in 1892 entitled *Female Suffrage*. In this he argued that women were 'generally indifferent' to the vote and that they already had sufficient power through their dominant position in the private sphere. Hostility towards greater equality for women was also strongly evident among working-class men and their attitudes were reflected in the labour movement, particularly in the trade unions. The heavy industries in which many men worked, such as coal mining, iron and steel making and engineering, had a dominant male culture; the trade unions which represented these workers gave no support for female suffrage or for greater employment opportunities for women. Such attitudes were reinforced by the male doctors who were prepared to argue that women were temperamentally unsuited for the world of politics since they were too emotional and prone to hysteria.

Tactical difficulties. The campaign for votes for women was faced with a difficult dilemma over the question of which women should qualify for the right to vote. Extensions of the franchise to different groups of men had been made on a step-by-step basis and, after the last extension of the franchise in 1884, there was still some 40 per cent of adult men who did not qualify for the right to vote. This was because the franchise was still based, not on the democratic concept of Parliament representing numbers of people, but on the concept of property and interests being represented. Thus the men who could vote in parliamentary elections were owners of property, or householders or lodgers with at least one year's residence.

The suffragists could not ignore these facts. If and when Parliament decided to grant the vote to women, it would do so on a step-by-step approach as it had with men. Many suffragists, therefore, believed that it was unrealistic to campaign for votes for all women and instead they limited their demand to the vote for women 'on the same terms as men'. This meant that they were calling for the right to vote for women householders or ratepayers; in practical terms this would restrict the franchise to about 1 million women, mostly spinsters and widows, and would exclude the vast majority of married women.

Tactically this strategy was fraught with difficulty. The suffragist movement exposed itself to the charge that it was undemocratic; politicians from the labour movement in particular accused the suffragists of only being concerned with the interests of a minority of wealthy women. There were also a number of anomalies that would arise from the householder franchise. It implied that a single woman who was a householder might then lose her vote if she married. **Anti-suffragists** were also keen to point out that a 'brothel madam' would qualify to vote as a householder whereas the respectable married woman would not.

This dilemma was never satisfactorily resolved either by the non-militant suffagists or the militant 'suffragettes'. Conscious of the need to win the backing of the main political parties and their leaders, they restricted their demands to those they believed had a realistic chance of success. But by not calling for a democratic franchise for all they lost the chance to broaden their campaign by making a direct appeal to working-class women and men.

Party politics. Extensions of the franchise in 1832, 1867 and 1884 all involved considerations of party political advantage when the details of the reform measures were being debated. The proposal to extend the vote to women involved the parties in calculations as to how this would affect their fortunes. The fact that the main parties, Liberal and Conservative, came to different conclusions about this

Lord Salisbury (1830–1903) was Conservative leader from 1881 until 1902 and served four terms as Prime Minister. Salisbury was a staunch opponent of democracy and almost certainly opposed in principle to the extension of the franchise to women. He could, however, see some tactical advantages for the Conservative Party in enfranchising women property owners. **Arthur Balfour (1848–1930)** was leader from 1902 until 1911 and Prime Minister 1902–5. **Andrew Bonar Law (1858–1923)** was leader from 1911 until 1923. He was more supportive of women's suffrage than his predecessors, mainly because he believed that a limited female franchise would benefit the Conservative Party.

James Keir Hardie (1856–1915) was a Scottish coal miner who became the first Labour MP in 1892. He was a founding member of the ILP and one of its leading figures until his death.

George Lansbury (1859–1940) was a Labour MP after 1906. His influence in the labour movement stemmed from his editorship of the *Daily Herald*, a newspaper that he founded in 1911.

meant that there was no cross-party consensus which would smooth the path to reform. The majority of MPs who supported women's suffrage were Liberals who believed that women voters would be natural supporters of **temperance reform**, social reform, free trade and cheap food, the issues which were closely associated with the Liberal Party. Gladstone, however, was very wary of the risks involved in such a strategy. He was already having difficulty in managing a party which was composed of so many different interest groups, each of which was determined to promote its own particular cause – a phenomenon known as 'faddism'. He believed that giving the vote to women might increase the influence of some 'faddists', particularly the temperance reformers, at a time when restrictions on the drink trade were already very unpopular with many male voters. There was also a strong belief within the Liberal Party that women property owners and householders would be more likely to vote Conservative.

For this same reason Conservative leaders tended to be more sympathetic to the idea of a limited extension of the franchise to women householders and ratepayers. **Salisbury**, **Balfour** and **Bonar Law**, the leaders of the Conservative Party between 1881 and 1914 all gave indications that they were not unsympathetic to the suffragists' case. Most Conservative backbench MPs, however, were hostile to the idea.

In 1900 a new Labour Party was established, built upon the foundations laid by socialist groups like the Independent Labour Party in the 1890s. Within the Labour movement there were many socialist women activists and leading male socialists, such as **Keir Hardie** and **George Lansbury**, who supported the cause of women's suffrage. The Labour Party, however, would not support a limited women's suffrage bill, preferring to campaign for full adult suffrage and to campaign on social and economic reforms. In any event, with only two MPs in 1900 and 29 after 1906, the Labour Party was not in a position to influence the outcome of parliamentary debates on the suffrage issue.

HOW HEALTHY WAS THE WOMEN'S SUFFRAGE MOVEMENT AT THE END OF THE NINETEENTH CENTURY?

During the late 1880s the women's suffrage movement appeared to be in a state of stagnation, if not of actual decline. Membership and incomes of the various suffrage groups were falling. A Bristol member of the suffrage campaign reported later that, between 1884 and 1904, supporters there were 'disheartened but kept working'. There were a number of problems that the suffrage movement was facing at this time:

- The 1884 Third Reform Act had extended the franchise to male householders and their lodgers in the countryside but the Liberal government that had introduced this reform refused to include women's suffrage in the legislation. Gladstone, the Prime Minister at the time, argued that to do so would provoke the House of Lords into rejecting the bill, although Gladstone himself was opposed to giving votes to women. The failure to secure women's suffrage in 1884 left women feeling, in the words of Sophia Jex-Blake, 'conspicuously isolated'. The passing of the Reform Act also deprived the suffrage campaign of the momentum that had been building up since 1867. It was clear that neither the Liberal nor the Conservative parties would sponsor any further reforms of the voting system for some time to come.
- Politically active women found, in the wake of the parliamentary reforms introduced between 1883 and 1885, that the parties were now encouraging their participation in party political work. The formation of the Primrose League in 1883 and of the Women's Liberal Federation (WLF) in 1887 gave women the opportunity to work within the 'pale of the constitution', even if they were not accepted as equals. This development contained two dangers for the suffrage movement. Firstly, participation in the political parties distracted attention from the suffrage issue. Secondly, the emergence of groups like the WLF threatened to undermine the non-party nature of the suffrage campaign. Many supporters of the cause of

women's suffrage joined the WLF, and in 1888 the WLF tried to affiliate to the Central Committee of the NSWS. This caused a split within the suffrage movement between those who believed that a link with one of the two main parties would give the campaign more influence and those who believed it would undermine the movement's claim to be independent of political parties.

- After 1886 British politics was dominated by the issue of granting Home Rule to Ireland. This issue caused a serious split in the Liberal Party in 1886, a split that contributed to a period of Conservative domination that lasted nearly 20 years. With Conservative governments in power for much of this period the pace of reform slackened considerably and the chances of a women's suffrage bill being adopted by the governments of the day were non-existent. The divisions over Home Rule also afflicted the suffrage movement. Mrs Fawcett left the Liberal Party in 1886, in common with many other Liberal Unionists, and antagonised her former Liberal colleagues in the 1890s by appearing on Conservative Party platforms to speak against Home Rule.
- The death of Lydia Becker in 1890 deprived the movement of its most prominent leader.

The suffrage campaign that had begun in the late 1860s had reached a low ebb by 1890. The campaign had appealed mainly to middle- and upper-class, educated women. Their campaign methods had been designed to demonstrate their respectability and the moderation of their demands. Lydia Becker had focused on winning the vote for single women who were householders in their own right, feeling that married women had a weaker claim to the vote.

This strategy had brought some success in placing the issue of women's suffrage on the political agenda and in securing advances for women's rights in local government and legal rights. But by 1890 this strategy was under increasing pressure from within the movement itself and the suffrage campaign was about to enter into a new phase in its development.

The National Union of Women's Suffrage Societies

In 1897 a new national organisation, The National Union of Women's Suffrage Societies, was formed to reunite the movement after the splits of the late 1880s. Led by Millicent Fawcett, the NUWSS was made up of 16 separate suffrage groups linked together in a federal structure. This structure was a recognition of the fact that the various suffrage groups in different parts of the country had developed their own distinctive identities. Some groups remained dominated by middle-class women who preferred the genteel tactics of the drawing room meeting and parliamentary petitions. Others were more radical in character and appealed more to working-class women. The federal structure of the NUWSS allowed the separate groups to retain their identities while co-operating on the central objective of campaigning for the right to vote.

Radical Suffragists

The development of a 'radical suffragist' movement in some parts of the country gave the campaign a renewed sense of vitality. As Liddington and Norris (1978) have shown, the most successful and effective group of 'radical suffragists' was active in the Lancashire textile towns but there were similar moves elsewhere. Radical suffragists had close links to the labour and socialist movements which were gaining in strength at this time. Interest in socialist ideas had begun to revive in the 1880s, and in 1893 a number of local socialist societies merged together in the Independent Labour Party. The first Independent Labour Member of Parliament was elected in 1892. Meanwhile, within the trade union movement there was the development of a more militant form of trade unionism among unskilled workers in the late 1880s and early 1890s. The involvement of women in trade unions was also beginning to increase. Moreover, many of the activists in the new socialist groups were women. Like their male counterparts they brought a crusading zeal to the task of building a mass movement, showing tireless energy in organising factory gate meetings, open-air meetings, visiting potential supporters in their own homes and

Esther Roper (1868–1939)
was the daughter of a factory
worker turned missionary.
Educated at Owens College,
Manchester (later Manchester
University), she became a
leading figure in the
Manchester women's suffrage
campaign after the death of
Lydia Becker. She was
involved in numerous
campaigns on behalf of
working women. In 1896 she
met **Eva Gore-Booth
(1870–1926)**, a daughter of
the aristocratic Sir Henry
Gore-Booth from Sligo,
Ireland. Gore-Booth was a
poet who became actively
involved in the suffrage
campaign and worked
alongside Roper.

**Selina Cooper
(1864–1946)** came from
Nelson, Lancashire. After
working in a local cotton mill
from the age of 10, she
became involved in the ILP
and the women's suffrage
campaign. She was a gifted
public speaker.

Helen Silcock (b.1866)
came originally from
Newcastle but started work in
a Wigan cotton mill at age
15. In 1894 she was elected
President of the Wigan
Weavers Union. She was
active in the socialist
movement and as a trade
union organiser. In 1901 and
1902 she appealed to the
TUC for support for
women's suffrage.

writing articles for socialist newspapers like *The Clarion*. As socialists they campaigned for social reforms to relieve poverty, improve health care and education for working-class children, or for an eight-hour working day. As women they campaigned equally passionately for the right to vote. Unlike the middle-class suffragists, however, they did not see the right to vote as an abstract symbol of their equality with men. The vote was the means of achieving improved working and living conditions for working women; for this reason they did not accept the limited demand of middle-class suffragists for the vote for women 'on the same terms as men'. Radical suffragists raised the demand for 'womanhood suffrage' and, since they understood that Parliament would not legislate to give all women the vote when many men were still excluded from the franchise, they were really campaigning for full adult suffrage.

The person who stands out as the mainspring of the radical suffragist movement in Manchester and South Lancashire was **Esther Roper**. The daughter of a factory worker turned missionary, Roper had had a middle-class upbringing and had taken a degree at Owens College, Manchester before becoming involved in charity work among the city's poor. As a campaigner for women's suffrage, however, she took the campaign to the working women of the city and out of the drawing rooms of the middle classes. In the words of Liddington and Norris (1978), Roper did 'more than anyone else [to] shift the Manchester suffrage campaign into a new gear from 1893 onwards'. After 1896 she was joined in her work by the woman who became her life-long companion, **Eva Gore-Booth**. Both of these women, however, came from privileged backgrounds and their efforts would not have been nearly as successful if there had not been a new generation of working women who were being drawn into the suffrage campaign through their involvement in the labour and socialist movements. Among these women, the contributions of **Selina Cooper**, **Helen Silcock** and **Ada Nield-Chew** were outstanding. Each of them had the skills of public speaking and of organising that were essential to the task of building a mass movement. They were members of the ILP and Helen Silcock was a trade union organiser, being President of the Wigan Weavers

Union. This gave her the opportunity to take the campaign for women's suffrage into the male-dominated Trades Union Congress. Working women such as these, in league with those such as Esther Roper, made the women's suffrage campaign in Lancashire a vigorous, relevant and well-supported movement by the turn of the century.

Although circumstances in Lancashire were favourable to the development of a radical suffragist mass movement, similar efforts were being made by other women in other parts of the country. **Enid Stacy**, for example, was a middle-class socialist and suffrage campaigner who became active in the struggles of working women in Bristol. She became involved in a strike by women at a cotton factory in Bristol in 1889 and in another strike by women in a confectionery factory in 1892. Like her counterparts in the north she was an exceptionally good public speaker but also a tireless campaigner and writer. Through her articles in *The Clarion* and through her work within the ILP she challenged that socialist organisation to give a greater priority to the cause of women's suffrage.

Similar stories could be told about women, either from middle-class backgrounds or, increasingly from the working classes, who were actively involved in building a campaign for women's suffrage that ran parallel to the campaign for social justice being waged by the ILP and the labour movement. The suffrage campaign at the turn of the century was undergoing a change of character but it was by no means moribund.

SUMMARY QUESTIONS

1 Summarise the main achievements of the women's suffrage movement during this period.

2 To what extent did the achievement of increased political rights in local government reflect the abandonment of the doctrine of 'separate spheres'?

3 What were the main obstacles in the way of achieving full political rights for women?

4 In what ways was the suffrage movement changing by the end of the nineteenth century?

CHAPTER 11

What were the origins of the militant suffragette movement?

WHO WERE THE SUFFRAGETTES?

The Women's Social and Political Union, the organisation which became better known by the name 'suffragettes', was formed in Manchester in 1903. It was led by Emmeline Pankhurst and her daughters, Christabel and Sylvia. The **Pankhurst family** had had earlier connections with the women's suffrage movement. Richard Pankhurst, husband of Emmeline, was a lawyer who in 1868 had been involved in a legal challenge to the ruling that women householders could not be included in the register of voters. He had also been involved in the establishment of the Women's Franchise League in the late 1880s. Mrs Pankhurst had become involved in politics through membership of the **Independent Labour Party** in Manchester, but by 1903 she had become disillusioned with the reluctance of the male-dominated organisation to make women's suffrage a priority. The founding of the WSPU, therefore, marked a break with labour politics. However, the influence of their early association with the labour movement can be seen in the suffragette marches and demonstrations which were a feature of the years 1905–14. The suffragette marches, with their colourful banners and accompanying bands, were modelled on labour demonstrations such as might be seen on the annual May Day parades.

Relations with the ILP

The breach with the ILP stemmed from a number of causes. The Pankhursts' frustration with a movement that seemed half-hearted in its commitment to women's suffrage was a major cause. The WSPU, under their leadership, embodied the single-minded determination – of Emmeline and Christabel in particular – to campaign on

KEY TERM

Suffragettes The name 'suffragettes' was adopted by the militant followers of the Women's Social and Political Union to distinguish them from the non-militant suffragists who supported the NUWSS.

KEY PEOPLE

The Pankhursts

Emmeline Pankhurst (1858–1928) was the daughter of a wealthy cotton manufacturer and prominent Liberal Party member in Manchester. She became involved in the ILP in the 1890s and served as a member of the Chorlton Board of Guardians (Poor Law).

Christabel Pankhurst (1880–1958) went to Manchester University to study law but was unable to practise as a lawyer because of her sex. Like her mother she had been a member of the ILP but was not very involved in the daily work of building the foundations of a new party.

KEY ORGANISATION

The ILP The Independent
Labour Party had been
founded in Bradford in 1893.
A socialist organisation, the
ILP was committed to
securing independent labour
representation in Parliament.
Many branches of the ILP
had been established around
the country since 1893,
including a strong base in the
Lancashire textile towns and
in the woollen towns of the
West Riding of Yorkshire.
The ILP was in favour of an
extension of the franchise but
its priorities were social
reforms.

the issue of votes for women to the exclusion of all other
causes. Theirs was a single-issue campaign that was based
on the belief that they could not rely on men in any of the
political parties to campaign for them. 'Women,' said Mrs
Pankhurst, 'we must do the work ourselves. We must have
our own independent women's movement.' Such an
approach would ultimately make co-operation between the
ILP and the WSPU impossible; nevertheless, co-operation
did continue until 1907 when it broke down under the
strain of repeated attacks on the ILP from the Pankhursts.

A militant strategy

Mrs Pankhurst later wrote that the justification for setting
up this new organisation, which would adopt more
militant tactics than the 'suffragists', was that: 'We had
exhausted argument. Therefore, either we had to give up
our agitation altogether, as the suffragists of the early
eighties virtually had done, or else we must act and go on
acting, until the selfishness and obstinacy of the
government was broken down, or the government
themselves destroyed'. In other words, the WSPU was

THE FORCES OF EVIL DENOUNCING
THE BEARERS OF LIGHT.

**The cover of 'The
Suffragette' for
17 October 1913.**

based on the belief that peaceful methods of persuasion had failed to achieve results and that the earlier suffragist movement was in decline. As we have seen, the non-militant suffragist movement had in fact made considerable progress in advancing the cause of women's suffrage and in securing a better legal position for women. There is some evidence that the various suffrage groups had lost their momentum in the late 1880s. The 1890s, however, were not barren years for the cause of women's suffrage. The right to vote in parish, rural district and urban district elections and to become councillors was given to women in 1894; a women's suffrage bill in 1897 achieved a Commons majority on its second reading. The divisions within the suffragist movement were healed in 1897 with the formation of the National Union of Women's Suffrage Societies. As we have seen, the claim that the suffragist movement was in decline before the WSPU's foundation was, therefore, largely suffragette propaganda. What the Pankhursts were justified in pointing out, however, was that all the women's suffrage bills put before Parliament had been private member's bills. Even though these bills had achieved Commons majorities, they had no chance of becoming law because the governments of the day would not allow enough parliamentary time for them to be fully debated. Only a government-sponsored suffrage bill had any realistic chance of becoming law. It therefore became the suffragettes' central objective to put pressure on the government to bring forward a women's suffrage bill.

In 1905 the Pankhursts moved to London and began to focus their activities on the forthcoming general election campaign. The general election of 1906 resulted in a Liberal landslide victory after nearly 20 years of Conservative dominance. A Liberal government was formed under **Henry Campbell-Bannerman**, who was then replaced as Prime Minister in 1908 by **Herbert Asquith**. Asquith was in office from 1908 until 1916. With Liberal governments in power the hopes of the women's suffrage campaigners increased since there was a large body of Liberal MPs who were sympathetic – these included leading Liberal ministers such as **David Lloyd George**. Asquith, on the other hand, was opposed. The suffragette tactic of putting pressure on the government to introduce a

Liberal leaders

Henry Campbell-Bannerman (1836–1908) served a brief term as Prime Minister, 1906–08, before he was forced to retire through ill-health. He was succeeded by **Herbert Asquith (1852–1928)** who served as Prime Minister until 1916. The Chancellor of the Exchequer in Asquith's Government was **David Lloyd George (1863–1945)** who was one of the more radical and reforming members of the cabinet.

HEINEMANN ADVANCED HISTORY

women's suffrage bill was therefore concentrated on Liberal ministers.

WHAT TACTICS DID THE SUFFRAGETTES USE?

In the early years of suffragette activity, between 1905 and 1908, their 'militant' tactics were confined to the heckling of ministers at public meetings, interventions in by-elections to encourage electors to vote against Liberal candidates, and marches and rallies. Breaches of the law were comparatively rare but both Christabel Pankhurst and **Annie Kenney** were arrested in Manchester for obstruction. Government ministers were unmoved by these tactics, pointing out that the suffragettes could only claim to speak for a minority of women. Also, at this stage their tactics were not very different from those of the non-militant suffragists who were organising public demonstrations of their own. For example, the suffragists organised a large open-air demonstration to coincide with the opening of Parliament in February 1907. This 'Mud March', as it became known, established a pattern for ordered, large-scale processions. Another NUWSS march in June 1908 was followed, a week later, by an even larger WSPU demonstration which attracted a crowd of around 30,000 women. Huge crowds watched these demonstrations and even larger numbers read about them in the press. The two demonstrations in the summer of 1908, however, coincided with Asquith becoming Prime Minister, and the size of the crowds was not enough to convince him that the majority of British women wanted the vote. **Emmeline Pethick-Lawrence**, another leading member of the WSPU, wrote in the suffragette journal *Votes for Women* in June 1908, 'We have touched the limit of public demonstration . . . Nothing but militant action is left to us now'.

Attacks on property. Orchestrated by Christabel Pankhurst, the suffragettes began a new, more militant phase of their campaign in 1909 with attacks on property. These included throwing stones at the windows of London clubs, setting fire to pillar boxes, attempts to set fire to the country houses of cabinet ministers and attacks on golf

KEY PEOPLE

Annie Kenney was a cotton factory worker from Oldham. Described as a charismatic speaker, she became a leading figure in the WSPU, taking over the role of organiser in the South-West before becoming a national organiser and staunch ally of Christabel.

Emmeline Pethick-Lawrence (1867–1954) was a wealthy sympathiser of the WSPU. After joining the WSPU in 1906 she raised £3 million for the organisation in six years. She was sent to prison four times for her activities as a suffragette and suffered force-feeding when she went on hunger strike. In 1912 she was expelled from the WSPU after disagreeing with Christabel over the increasingly violent tactics being used.

Mrs Pankhurst and her daughter in prison clothes, a staged photograph for propaganda purposes.

greens. Public demonstrations continued but now involved attempts to storm the lobby of the House of Commons and Downing Street. After a battle with police outside the Houses of Parliament in November 1910, known as 'Black Friday', several suffragettes were arrested including Emmeline and Christabel Pankhurst. Those who were jailed for their activities kept themselves in the public eye by going on hunger strike.

The Conciliation Bill, 1911–12. In 1911 a **Conciliation Bill** was introduced into Parliament which would have given the vote to a limited number of wealthy women. This had the support of the suffragettes because it was a measure for women only and their militant campaign was suspended to give the parliamentary supporters of women's suffrage a breathing space in which to win a parliamentary majority.

KEY TERM

Conciliation Bill The Bill was so called because Asquith's government was attempting to find a compromise solution, acceptable to all parties, to the controversy surrounding the issue of women's suffrage. An all-party Conciliation Committee of MPs was set up to consider the matter, but an acceptable compromise proved elusive.

HEINEMANN ADVANCED HISTORY

After passing its second reading in the Commons, the Bill was killed through lack of parliamentary time, but Asquith's government announced its intention of introducing its own franchise reform. This Franchise and Redistribution Bill would have extended the male franchise only, but Asquith indicated the government would be open to amendments that would extend the franchise to women also. The suffragettes regarded this as unacceptable since the issue of women's suffrage would be tacked onto a male suffrage bill. In any event the Government abandoned its own Bill after the Speaker ruled that a female suffrage amendment could not be added to it. The WSPU decided to resume its militant campaign.

Renewed violence. After 1912 the miltancy became more organised and more extensive. Attacks on property included the breaking of windows of West End stores and arson attacks on buildings. A famous painting in the National Gallery, the *Rokeby Venus* by Velasquez, was slashed with a knife. Asquith and his ministers were assaulted or threatened with assault. These attacks were not confined to London. In Bristol, for example, suffragettes burned a timber yard, two mansions and the University sports pavilion, although students retaliated against the latter by burning down the WSPU office in the city. Many more suffragettes were arrested and hunger strikes resumed. In response the prison authorities resorted to force-feeding but a number of high profile cases, including that of **Lady Constance Lytton**, discredited this practice as being oppressive and a danger to the lives of those who were force-fed. As an alternative, the government passed the **Prisoners' Temporary Discharge Act** which allowed hunger strikers to be released on licence if their health was threatened and then subsequently rearrested when their health improved. In the midst of this stand-off between suffragettes and government, **Emily Wilding Davison** was killed when she threw herself in front of the King's horse, Anmer, at the Derby races in 1913.

FUNERAL OF MISS E.W. DAVISON 1913

HOW EFFECTIVE WAS THE SUFFRAGETTE CAMPAIGN?

Successes

By the time war broke out in 1914 the vote for women in parliamentary elections had still not been won. Had the militant campaign of the WSPU, however, advanced the cause of women's suffrage in any way? It is possible to identify four positive effects of their campaign.

- Militancy attracted publicity, as it was intended to do. Marches and demonstrations, battles with the police and attacks on property were all extensively reported by the press. More publicity made recruitment easier and attracted more funds.
- The anti-suffragists were forced to become more organised in order to counter the propaganda and impact of the suffragette campaign. For example, a National League for Opposing Woman Suffrage was founded in 1911. Although led by men like Lords Curzon and Cromer, the League involved many women in its work. This in itself contradicted the argument of the 'antis' that women should confine themselves to the private sphere.

This photograph shows how effectively the suffragettes turned Emily Davison's funeral into a political demonstration.

The death of Emily Wilding Davison Davison was killed after being trampled by the king's horse during the 1913 Derby. Although the inquest verdict was that she committed suicide, some have questioned this version and have argued that she may have simply slipped under the railing at the edge of the course and fallen into the horse's path. Her funeral was the occasion for an enormous suffragette demonstration as the organisation used her death for propaganda purposes. Davison came from a Northumbrian family and was educated at Oxford.

A suffragette propaganda poster highlighting the inhumanity of force-feeding methods in prison.

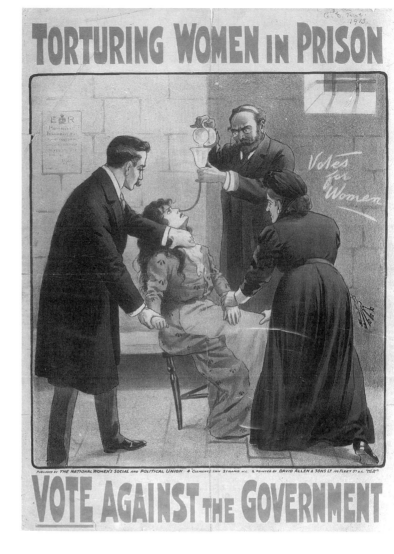

- There was a succession of parliamentary bills brought forward by backbench MPs in the years 1908–11. This followed the pattern set by the earlier suffragist campaign in the period 1867–84. The issue of women's suffrage had returned to the parliamentary agenda after a lull during the period 1897–1907. Credit for this, however, should be shared between the WSPU and the long-standing campaign of the NUWSS.
- An indirect effect of the militant campaign was to boost membership of the non-militant NUWSS. This was partly because the NUWSS now faced serious competition and had to become more active in its recruiting. It was also due to the fact that the WSPU stimulated growing interest in the cause of women's

suffrage, even if many women preferred to join a non-militant organisation. Membership of the NUWSS grew from 12,000 in 1909 to 50,000 by 1914.

Overall failure

The overall effect of the suffragette militancy, however, was to set back the cause of women's suffrage. For women to gain the right to vote it was necessary to demonstrate that they had public opinion on their side, to build and consolidate a parliamentary majority in favour of women's suffrage and to persuade or pressurise the government to introduce its own franchise reform. None of these objectives was achieved.

- Suffragette demonstrations attracted large crowds but this does not necessarily imply that the onlookers were sympathetic. Indeed, the militancy of the years 1912–14 appears to have provoked a backlash. There was anti-suffragette violence during WSPU marches in 1912, and by 1913 it was dangerous for any suffrage supporter, militant or non-militant, to get on a soapbox to make a speech at the well-known Speakers' Corner in Hyde Park. One crucial test of public opinion in 1912 showed the extent of feeling against the movement. The Labour MP and suffrage supporter, George Lansbury, resigned his seat in Parliament to fight a by-election on the issue.

KEY STATISTICS

Parliamentary votes on women's suffrage bills

	Votes	
	for	against
1911 (Conciliation Bill)	255	88
1912 (Conciliation Bill)	208	222
1913	221	268

A WSPU procession in 1908.

HEINEMANN ADVANCED HISTORY

He represented the mainly working-class constituency of Bow and Bromley in the East End of London. The WSPU concentrated its resources on the campaign but the working-class male voters in the constituency had become so alienated from their campaign that Lansbury was defeated by his Conservative opponent.

- In Parliament the pro-suffrage majority which had gradually been cultivated and built up since the 1880s was turned into an anti-suffrage majority. The suffrage bills of 1897, 1904 and 1908 had all achieved majorities on their second readings and the size of the majority had increased after the Liberal election victory of 1906. The 1911 Conciliation Bill also had a majority of MPs in favour. In 1912, however, the Conciliation Bill was defeated by a small majority and another private member's bill in 1913 was rejected by an even larger margin.

- Despite the increasing intensity of the suffragette campaign the government remained unmoved on the issue. Asquith was irritated and embarrassed by the militancy but he was not forced to make concessions. There were serious difficulties facing a Liberal government in tackling the issue of women's suffrage that the WSPU, through its tactical ineptness, did nothing to alleviate. It was unlikely that a Liberal government would agree to the suffragettes' demands for a dedicated women's suffrage bill which would enfranchise women property owners. This would give an electoral advantage to the Conservative Party. The WSPU, for their part, would not accept the alternative strategy of introducing a more wide-ranging franchise bill that would extend the franchise to more adult men as well as to some women. The result was an impasse from which the WSPU derived no benefit. In any event, Asquith's government in the years 1910–14 had many serious problems to contend with and the issue of women's suffrage was not at the top of the agenda.

WHY DID THE WSPU NOT ACHIEVE MORE?

There were many weaknesses in the WSPU organisation, leadership and tactics which limited its effectiveness.

- The leadership style of Emmeline and Christabel Pankhurst was autocratic and alienated many of the organisation's members. The WSPU had no constitution, no annual meetings and no accounts. They demanded unquestioning obedience to their decisions. One suffragette complained that although 'Mrs Pankhurst wishes women to have votes, she will not allow them to have opinions'.

- This style of leadership provoked many splits in the organisation as other leading suffragettes were forced to leave. In 1907 Charlotte Despard and many of the more left-wing members left to form the **Women's Freedom League**. In 1912 Emmeline and Frederick Pethick-Lawrence, who had financed the WSPU and run its newspaper, left to form the United Suffragists. Finally, in 1913, Sylvia Pankhurst herself broke away to form the East London Suffrage Federation and concentrate on building up support among working-class women. According to Sylvia Pankhurst, her sister Christabel expelled her from the WSPU on the grounds that 'You have a democratic constitution for your East London Federation; we do not agree with that ... You have your own ideas. We do not want that'.

- The militant tactics provoked a backlash against the suffrage campaign and polarised opinion. Militancy became the issue and diverted attention away from women's suffrage. Liddington and Norris (1978) have

A Women's Freedom League caravan used to carry speakers on campaigns around the country.

written that militancy carried within itself 'the seeds of its own destruction; each act had to be more militant than the previous one in order to hold public attention; and while violence attracted public interest it also forfeited mass support from women who preferred to join the constitutional, democratic NUWSS'.

- Historians generally have argued that the WSPU was dominated by upper- and middle-class women who made little attempt to build a mass following among working-class women. Liddington and Norris have written about the degree of hostility and suspicion which was shown towards the Pankhursts by Lancashire mill girls. More recently, however, Paula Bartley (1998) has tried to correct this impression by pointing out that a number of prominent suffragettes came from working-class backgrounds – Annie Kenney was a Lancashire textile worker, for example – and that the WSPU built up strong branches in working-class areas of London. She also points to the successful campaign by the WSPU to challenge the threat to the jobs of the pit-brow lasses in the coal mining industry during 1911 as evidence that the organisation did not neglect the issues which were of immediate relevance to working-class women. The evidence on the amount of support the suffragettes had from working-class women is, therefore, rather inconclusive. June Hannam in Purvis and Holton (eds) (2000) has written that 'working-class women were more likely to be involved in the suffrage movement as members of the WSPU, rather than the NUWSS, in particular in towns such as Glasgow and Liverpool ...'. Feminists in these areas tended also to be socialists who made strenuous efforts to link the campaign for women's rights with broader issues of equality and poverty. Hannam points out that although the London-based leadership of the WSPU received most of the attention from contemporaries and historians alike, it was the local branches that provided the movement with its vitality and that each local group had a distinctive character.
- The WSPU offended virtually all the allies on whom their success ultimately depended. Among the more sympathetic ministers in the Liberal government was Lloyd George, yet the WSPU heckled him at public meetings in exactly the same way as they directed their

fire at known opponents of women's suffrage such as Asquith. They also attacked Lloyd George's country house. At by-elections in 1906 WSPU speakers accepted hospitality from local ILP activists and then spoke out against the ILP at election meetings. There were parliamentary supporters of women's suffrage, albeit many of whom were lukewarm supporters who did not expect a reform to be passed. Instead of working to build a parliamentary coalition of suffrage supporters, the WSPU alienated many of the MPs who were on the side of votes for women.

WHAT HAPPENED TO THE NON-MILITANT SUFFRAGIST MOVEMENT DURING THIS PERIOD?

As we have already seen, the actions of the WSPU did have an impact on the non-militant NUWSS. During the years 1908–13 it was the WSPU that was claiming all the attention in the press and this, to some extent, marginalised the NUWSS. On the other hand, the NUWSS was also growing in membership and income and there is evidence that it was having some success in attracting support from working-class women.

Pact with the Labour Party

By 1912 the NUWSS was making a significant change in its non-party strategy. Asquith was considered by both the WSPU and the NUWSS to have been obstructive and devious in his behaviour towards the suffrage campaign and many suffragists came to the conclusion that the Liberal government would not give any priority to the issue. The Labour Party, on the other hand, had given more consistent support to women's suffrage, despite being unwilling to detach the issue of votes for women from the more general demand for full adult suffrage. The NUWSS, therefore, made a pact with the Labour Party under which the women's organisation set up an electoral fighting fund and pledged itself to support Labour candidates in elections where they were fighting against known opponents of women's suffrage. Through this pact the NUWSS became involved in a number of by-elections between 1912–14 in which the Liberals lost a number of seats.

Impact on the government

The impact of this new strategy should not be exaggerated. The Labour Party was still small in parliamentary terms and its leader, Ramsay MacDonald, was determined to maintain the electoral co-operation with the Liberals which had begun in 1903. Nevertheless, the intervention of the NUWSS in elections did put pressure on the Liberal government at a time when it had lost its overall majority in Parliament. Asquith met deputations from the NUWSS in 1913 and from Sylvia Pankhurst's East London Suffrage Federation in 1914. To the latter group he gave a hint that he had come round to the idea of votes for women and that this would have to be on the same basis as an extension of the male franchise. It is entirely possible that Asquith was once again playing for time but it is also possible that he was taking the first steps towards a more sympathetic line on the issue.

SUMMARY QUESTIONS

1 What was the WSPU's justification for using militant tactics?

2 What had the suffragette campaign achieved by 1914?

3 What were the main obstacles in the way of their achieving more?

4 How effective was the leadership of the Pankhursts?

CHAPTER 12

How did the First World War affect the campaign for women's suffrage?

INTRODUCTION

In the summer of 1914, as Asquith was giving his first hints that he was modifying his opposition to votes for women, the suffragette militant campaign was reaching new heights of intensity. During July and early August, however, the international situation was rapidly deteriorating as Europe began to move towards war. Great Britain joined the war on 4 August after Germany invaded Belgium. In the last days of peace, various anti-war demonstrations were organised by pacifist organisations, the labour movement and by women. On the very day that war was declared, a women's protest meeting was held in London at which Mrs Fawcett was the principal speaker. Once the war had started, however, both the non-militant NUWSS and the militant WSPU began to come out in support of the war effort.

Patriotism

The change of tone and policy by the WSPU was the most dramatic. Mrs Pankhurst was strongly anti-German and patriotic and very quickly suspended the WSPU militancy. This decision was helped by the offer of the Home Secretary to release suffragette prisoners, part of a general move towards political reconciliation which was bringing about the cessation of normal political conflicts. The Pankhursts turned the WSPU into a patriotic, pro-war organisation which was committed to supporting the war effort through encouraging women to do war work and exhorting men to enlist. A sign of this change was the renaming of the WSPU newspaper from *The Suffragette* to *The Britannia*.

From a WSPU circular written by Mrs Pankhurst in 1914: 'It is obvious that even the most vigorous militancy of the WSPU is for the time being rendered less effective by the contrast with the infinitely greater violence done in the present war not to mere property alone but to human life.'

Split in the NUWSS

The NUWSS took longer to arrive at a pro-war consensus. Many of the rank and file and of the leading figures within the NUWSS were themselves pacifists, particularly those who came from Quaker backgrounds. After her initial doubts, however, Mrs Fawcett came out strongly in favour of the war and worked to persuade the organisation to follow her lead. It was only after she carried out a purge of the anti-war members of the NUWSS executive in 1915 that the organisation was fully behind her policy. These events led to a split in the NUWSS as the pacifists broke away and concentrated their efforts on campaigning for the rights of conscientious objectors and for a negotiated peace. Many of them were prominent in the **No-Conscription Fellowship** after 1915; indeed, as the male members of the N-CF were imprisoned for refusing to join the armed forces, the organisation was kept going by the work of these women.

The war had, therefore, forced the issue of women's suffrage off the immediate political agenda and brought significant changes to the organisations that were campaigning for women's votes. In the long term, however, the war had a positive effect on the campaign.

KEY ORGANISATION

The No-Conscription Fellowship The N-CF was an organisation set up to resist the introduction of military conscription. Once conscription had been introduced, the N-CF concentrated on supporting conscientious objectors whose appeals against conscription orders had been disallowed. Its members consisted of pacifists, many of whom were Quakers.

HOW DID WOMEN CONTRIBUTE TO THE WAR EFFORT?

The war brought new employment opportunities for women of all classes, and women workers became vital to the production efforts of key industries such as munitions. 'It would have been utterly impossible for us to have waged a successful war', wrote Lloyd George, 'had it not been for the skill and ardour, enthusiasm and industry which the women of this country have thrown into the war.' The war years, 1914–18, therefore, mark a significant turning point in the history of women.

'Business as usual'

During the first year of the war, however, change was very slow. Although many men volunteered for service in the army or navy, the government saw little need to fill the

gaps left in industry or agriculture with women workers. Nor did the government recognise the role that women could play in suppporting the armed forces. When Dr Elsie Inglish, the founder of the Scottish Women's Suffrage Federation, suggested to the War Office that Scottish Women's Hospital Units be formed for service overseas, her proposal was rejected. Undaunted, she formed her own Hospital Unit anyway and took it to Serbia. A similar experience was meted out to the Women's Volunteer Reserve, a body of upper-class women which was formed in February 1915 to support the armed forces. Very little work was found for them. During the early months of 1915 there were some moves at a local level towards women taking over jobs formerly done by men but this did not become a general trend until much later in the year. Indeed, so frustrated had many women become by the refusal of the government to recognise the role that they could play in the war that, in July 1915, the WSPU organised a march of 30,000 women through London to demand 'the woman's right to serve'.

Dilution of labour

By the autumn of 1915, however, the situation had begun to change. The scandal of the shell shortage on the Western Front in the spring had provoked the government into a more interventionist industrial policy. A Ministry of Munitions had been set up under Lloyd George; a Treasury Agreement between government and the trade unions had persuaded the unions to accept the **'dilution' of labour** in the munitions factories and a Munitions of War Act had given the agreement the force of law. Production of weapons, munitions and military equipment had to be increased massively and this could only be achieved through the employment of more women workers. The introduction of conscription in 1916 took many more men away from their employment and the government launched a major effort to fill the jobs left vacant with women workers. By the end of the war some 60 per cent of those employed in shell factories were women.

KEY TERM

Dilution of labour The term 'dilution' was used to describe the practice of getting unskilled and semi-skilled workers to do work which had previously been the exclusive preserve of skilled workers. Many of the 'dilutees' were women workers.

KEY STATISTICS

Women employed in the munitions industry

July 1914	212,000
July 1915	256,000
July 1916	520,000
July 1917	819,000

Women operating machine tools in a war-time armament factory.

Munitions industry. It was in the munitions industry that women made the most direct contribution to the war effort. Under the pressure of patriotic appeals and the demands of the military for large quantities of munitions, the women often worked 12-hour shifts for seven days a week in conditions of some danger. Women proved that they could perform engineering tasks as efficiently as men and, where manual dexterity was required, they could do the work more efficiently. Although they did not have the same level of training as skilled male workers, the work they performed could be done on machines that did not require their operators to be highly skilled. The employment of women workers in engineering, therefore, speeded up the introduction of mass-production techniques. Few women, however, became supervisors or managers. Women usually worked under the supervision of men and few managed to get any extended training, although the NUWSS did establish its own training school for oxy-acetylene welders.

Transport. Starting in Glasgow in 1915, where the municipal tramways took on a few women conductresses as an experiment, the urban transport system came to rely increasingly on women workers as the war progressed. By 1917 there were about 2500 women employed as conductresses on trams and buses. Many of these women were former domestic servants who had taken the opportunity to find better-paid employment.

Commerce and administration. Before the war, the employment of women in clerical and administrative jobs had been increasing; the war brought an even greater increase in this type of employment. The expansion of the government's bureaucracy as both central and local government took on more functions, and the shortage of men, led to a very large increase in the number of women employed in administration, particularly shorthand typists. Two of Lloyd George's secretaries were women.

Medicine. The nursing profession had already become a respectable calling for middle-class women in the late nineteenth century. The war increased demand for nurses and gave large numbers of middle- and upper-class women the chance to make a contribution. By 1917 there were 45,000 women nurses, many of whom had joined the Voluntary Aid Detachments and were working at military hospitals in France.

Police. The appearance of women police officers was a direct consequence of wartime conditions. Originally women's police services were established in garrison towns, to protect the morals of local young women from the large numbers of young men who were away from home for the first time in their lives. There were also the prostitutes which military camps usually attracted. Women police officers had the responsibility for discouraging 'provocative loitering' on the streets, and indecent behaviour in cinemas, parks and public houses. By 1916 most police forces had established women's divisions and the female police officers were being given wider responsibilities, including the controlling of crowds during air raids.

Armed forces. The armed forces were slow to accept that women in uniform could make a useful contribution but the setting up of the Women's Army Auxiliary Corps in 1917 was followed by the Women's Royal Naval Service and the Women's Royal Air Force. In the forces, women were used in support roles, such as helping to maintain lines of communication, ambulance drivers, office workers

Women in the armed forces by 1918

WAAC	57,000
WRNS	3,000
WRAF	32,000

or kitchen workers. The WAAC, by the end of the war, was operating behind the front lines in France and Belgium.

WHAT WERE THE CONSEQUENCES OF THE INCREASED EMPLOYMENT OF WOMEN?

Independence and freedom

- Many women began to experience greater economic independence. The change was perhaps greatest for those middle-class young women who had been financially dependent on their parents before the war and who started to earn an income on their own account. Although women were still not paid the same as men, the incomes which could be earned by shorthand typists or by munitions workers were far higher than most women could aspire to in the pre-war years.

- For some women there was a greater sense of social independence. Those women who went into nursing or the armed forces, and many of the munitions workers, had to work away from home where they experienced a sense of liberation from their restricted home lives. Chaperones disappeared. Self-reliance had to take the place of parental protection.

- Factories and workshops had to pay more attention to the needs of their employees. Factory inspectors and other agencies urged employers to provide canteens for their workers, nurseries for working mothers and medical facilities.

- Despite resistance from trade unions to the dilution of labour, the unions recruited many more women into membership during the war, particularly in the last two years. The number of women who were trade union members increased from around 350,000 in 1914 to some 600,000 in 1917.

- Women began to grow in confidence and self-respect. *The New Statesman* of June 1917 commented that 'They appear more alert, more critical of the conditions under which they work, more ready to make a stand against injustice than their pre-war selves . . . They have a keener appetite for experience and pleasure and a tendency quite new to their class to protest against wrongs even before they become intolerable'.

Changing attitudes

The outward signs of this greater sense of independence and freedom were seen in behaviour and in fashion. Many more women used cosmetics, more women smoked cigarettes and went to public houses. The wearing of shorter skirts and brassieres became more common and trousers became the normal form of workwear for Land Girls and many engineering workers. From these experiences women gained a greater sense of independence and a growing sense of their own worth. One upper-class woman commented: 'The war turned one topsy-turvy, altered one's whole outlook on life. I felt I could never be 'pre-war' again. None of us ought ever to have been like that.' Such a change in attitudes would have to be acknowledged and recognised when the nation returned to the question of votes for women.

HOW WERE VOTES FOR WOMEN FINALLY WON?

Political truce

All normal political activity had been suspended in 1914 in a political truce. The issue of votes for women had been put to one side along with the many other issues that had been the subjects of so much debate in the pre-war years, such as Irish home rule. The year 1915 should have been an election year but, by agreement between the political parties, the general election was postponed until after the war. When that election was held, however, there would be serious problems arising from the outdated electoral register. Most adult males who had the right to vote qualified under the householder franchise which required that they had been in residence at a given address for at least 12 months. This stipulation would have disqualified the men who had left home to fight in the war. To disqualify servicemen from voting on the grounds that they had been away fighting was clearly unacceptable, and so in 1915 Asquith's government began to consider changes in the voter registration requirements in order to restore servicemen to the lists. In doing so the government began a process in which the whole basis of the franchise came under renewed scrutiny. If the registration requirements for men were to be changed, should there not be a thorough reform of the whole system that should include allowing women to vote as well?

Changing climate of opinion

By 1916 there were definite signs that much of the opposition to votes for women was beginning to fade. The ending of suffragette militancy, which had reinforced many male prejudices against women's suffrage, was a helpful factor. More important was the fact that the circumstances of wartime had undermined many of the arguments that had been used to exclude women from the franchise. Many anti-suffragists had argued that since women could not fight or contribute to a war effort they should not have a role in choosing governments which have to make decisions about war and peace. By 1916 many former anti-suffragists were announcing their conversion to votes for women on the grounds that women had demonstrated their courage in many ways. Although die-hard anti-suffragists such as Lord Curzon did not change their minds, there was a notable change of tone on the issue of women's suffrage from the government and from important sections of the press. From May 1915 the government consisted of a coalition made up of politicians from Liberal, Conservative and Labour parties; this had brought into the government politicians like Bonar Law and Arthur Henderson who were sympathetic to the women's cause. Finally, by 1916 there was much debate about the issue of post-war reconstruction, and as politicians and others began to consider the changes that peace should bring, the 'woman question' featured prominently in their deliberations.

Electoral reform

In May 1916, prompted by reports that Asquith's government was considering changes to the registration qualification for male voters, Mrs Fawcett wrote to the Prime Minister to urge him to include the enfranchisement of women in any reform that he might introduce. In July and August 1916 the NUWSS followed this up with deputations to Asquith and to the Conservative leader

Bonar Law. The organisation also began to meet with sympathetic MPs to co-ordinate their tactics for the parliamentary battles that lay ahead.

In October 1916 Asquith's government referred the question of electoral reform to an all-party committee of MPs under the chairmanship of the Speaker. The NUWSS was not allowed to present evidence to this committee but it was able to initiate a series of motions in favour of women's suffrage from political organisations, trade unions and women's societies which were sent to the Speaker as evidence of public backing for their demands. The Speaker's Conference produced its report in January 1917 in which it proposed a simplification of the franchise based on residence alone and the introduction of proportional representation. On the issue of women's suffrage the Speaker's Conference was not so emphatic in its recommendations but it did propose 'that some measure of woman suffrage should be conferred' on 'any woman who has attained a specified age.' For this 'specified age' the report suggested 30 or 35.

Following the report, the government, which since December 1916 had been led by Lloyd George, introduced a Representation of the People Bill. This Bill gave the vote to all adult males and to women over 30. It passed easily through the House of Commons and even the die-hard anti-suffragists in the House of Lords abstained rather than vote against the Bill. The Representation of the People Act, giving women the vote in parliamentary elections, was passed into law in February 1918.

The enfranchisement of women

Women had won the right to vote but not on the same terms as men. There were a number of reasons why the male politicians would not agree to the franchise for all adult women. Firstly, there was still a great deal of prejudice on the subject, which now found expression in the notion that younger women – nicknamed '**flappers**' – were less mature and less capable of exercising rational choices as voters than their male counterparts. There were also considerations of party political advantage to be taken into account. If all adult women had gained the vote

Mrs Fawcett, writing to Asquith in May 1916: 'Our movement has received very great accessions of strength during recent months, former opponents now declaring themselves on our side, or at any rate withdrawing their opposition. The change of tone in the press is most marked … The view has been widely expressed in a great variety of organs of public opinion that the continued exclusion of women from representation will … be an impossibility after the war.'

KEY TERM

'**Flappers**' was the disparaging term used to describe young, single women. It was used by newspapers and politicians to justify the decision not to enfranchise women under the age of 30. 'Flappers' were thought to be rebellious because of their free social life and their perceived rejection of marriage, whereas married women were believed to be more domesticated and would therefore bring a stabilising influence to politics.

A woman voting for the first time in 1918, illustrating the fact that it was mainly married women who had gained the vote.

females would have been in a majority in the total electorate and it was widely assumed that this would favour the Conservatives. Women over 30 were more likely than their younger sisters to be wives and mothers and therefore could be a stabilising influence within the political system. Thus, despite the fact that the majority of the women war workers were younger, single women, the Act discriminated against this group. The NUWSS, for its part, was prepared to accept the age bar for women on the grounds that once women had the chance to exercise the right to vote the prejudice against younger women would disappear.

SUMMARY QUESTIONS

1 How did the women's suffrage organisations react to the declaration of war in 1914?

2 Summarise the contribution made by women to the war effort.

3 To what extent did women achieve greater equality in the workplace during the war?

4 What were the main factors that led to the introduction of women's suffrage in 1918?

CHAPTER 13

What was the impact on British society of the enfranchisement of women?

THE CAMPAIGNERS

The winning of the right to vote in parliamentary elections for some women was, despite its limitations, a major victory for the suffrage campaigners. There still remained many inequalities and barriers to the advancement of women, and former suffragists continued to campaign against them. The WSPU, however, was disbanded after the Representation of the People Act. Mrs Pankhurst continued to be involved in politics as a member of the Tory Party and a candidate for the Whitechapel constituency. Christabel moved to the United States and became involved in a fringe religious group. Sylvia moved further to the left and became a founder-member of the British Communist Party. By contrast, the NUWSS adopted a new name, the National Union for Equal Citizenship, and continued to campaign on other issues of female equality such as equal pay, and against the practice of dismissing women teachers when they married.

WOMEN IN PARLIAMENT

After the Act that granted the right to vote to women over 30, Parliament passed another reform that allowed women to become MPs. There was not an immediate flood of women being elected to Parliament mainly because there was still resistance within party organisations towards adopting women as official candidates. There were seven female candidates in the general election of 1918, of whom only one was elected. Since the only successful woman, the **Countess Markiewicz**, was a candidate for the Sinn Fein Party in Ireland, she never took her seat in the House of Commons.

The first woman to be elected to Parliament and to take her seat was **Lady Astor** who took over her husband's Plymouth constituency when he moved to the House of Lords. Over the course of the next ten years the number of women MPs gradually increased but even in 1929 the 14 women who entered the House of Commons were heavily outnumbered by men in a House of 615 members. Few women were elected because local constituency parties were reluctant to adopt them as candidates, and many of those who were adopted were in seats that the party concerned could not possibly win. The Palace of Westminster, itself, was hardly prepared for the influx of even a small number of women. In 1922 the five women MPs had to share one office and there was no ladies' lavatory in the building.

Another significant political milestone for women was passed in 1929 when **Margaret Bondfield** became the first female cabinet minister. She served as Minister of Labour in the second Labour government between 1929 and 1931.

POLITICAL PARTIES

Although Christabel Pankhurst attempted to establish a separate women's party, her efforts were unsuccessful and the impact of the new women voters on the political scene was channelled through the existing political parties. The parties themselves had to adapt their organisations to accommodate women as full members rather than in the ancillary role which women had held since the 1880s. The Labour Party established a Women's Section, the Liberals had their Women's Liberal Federation and the Conservatives recruited women into their branch structure. The parties began to hold annual women's conferences and to employ professional women organisers. By 1929 the Conservatives were claiming to have recruited 1 million female members while the Labour Party estimated a female membership of between 250,000 and 300,000.

Clearly, then, the enfranchisement of women had brought about some changes within party structures; and the need to appeal to the 8.4 million women who had gained the vote in 1918 had an effect on the policies of the parties.

The Conservatives, for example, made a clear bid for women's support during Baldwin's ministry, 1925–9, when they introduced pensions for widows. In general it seems that the older parties, particularly the Conservatives, became more interested in social reforms and that this was partly motivated by the desire to appeal to women voters. Such an approach, however, was based on a very traditional view of women as being mainly concerned with domestic issues. Parties continued to be dominated by men and no party was prepared to adopt a distinctively feminist agenda. Even the creation of separate structures for women was a double-edged sword. On the one hand it gave women a distinctive place within party structures but on the other hand it was also a way of marginalising women.

These effects should not be exaggerated, however. None of the parties considered it necessary to make any major changes in policies or image to attract the new female voters. Only in one of the elections held during the years 1919–29 were women voters thought to have made a significant impact. That was in 1923 when the Conservative leader, Stanley Baldwin, proposed to reintroduce tariffs on the import of foreign goods. This had implications for higher prices of imported food and other items and it was believed at the time that many women voted against this policy, thereby swinging the result of the election which was a defeat for the Conservatives.

EMPLOYMENT

Although employment opportunities for women generally continued to increase, and female membership of trade unions had reached a peak by the end of the war, there was still staunch resistance within the unions, amongst employers and in Parliament to equal pay and equal opportunities. The Treasury Agreement, which Lloyd George had negotiated with the unions in 1915 to allow dilution of labour, had contained the commitment to restore the pre-war position once the war was over. In 1919, as men returned from the forces and found women still doing the jobs that they had previously considered to be their own, there were demands for the removal of women workers. In Bristol these demands turned to violence when unemployed ex-servicemen rioted and overturned trams in a bid to force the Tramways Company to dismiss the women conductresses and employ men in their place. Such disturbances led to the passing of the Restoration of Pre-War Practices Act that led to the rapid expulsion of many women from their wartime jobs.

OTHER REFORMS

After the enfranchisement of women, there were a number of other reforms to remove some of the more glaring inequalities.

- In 1919 there was a Sex Disqualification (Removal) Act. This gave women the right to become jurors and magistrates and also to become barristers and to enter the higher ranks of the civil service. It also removed the legal barriers to women becoming full graduate members of the universities of Oxford and Cambridge.
- In 1923 a Matrimonial Causes Act gave women the same rights in divorce cases as their husbands.
- In 1925 a Guardianship of Infants Act gave mothers the same rights of custody over their children as fathers.
- In 1928 the Equal Franchise Act finally gave women the right to vote on the same terms as men. Women over the age of 21 could now vote, adding a further 5 million women to the voting register and putting women in a majority in the voting population.

These reforms removed some of the legal discrimination against women; but the National Union for Equal Citizenship continued to press for further reforms. In particular, the issues of equal pay and an end to discrimination in employment were not tackled by governments at this time and the parties were generally agreed that they would not go any further. In 1919, for example, the Labour Party had introduced a Women's Emancipation Bill into Parliament that proposed the removal of all legal inequalities experienced by women. This Bill was blocked and the Sex Disqualification

(Removal) Act that was passed was a much more timid measure. After the passing of the Equal Franchise Act in 1928 progress towards greater legal and civil equality for women via legislation came to a temporary halt. Equal pay and equal opportunities legislation would not come for nearly 50 years.

SUMMARY QUESTIONS

1 To what extent did the enfranchisement of women lead to further advances for women in

(a) political life?

(b) legal rights?

(c) employment opportunities?

2 Why did women not make a greater impact on the political scene in the 1920s?

AS ASSESSMENT: VOTES FOR WOMEN, 1867–1928

STRUCTURED, SOURCE-BASED QUESTIONS IN THE STYLE OF EDEXCEL

Study Sources 1–5 below and then answer the questions which follow:

Source 1. *From a pamphlet written by Millicent Fawcett in 1886.*

Women's suffrage will not come, when it does, as an isolated phenomenon; it will come as a result of other changes which have been gradually and steadily modifying during the century the social history of our country. It will be a political change based upon social, educational and economic changes which have already taken place.

Source 2. *From an article written by Christabel Pankhurst in* ILP News, *the newspaper of the Independent Labour Party, August 1903.*

As a rule, Socialists are silent on the question of women. If not actually antagonistic to the movement for women's rights, they hold aloof from it. One gathers that, some day, when the Socialists are in power, and have nothing better to do, they will give women votes as a finishing touch to their arrangements, but for the present they profess no interest in the subject. Why are women expected to have such confidence in the men of the Labour Party?

Working men are just as unjust to women as are those of other classes.

Source 3. *From a letter written by Millicent Fawcett to the Prime Minister, Herbert Asquith, in May 1916.*

When the government deals with the franchise, an opportunity will present itself of dealing with it on wider lines than the simple removal of what may be called the accidental disqualification of a large body of the best men in the country, and we trust that you would include in your Bill clauses which would remove the disability under which women now labour.

An agreed Bill on these lines would, we are confident, receive a very wide measure of support throughout the country. Our movement has received very great increases of strength during recent months, former opponents now declaring themselves on our side, or at any rate, withdrawing their opposition. The change in the Press is most marked. The view has been widely expressed in a great variety of organs of public opinion that the continued exclusion of women from representation will be an impossibility after the war.

Source 4. *A poster produced by the NUWSS in 1908.*

Source 5. *From Arthur Marwick,* Women at War, 1914–1918 *(1977).*

To say that war brought votes for women is to make a very crude generalisation, yet one which contains an essential truth. One must see the question of women's rights not in isolation, but as part of a wider context of social relationships and political change. A broad liberal-democratic movement starting in the late nineteenth century had come near to achieving votes for women before 1914. Yet the political advance of women in 1914 was still blocked by the vigorous hostility of men, and the often fearful reluctance and opposition of many women. [The War] brought a new confidence to women, removed apathy, silenced the female anti-suffragists. Asquith was only the most prominent of the converts among men. Undoubtedly the replacement of militant suffragette activity by frantic patriotic endeavour played its part well.

(a) Study Source 2.

   What evidence in this source suggests that Christabel Pankhurst did not
   believe that it was a priority for men to give women votes?   (3)

(b) Use your own knowledge to identify Millicent Fawcett, the author of
   Sources 1 and 3, and explain why she was important in the history of the
   women's suffrage movement.   (5)

(c) Study Sources 1 and 5.

   To what extent do Millicent Fawcett and Arthur Marwick agree about how
   to explain the significance of the question of women's rights in the late
   nineteenth century?   (5)

(d) Study Sources 3 and 4.

   Assess the value of these two sources to a historian studying the history of
   the women's suffrage campaign in the years 1911–18.   (5)

(e) Study Sources 3 and 5 and use your own knowledge.

   Do you agree with Arthur Marwick that it was essentially true that war
   brought votes for women? Explain your answer using these two sources and
   your own knowledge.   (12)

Reading
In order to answer these questions you will need to read Chapters 9, 10, 11 and 12 in
this book.

How to answer these questions
Question (a). This is a straightforward question asking you to glean information from
the source and draw inferences from it. Note that the source refers to the attitude of
the men in the Labour Party towards women's suffrage, while the question asks about
Christabel Pankhurst's belief that it was not a priority for men in general. It is
possible to infer from the source that if a progressive organisation like the Labour
Party did not see women's votes as a priority then male politicians as a whole would
not have been very supportive.

Question (b). This is also a straightforward question about the importance of
Millicent Fawcett in the history of the women's suffrage movement. You need to be
able to outline the work of Fawcett within the NUWSS, her beliefs and her

opposition to the methods of the WSPU. Better answers will show an awareness that the NUWSS continued to flourish during the years of the suffragette agitation and that Millicent Fawcett played an important role in lobbying government ministers in the final stages of the struggle for women's suffrage, 1916–18.

Question (c). This question asks you to cross-reference between sources and find similarities and differences. The similarities are quite easy to find. Both agree that the issue of votes for women needs to be put in a wider context in which social and economic factors played a vital part. Note that the question is phrased in terms of 'To what extent . . . agree' and you will need to address this aspect of the question directly and explicitly in order to gain higher marks. You could point to the fact that Fawcett mentions education whereas Marwick does not, as evidence of a difference in *emphasis* between the two sources. You could also note that Marwick mentions the political factor of 'a broad liberal-democratic movement' and Fawcett does not.

Question (d). Questions about the value of sources can be approached from two angles: how much useful information does the source provide, and how reliable is it? Both of these need to be addressed in your answer. Clearly the letter (Source 4) provides more information than the poster; and the poster, as a form of propaganda, is inevitably a highly biased source of information. The fact that the letter was written by Millicent Fawcett, who was a key figure in the suffrage struggle, and that it was written at a crucial stage in the story, gives it a great deal of value as a source of information about the suffragists' tactics and ideas. To gain the higher marks on this question you will need to be able to infer from the sources. For example, the poster gives an insight into the methods of the NUWSS and, from its date, into the fact that the non-violent campaign was flourishing at the time when the WSPU was gaining all the attention.

Question (e). This question carries the most marks and requires the longest answer. Note that you are asked to base your answer on the two sources and on your own knowledge. Appropriately selected quotes from the sources are essential but you will need to place the sources in their context using your background knowledge. Decide on your line of argument before you start and maintain this theme through your answer.

An important part of your answer will be about the impact of the war on the campaign for women's votes. You will need to explain how the war brought new opportunities for women and changed the climate in which the issue of votes for women was discussed. You can infer from Source 4 that there had been significant conversions to the cause of votes for women, including Prime Minister Asquith himself.

You will also need, however, to place the events of the First World War in the context of the whole campaign for votes for women. What were the social, economic and educational factors that led to the growing demand for women's suffrage? How successful had the women's suffrage campaigns been before 1914? Is it possible to argue that the argument in favour of votes for women had been won by 1914 and that women would have gained the right to vote even without the war? In other words, you need to assess the *relative* importance of the war in the overall story of women's suffrage.

A2 SECTION: REPRESENTATION AND DEMOCRACY, 1830–1931

INTRODUCTION

Change

This section of the book is concerned with the changes that were made in the parliamentary system during the period 1830–1931. Beginning with the Great Reform Act in 1832, which made the first change in the system of parliamentary elections since the seventeenth century, there were a series of further reforms in the franchise, the distribution of parliamentary seats, the rules for the conduct of elections and the powers of the House of Lords. A system that was in 1830 dominated by the landed classes, elected on a restricted franchise and was criticised for being unrepresentative and out of touch with society at large, was gradually transformed so that by 1931 it was possible to describe the British political system as democratic. The main theme of this section, therefore, is change over a long period of time. The changes that were made happened in a piecemeal, step-by-step fashion; change was more rapid at some stages in this process than at others. There were numerous pressures that drove the changes forward and many underlying factors that made those changes necessary. Although it would not be accurate to argue that the changes happened in an accidental way, it is nevertheless true that few, if any, of those campaigning for democratic change in the 1820s could have predicted the way that the system adapted and evolved during this period.

Continuity

Although often subject to pressures from outside Parliament, the political parties which introduced these changes remained in control of the political agenda. As a result, the process of political evolution was remarkable, as much for the degree of continuity that was ensured as for the extent of the changes. Aristocratic influence remained strong throughout the nineteenth century; as late as 1900 the British government was led by a member of the landowning aristocracy, Lord Salisbury. The House of Lords, based largely on the hereditary principle, retained formidable powers until 1911 and considerable powers thereafter. The monarchy survived, although the powers of George V in the 1920s were not the same as those assumed by William IV on his accession in 1830. Above all, through all of these changes, the political system itself remained remarkably stable.

Impact

Although we must give due attention to the continuity within the system, we must also acknowledge the impact that changes in the system of parliamentary representation had on other institutions. Local government could not remain an aristocratic preserve after Parliament was opened up to new forces in society. The monarchy had to adapt, and eventually the House of Lords had to be forced to relinquish some of its powers. Political parties were transformed from the narrow, aristocratic, parliamentary cliques which adopted party labels at the beginning of the nineteenth century into the mass political parties with branches in the constituencies and professional agents that had emerged by the end of the century. The role of the state also underwent significant change. By the 1920s the state was involved in areas of the social and economic lives of individuals in ways that would have been unthinkable – and also impracticable – in the 1820s. Part of the reason why these changes had come about was the extension of the franchise to the middle classes and later to the working classes, a process that can be called the transition to democracy.

SECTION 1

Why democracy?

The term 'democracy' derives from the ancient Greek concept of government by the people but only came into common usage in Britain at the time of the American and French revolutions at the end of the eighteenth century. Both the American Declaration of Independence of 1776 and the French Declaration of the Rights of Man and the Citizen of 1790 contained statements of democratic rights and principles which had a relevance far beyond the states in which they originated. The publication of *The Rights of Man* by Tom Paine in 1792 brought these ideas to a British audience. Some British radicals of the 1790s enthusiastically embraced the revolutionary idea that it was the people who had sovereign power, not the monarch, and that the people had natural, inalienable rights which should be enshrined in a written constitution. During the 1790s some radical groups began to make reference to the French Revolution in their speeches and slogans and to adopt French **revolutionary symbols** such as the *tricolore* flag and the 'cap of liberty'. Although the ideas of the French Revolution were wholeheartedly embraced by only a small minority of the people in Britain, the impact of the Revolution coloured the debate over Parliamentary reform in the years preceding the First Reform Act of 1832. Whereas for many radicals, the example of the French in sweeping away the hereditary rights of monarchy and aristocracy and asserting that government should represent the 'general will' of the people, provided an inspiration, the anti-reformers were equally certain that the excesses of the Revolution and its degeneration into the military dictatorship of Napoleon Bonaparte proved that democracy inevitably led to tyranny. In the debates over Parliamentary reform in Britain in the nineteenth century, therefore, democracy was either an ideal to be worked towards or an evil to be avoided at all costs.

A radical political movement, campaigning for democratic reform, began to develop in Britain towards the end of the eighteenth century. For most British radicals a revolutionary overthrow of the existing system was not necessary, unlike the situation in France before 1789. Britain already had a form of constitutional rule that imposed limits on the powers of the monarchy. In their struggle for freedom of speech, of the press and of assembly, which was fought alongside the struggle for representative democracy, the radicals made frequent references to 'the rights of free-born Englishmen'. Tom Paine harked back to an idealised Anglo-Saxon period before English liberties were destroyed by the Normans.

KEY TERM

Revolutionary symbols The red, white and blue colours in the *tricolore* flag that was adopted as the standard of the French Revolution symbolised the people of Paris (red and blue colours of the city) establishing their control over the monarchy (white was the colour of the Bourbon royal family). The 'cap of liberty' was worn by the revolutionary crowds in Paris.

The Rights of Man

The basic principles, as set out in the French Declaration of the Rights of Man in 1790, were as follows:

- 'Men are born and remain free and equal in rights.' Democracy is based on the concept of natural rights that should be guaranteed in law through a written constitution. (Although the Declaration of the Rights of Man ignored the position of women, subsequent declarations of democratic principles have been more inclusive, using the term 'human rights'.)

- The rights of the individual included freedom of speech and of the press, freedom of assembly and of association (the right to demonstrate and to join political parties), freedom of conscience and freedom from arbitrary arrest and punishment. The rights of property owners to keep their property were also included.

- 'The principle of all sovereignty rests essentially in the people.' This was a rejection of the rights of hereditary monarchs to exercise absolute power and an assertion of the right of the people to decide how to govern themselves.

- 'Law is the expression of the general will.' In other words, laws should reflect the interests and the wishes of the majority of the people. In practical terms, this could only be achieved through free elections of representatives to a parliamentary assembly that could claim to represent the will of the people. Although the framers of the Declaration of the Rights of Man did not advocate universal suffrage, over the course of the past two centuries democracy has come to be equated with a system of 'one person, one vote'.

KEY PERSON

Major John Cartwright (1740–1824) was an army officer who became one of the leading radical politicians in the years 1812–20. He was the founder of the Hampden Clubs and went on tours of the industrial areas to rally support for radical politics.

Paine's recipe for the restoration of these ancient liberties was a reformed Parliament elected by universal suffrage. Similarly, **Major Cartwright** in 1776 advocated a series of reform measures that became the stock-in-trade of the radical movement in Britain until the 1850s and were encapsulated in the Six Points of the People's Charter in 1836.

- Universal suffrage.
- Annual parliaments (a general election every year).
- Secret ballot.
- Payment of MPs.
- Equal electoral districts (every constituency to have roughly the same number of voters).
- Abolition of the property qualification for MPs.

Although influenced and inspired by the examples of the American and French revolutions, British radicals drew upon British traditions when presenting their case for democratic change. There were ancient liberties to be restored or defended as well as new rights to be won. There was a parliamentary system that could be reformed and improved rather than a new form of representative government that needed to be invented.

SECTION 2

How undemocratic was the British political system?

A 'BALANCED CONSTITUTION'?

The monarch. The constitutional settlement between Crown and Parliament which had been established after the 'Glorious Revolution' of 1688 created a 'balanced' constitution in which the monarch and Parliament shared power and each acted as a check on the other. Within this arrangement there were both hereditary and elected institutions.

The hereditary part of the constitution consisted of the monarch and the House of Lords, each of which retained considerable powers. The monarch's 'prerogative' powers included the right to appoint and dismiss ministers and the right to veto legislation passed by Parliament, although the last monarch actually to exercise the latter was Queen Anne (1702–14). The monarch could not collect taxes nor keep a standing army in peacetime without the consent of Parliament. But despite these limitations the monarch remained very powerful. Ministers owed their positions to the Crown; civil servants were the servants of the Crown. This placed in the monarch's personal gift a vast array of appointments and patronage which was used to ensure that not only the executive branch of government, i.e. ministers, but also the legislative branch, i.e. Parliament, were subject to the influence of the Crown.

The House of Lords. Membership of the House of Lords was also based on the hereditary principle – apart from the bishops and archbishops of the Church of England who held seats in the House of Lords by virtue of their position in the church. The 'Upper House' still retained the power of veto over legislation passed by the House of Commons, and its members included the most wealthy and powerful men in the country, who filled most of the senior positions within any administration. Many aristocrats also controlled the elections in borough seats to the House of Commons, thereby giving peers a powerful influence in the 'Lower House'.

The House of Commons. The House of Commons, on the other hand, was the elected branch of the constitution. Unlike the situation in most continental European countries, where representative assemblies were either non-existent or met only at the instigation of the monarch, the

British House of Commons had a permanent position within the constitutional framework and very real powers. The Septennial Act of 1716 limited the length of a Parliament to seven years. Annual Mutiny Acts – which limited the monarch's power to maintain a standing army to one year at a time – and annual budgets – which limited the monarch's power to collect taxes and customs revenues to one year – guaranteed that Parliaments would be called into session annually. The House of Commons had established its primacy over the House of Lords and the Crown in matters of finance, which enabled the Lower House to exercise a powerful influence over the government of the day. Although the monarch chose the ministers, no administration could survive which did not have the support of a majority of Members of Parliament. The Commons' claim to its power over ministers, finance and legislation and as a check on the power of the Crown, lay in its representative function. The fact that Members of Parliament could claim – however unjustified that claim might be in reality – to speak on behalf of the nation was the basis of the power of the Commons.

The rights of 'free-born Englishmen'

The system described above was a very long way from being democratic but it was equally far from the system of absolute monarchy which had been overthrown in France after 1789 and which still survived in many European countries. Not only did the British system of constitutional monarchy include a representative assembly with genuine powers but important individual rights were also enshrined in English law. The legal device of habeas corpus was a protection against arbitrary arrest; the independence of the judiciary from the Crown, and trial by jury, aided the fairness of trials. There were no legal guarantees of the freedom of speech, of the press, of assembly or of conscience but in practice all of these existed to some degree. Nonconformists and Roman Catholics were free to worship in their own ways, although there was discrimination against them in public life. There was a vigorous press, public meetings were held and, at least towards the end of the eighteenth century, increasingly critical views of the system of government were being expressed. As the experiences of radical groups in the 1790s and in the post-war years were to show, however, repressive legislation by governments which were fearful of popular unrest could set aside ancient rights such as habeas corpus and place severe restrictions on the freedoms of speech, the press and assembly. Without a written constitution, argued many democratic radicals, the freedom of the individual was subject to the whim of the government of the day.

How representative was the House of Commons?

The basis of the power of the House of Commons was that it was the representative element in the constitution. The claim to be representative of the nation as a whole, however, was coming under severe criticism.

Critics could point to a number of flaws in the system for electing Members of Parliament.

- The franchise was limited to a small minority. In 1800 about 3 per cent of the adult male population could vote. Although the franchise qualification in the boroughs varied from place to place and in some towns the right to vote was held by a majority of the adult male population, over the country as a whole the franchise was the privilege of a minority of the population, not the right of the majority.

A Cruikshank cartoon of 1819 making an ironic comment on how the rights of 'free-born Englishmen' were being trampled on by the post-war Tory government.

- The system of elections was distorted by corruption and influence. The representation of many boroughs was controlled either by the Crown or by wealthy aristocratic patrons. Large sums of money were spent in bribing electors or in employing thugs to intimidate opponents.
- Many elections were not contested at all; instead the parliamentary representation for many constituencies was settled by agreements between the leading families of the district.
- The distribution of parliamentary seats did not reflect the social and economic structure of the country. Rural areas in the southern part of England were overrepresented whilst the growing industrial areas in the north were underrepresented.

From a democratic perspective this system had obvious flaws and was in need of reform. There was a balanced constitution that imposed checks on the power of the Crown, but Crown patronage was used to manage majorities in the House of Commons for ministers. There was an elected element in the constitution, but the claim of the House of Commons to be representative of the nation was increasingly seen to be untenable. However, those radicals who advocated a democratic system of government were conscious that, unlike in France, a revolutionary overthrow of the existing system was not necessary. There was a historical tradition on which to build.

WHO OPPOSED DEMOCRACY AND WHY?

The system for electing the House of Commons was, therefore, subject to growing criticism by the beginning of the nineteenth century. Not all of those who advocated parliamentary reform, however, argued their case from a democratic perspective. When the Whigs introduced the Reform Bill into Parliament in 1831 their main aim was to defend the existing system against demands for democratic change. A thoroughly aristocratic party themselves, the Whigs sought to defend and strengthen aristocratic rule. In proposing to give the vote in borough elections to middle-class property owners the Whigs were trying to give the existing system more legitimacy by broadening the basis of representation. But under the Whig proposals, the House of Commons would still represent interests and property owners rather than numbers of people. The Whigs' main concerns were to restore the balance of the constitution by reducing the influence of the Crown over parliamentary elections, thereby making the House of Commons more independent, and to prevent a revolution by encouraging the middle classes to ally themselves with the aristocracy.

Virtual representation

It is important to recognise that the existing system of representation received much praise as well as criticism. In the eighteenth century, representation in Parliament was viewed differently. Parliament represented 'interests' rather than numbers, with interests being defined in economic terms. The main interests, therefore, were landowners, farmers, merchants, manufacturers, shopkeepers, bankers etc. Tory defenders of the unreformed system of election argued that all of the main interests were represented in Parliament and, since landownership was the most important interest, it was right that landowners should predominate. The existence of some MPs from commercial backgrounds was a sign that these interests were not neglected and other interests enjoyed 'virtual representation' through the fact that there were MPs who would speak on their behalf. The lack of a vote in parliamentary elections did not in itself prevent people from participating in an election campaign and making their views known to the candidates. Elections on the open hustings were lively affairs with voters and non-voters alike making their presence felt; through open voting the minority who did have the right to vote could be held accountable to the community as a whole for the way in which their votes were cast. Once elected, MPs needed to 'maintain the interest' in a constituency which involved taking note of the concerns of the inhabitants, voters and non-voters alike. Despite corruption and the weight of aristocratic influence on the electoral system, therefore, there was a vigorous political culture at constituency level that involved a wider cross-section of the population than the small minority who actually qualified for the franchise.

The anti-reformers

Both Whig reformers and Tory anti-reformers agreed that democracy was an evil to be avoided at all costs. In their eyes democracy was equated with 'mob rule' and democrats were regarded as dangerous and subversive agitators. In the words of **Edmund Burke** in his *Reflections on the French Revolution* (1790) democrats had 'nothing of politics but the passions they excite'. Burke rejected the doctrine of natural rights and stressed the need for any rights to be based on precedent and tradition. In other words, Burke defended the hereditary principle and the existing constitution. Aristocrats were best suited to rule because of their upbringing and their experience; whereas he believed that democracy would inevitably lead to the tyranny of the majority over the minority, aristocratic rule produced harmony in society and stable government.

Just as radical reformers looked to France and the USA for their inspiration, the anti-reformers pointed to the ways in which democracy worked in those countries as evidence in support of their opposition. As late as 1867, during the debates on the Second Reform Bill, **Lord Cranborne** used the American experience to warn of the dangers of

Edmund Burke (1729–97) was a leading politician who came from an Irish middle-class background. He represented Bristol in Parliament. A man of great ability, he wrote many political pamphlets. His *Reflections* became a basis of Conservative political theory, although he entered politics as a Whig.

Lord Cranborne (1830–1903) was Foreign Secretary in Disraeli's government 1867–8. He resigned over Disraeli's decision to introduce a parliamentary Reform Bill giving the vote to some working-class men. Cranborne later succeeded to the title of Lord Salisbury and led the Conservative Party after Disraeli's death.

unmitigated democracy. His main argument was that, in a system in which large numbers of voters were involved, political parties became little more than electoral 'machines' designed to maximise their vote on polling day. The successful politicians would be those who pandered to the prejudices of the electorate and entered into a competitive auction to win the voters' loyalty through promising to promote their economic interests. Aristocratic government, in the view of its apologists such as Cranborne, gave the country the benefits of rule by men of independent judgement and incorruptible standing.

Middle-class attitudes

Fears of democracy were not confined to the landowning classes. Middle-class property owners, who increasingly came to the conclusion that a reform of Parliament was necessary, were equally fearful of the consequences of universal suffrage. If the 'lower orders' were to gain the vote, the middle classes would be in a minority and their interests would be ignored. There was a fear that, since the working classes had no property or stake in society, they would vote for politicians who promised to confiscate the property of the middle and upper classes and redistribute the wealth. They also believed that the working classes did not have the education or the knowledge to use their votes in a rational way. However much a growing number of the middle classes resented aristocratic rule, democracy and revolution from below were feared even more.

KEY QUOTE

Lord Cranborne, speaking in Parliament in 1867: 'We are in danger of drifting into a system of nomination caucuses such as are to be seen in America and such as will arise when there are large multitudes of people in each constituency. Wherever the multitude is so large that it swamps every special local influence, that it destroys every special local interest, what happens is the introduction of the hard machinery of local party organisation conducted by managers, men who give up their lives to the task – not usually men of the purest motives or the highest character.'

Lord Randolph Churchill (1849–95) The third son of the Duke of Marlborough, Churchill became the *enfant terrible* of the Tory Party in the 1880s. A highly ambitious man, he adopted the cause of 'Tory Democracy' – i.e. demanding a greater role for the rank-and-file members in discussions over policy, and adopting policies that would appeal to working-class voters – as a springboard for his own ambitions. He was associated with a small clique within the Tory Party known as the 'Fourth Party' and conducted a long campaign to undermine the party's leader in the House of Commons, Sir Stafford Northcote. Salisbury referred to Churchill as 'a boil on his neck'. His great strengths were his style and panache, his skill as an orator and his ability to make Gladstone look ridiculous.

SECTION 3

How did the electoral system become more democratic?

INTRODUCTION

Between 1832 and 1928 there were a series of reforms of the franchise, of the distribution of parliamentary seats and of the rules for the conduct of elections, that resulted in the system gradually becoming more democratic. There were also reductions in the powers of the House of Lords which confirmed the predominance of the elected House of Commons over the unelected Upper House. Taking an overview of the period it is clear that many of the reforms advocated by the radical reformers of the early nineteenth century such as Major Cartwright and the Chartists, were actually implemented by 1928 and that the parliamentary system had become more democratic. It is also clear that political parties became more broadly based and that those parties which were adamantly opposed to democracy in the 1830s were at least paying lip-service to it by the 1880s. Thus Sir Robert Peel, in the debate on the First Reform Act in 1831, declared that he would 'oppose to the last the undue encroachments of that democratic spirit to which we are advised to yield without resistance'. Contrast this with the use of the term 'Tory Democracy' by **Lord Randolph Churchill** in the 1880s to describe the popular Conservatism which he was trying to encourage. Although Churchill himself had no sympathy whatsoever for genuine democracy, in common with his party leader Lord Salisbury, the fact that the term 'Tory Democracy' was used at all suggests a change in the political climate.

THE PROCESS OF REFORM

Generalisations about historical changes over a period of a century are fraught with difficulty and need to be approached with caution. What can be said with certainty is that the transition to democracy happened on a piecemeal, step-by-step basis. At every stage there was pressure from the disenfranchised for an extension of the right to vote and a fairer distribution of parliamentary seats, but all of the reforms which were implemented were under the control of the politicians. Their main priority was not so much to create a more democratic system as to maintain the stability of the political system and to ensure that their own party gained an advantage from the reforms. Although it is clear that social and economic change was pushing the political system gradually in the direction of transferring power from the aristocracy to the middle and working classes, and that timely concessions by the aristocratic parties avoided the build-up of tensions which could have led to revolution, we need to avoid the assumption that this process was inevitable. Democracy was the eventual outcome of a series of piecemeal reform measures; but at the very beginning of this process reform was seen by its Whig advocates as their most effective defence against the forces of democracy. Even in the 1880s, when a form of limited democracy was achieved, the two main party leaders of the time, Gladstone and Salisbury, were both opposed to full democracy. Nevertheless, the cumulative long-term effect of the series of parliamentary reform measures was the creation of a democratic political system.

What were these measures and what were their effects? The main parliamentary reforms can best be summarised in the form of a table.

Summary of the main parliamentary reforms, 1832–1928

Date	Title of Reform	Details of changes
1832	First Reform Act	*Franchise:* In boroughs, a uniform franchise was introduced, based on the £10 householder qualification. In effect, this gave the vote to middle-class, adult males. In the counties, the right to vote was kept by the 40-shilling freeholders (landowners) and extended to tenant farmers.
		Seats: 56 small boroughs lost both seats in Parliament, 30 lost one seat. 42 new boroughs were created, including the larger industrial towns of Manchester, Birmingham, Leeds etc. County constituencies also gained extra seats.
		Registration: Voters now had to be properly registered before they could exercise their right to vote.
1867	Second Reform Act	*Franchise:* In boroughs, the vote was given to householders and lodgers who had been resident for at least 12 months. In effect, this gave the vote to the skilled

artisans. In the counties, more landowners and tenant farmers were added to the electoral register.

Seats: 38 small boroughs lost one member. Four boroughs lost both members because of corruption. 19 seats given to boroughs, 26 seats given to counties.

1872	Secret Ballot Act	Voting to be conducted by a secret ballot, replacing the old, open voting system.
1883	Corrupt Practices Act	Corrupt practices in election campaigns – defined as 'bribery, treating, undue influence, assaulting, abducting or impersonating' – were banned, punishable with imprisonment or a fine and a ban from membership of Parliament for seven years. Limits were set on the amounts candidates could spend on election campaigns and proper accounts had to be kept.
1884	Third Reform Act	*Franchise:* A uniform franchise for counties and boroughs; all adult males occupying land or 'tenements' worth £10 a year or more.
1885	Redistribution Act	107 boroughs lost representation in Parliament. Seats gained were redistributed to largest cities and counties.

A radical redrawing of constituency boundaries. Most large cities and all counties were divided into separate constituencies, each with one Member of Parliament. (24 boroughs still had two members.) Principle of electoral districts (constituencies) having roughly equal populations now accepted, and an independent body, the Boundary Commissioners, set up to oversee future changes in constituency boundaries.

How did the electoral system become more democratic?   199

1911	Parliament Act	Powers of House of Lords severely reduced. Power of veto over legislation passed by House of Commons was abolished and replaced by power to amend or delay legislation for up to two years. House of Lords to have no powers over finance bills passed by Commons. Parliamentary elections to be held at least every five years. MPs to be paid a salary.
1918	Representation of the People Act	*Franchise:* All adult males (over 21), with at least six months residence, entitled to vote. Women over age of 30 able to vote if (a) they were local government electors, or (b) they were householders, or (c) their husbands were entitled to vote.
		Seats: An extensive redistribution of seats to larger cities and towns
1928	Equal Franchise Act	Women over the age of 21 were given the vote on the same terms as men.

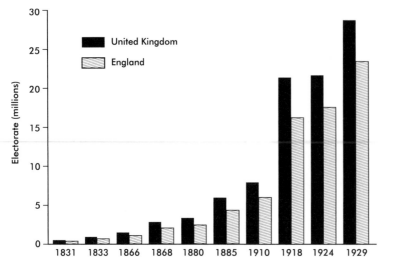

A bar graph to show the growth of the electorate between 1831 and 1929.

What was the significance of these reforms?

OPENING THE DOOR: THE FIRST REFORM ACT, 1832

The significance of the First Reform Act of 1832 continues to provoke controversy between historians. No modern historian would agree with the view of **J. R. M. Butler** in *The Passing of the Great Reform Bill* (1914) that the Reform Act 'placed the feet of the nation firmly in the direction of democracy'. As **Evans** (2000) has pointed out, this is to view history from the wrong end of the historical process, using the benefit of hindsight to impose an interpretation on a historical event which cannot be supported by a detailed study of its actual context. The Whigs who introduced the Reform Act were seeking to strengthen the defences of the existing political system against the demands of those who wanted democracy; they were attempting to 'reform in order to preserve'. A number of historians have in fact argued that the Reform Act of 1832 changed very little and left the political system riddled with all of the abuses and anomalies which had exposed the unreformed system to much criticism. Thus **Gash** (1979) has written that the Reform Act was 'no more than a clumsy but vigorous hacking at the old structure to make it roughly more acceptable'. **Vernon** (1993) has gone even further in arguing that the Reform Act did not represent any real advance towards democracy. 'English politics', he has written, 'became progressively less democratic during this period as political subjectivities and the public political sphere were defined in increasingly restrictive and exclusive fashions.' **Evans** (2000), on the other hand, has attempted to reinstate the view that the Reform Act did have a significant impact on the politics of the post-reform era.

Continuity with the pre-1832 system

A detailed examination of the results of the 1832 Reform Act has already been given in an earlier chapter (see Chapter 5) and a summary of the main points will suffice here. It is clear that the Reform Act of 1832 made many changes in the franchise qualification in both borough and county constituencies and also redistributed a number of seats from the smaller boroughs to the larger industrial and commercial towns and to the counties. It is also clear that the electoral system after 1832 still contained many of the abuses for which the unreformed system had been criticised.

- The electorate had been increased from 478,000 to 813,000 (United Kingdom total figures) but this still represented only 8 per cent of the total adult population. The franchise was still very restrictive, and confined to owners of property. Only males could vote.
- There had been an extensive redistribution of parliamentary seats, and growing industrial towns such as Birmingham, Manchester and Leeds gained direct representation in Parliament for the first time. The distribution of parliamentary seats after 1832 was still heavily weighted in favour of the more rural, southern half of England. Smaller boroughs still had the same parliamentary representation as the large industrial centres. The principle of equal electoral districts had not been conceded.
- Voting was still conducted by open declaration and voters were therefore subject to pressure and influence. Bribery, intimidation and violence were just as prevalent in elections held after 1832 as they had been before.
- MPs were not paid a salary and still had to satisfy a property qualification. The majority of MPs still came from the landed classes. There were not significantly more middle-class MPs in parliaments elected after 1832 than there had been before and it was still impossible for any man of working-class origin to enter Parliament.

On one level, then, the Reform Act of 1832 had changed very little. Parliament still represented 'interests' rather than numbers. The franchise was restricted to owners of property, and the landed elite continued to dominate political life. Indeed, for working-class radicals who had been campaigning for a more democratic system, the Reform Act in many ways represented a step backwards. Some boroughs had had a relatively open franchise qualification before 1832 which entitled many working-class males to vote; under the Reform Act these men kept the right to vote for their own lifetimes but could not pass it on to their descendants. The result was that in the longer term there were fewer working-class voters after 1832 than there had been before. This was the basis for Vernon's claim that the post-reform era was less democratic, not more.

Impact of the Reform Act

As has been shown in an earlier chapter (see Chapter 5), however, the 1832 Reform Act did have a significant impact on political life.

- There were more contested elections after 1832. Voters could therefore have more influence over the composition of the House of Commons.
- Party organisation and the domination of politics by parties were given a significant boost by the Reform Act.
- Because of the manner in which the Reform Act was passed, the House of Commons had established a clear predominance over the House of Lords.

KEY PEOPLE

Lord Derby (1799–1869)
Known as Lord Stanley until he succeeded to the family title in 1851, he entered politics in the 1820s and served in Grey's Whig government 1830–4. He joined Peel's government in 1841 but resigned over Peel's decision to repeal the Corn Laws. Derby was very able but rather lazy. He was leader of the Conservative Party until 1867, and served as Prime Minister three times, in 1852, 1858–9, and 1866–7.

Benjamin Disraeli (1804–81) also opposed the repeal of the Corn Laws in 1846. Although he was one of the most able Conservative politicians after the split of 1846, he was denied the leadership because of prejudice against his Jewish origins and his flamboyant style. He served as Chancellor of the Exchequer under

Derby in 1866–7, and became Prime Minister for the first time after Derby's retirement from politics.

William Gladstone (1809–98)

Gladstone was the son of a Liverpool merchant who entered politics as a staunch Tory and defender of the Anglican Church. He supported Peel in the split of 1846 and became a leading figure in the Peelite group of MPs. He served as Chancellor of the Exchequer in Whig-Liberal governments in the 1850s and 1860s, showing himself to be committed to free trade, low taxation and low government expenditure. He became Liberal leader after the retirement of Russell in 1867 and Prime Minister for the first time in 1868.

- The influence of the monarchy, particularly over the choice of ministers and over the outcome of general elections, was shown to be much reduced in the post-reform era.
- Local government was reformed, breaking the monopoly of Tory landowners over the government of the towns.
- General elections began to become the means by which governments were chosen. Public opinion became a more important factor in political calculations.

Political life in the years after 1832 was different in many ways from the preceding era but aristocratic dominance of parliamentary representation and of government continued, just as the Whig architects of the Reform Act intended. Indeed, the Whig strategy of forging a new alliance between middle-class property owners and aristocratic landowners was seen to have been successful when the bulk of the middle classes supported the government against the Chartists during the years 1837–48. Neither the Whigs nor the newly enfranchised middle classes believed that further extensions of the franchise or other democratic reforms were necessary or desirable. But once the principle had been accepted that 'Old Corruption' was unacceptable and that the constitution was in need of reform, a precedent had been set. This was never the intention of the Whigs, but the fear that the Reform Act would lead inevitably to further parliamentary reforms was one of the main reasons why the Tories opposed it. 'I have been uniformly opposed to reform on principle', stated Peel, ' because I was unwilling to open a door which I saw no prospect of being able to close.'

LEAPING IN THE DARK: THE SECOND REFORM ACT, 1867

The Second Reform Act was passed by a Conservative government led by **Lord Derby** but in which **Benjamin Disraeli** was the dominant influence. It had been the Conservatives' intention to construct a Reform Act that was 'extensive, safe and satisfactory'. What was finally passed in the summer of 1867 was certainly extensive in the way that it increased the size of the electorate, but whether the Conservatives and their supporters could feel that it was safe and satisfactory was open to doubt.

Gladstone's Bill, 1866

Proposals to reform the parliamentary election system were first put before Parliament by **William Gladstone**, a leading Liberal, in 1866. Pressure for reform from outside Parliament had been gradually building since 1864 when the **National Reform Union** and the **Reform League** had been founded. Gladstone's Bill was far from radical. He proposed lowering the £10 rental qualification for householders, adopted in 1832, to £7, thereby giving the vote to an estimated 200,000 extra men, most of whom would be skilled artisans. This was the first time that any members of the working classes had been considered fit to exercise the franchise; and because Gladstone was aware of the opposition this would provoke, he proposed only to enfranchise the better-paid, better-educated and (by implication) more respectable artisans. The rest of the working classes – referred to as the 'residuum' in the debates on the Bill – were still considered to be unfit to exercise the franchise. Nevertheless, Gladstone's proposals were too radical for many of his fellow Liberals and the Bill was defeated after the Liberal Party split.

Disraeli's Bill, 1867

A Conservative government led by Lord Derby now took office and proceeded to introduce its own Reform Bill with Benjamin Disraeli as the main architect of the measure. The Conservatives took office in an atmosphere of crisis as the NRU and the RL united in a campaign of protest meetings that culminated in the Hyde Park riots of July 1866. There was also a series of reform demonstrations in the north of England in the autumn. The strength of feeling displayed on the reform issue showed the new government that it was not an issue that could be quietly dropped. But Disraeli's motives in taking up the cause of reform were more to do with exploiting the divisions in the Liberal Party, and with gaining the credit for himself and the Conservative Party in succeeding where Gladstone had failed. Disraeli's Reform Bill proposed to give the vote to all male householders in the boroughs but the effects of this seemingly radical measure were to be limited by a number of restrictions, including a two-year residence qualification and the stipulation that householders must pay their own rates. It would have resulted in a modest expansion of the electorate – by about 400,000 men. During the course of the parliamentary debates on the Bill, however, Disraeli accepted a number of amendments which resulted in the extension of the franchise being much greater than originally intended. The two-year residence qualification was reduced to one year and '**compounders**' were allowed to vote. In its final form, therefore, the Second Reform Act increased the size of the electorate in the boroughs by about 700,000 men.

Borough electorate

The increase in the size of the electorate brought about by the Second Reform Act was huge in comparison with the First Reform Act. Most of this increase was concentrated in the boroughs. The table shows how the size of the electorates in some of the industrial towns grew dramatically after the Act was passed.

KEY ORGANISATIONS

The **National Reform Union** was essentially a middle-class body. Based in Manchester, and including many former members of the Anti-Corn Law League, it campaigned for a limited extension of the franchise to include all male ratepayers. The **Reform League** was more working-class in composition and had close links with trade unions. Its aims were more radical than the NRU since it campaigned for manhood suffrage.

KEY TERM

Compounders were tenants who paid their rates (local government taxes) with the rent they paid to their landlord, rather than directly to local councils as houseowners did.

Examples of the growth in the size of the electorate as a result of the Second Reform Act

Town	Number of voters in 1866	Number of voters after 1867
Birmingham	15,500	42,000
Blackburn	1,800	9,700
Bradford	5,708	21,518
Leeds	7,217	35,510
Manchester	21,542	48,256
Newcastle	6,630	21,400

Even more significant was the fact that in many of these boroughs working-class voters were in a majority after 1867. The enfranchisement of part of the working classes was viewed with alarm by politicians in both major parties and prompted resignations from Derby's cabinet when Disraeli's Bill was first published. Lord Cranborne accused Disraeli of betraying his party and conceding the principle of a democratic political system which would sweep away the aristocracy. Clearly, the conceding of votes to some working men could not be accomplished without some repercussions for the political system, but the seemingly radical gesture made in the Second Reform Act was hedged around with so many restrictions and safeguards for the property-owning classes that genuine democracy was no more than a distant point on the horizon.

Continuity with the past

The undemocratic features of the post-1867 system were as follows:

- The limited redistribution of seats in the 1867 Act still left London, the Midlands and the north underrepresented in Parliament. There was still an imbalance in the system which allowed the rural south and west of England to be overrepresented in terms of size of population. Thus the South-West, with 76,612 borough electors, had 45 MPs while the North-East, with 232,431 electors, had a mere 32. Such an uneven distribution of seats favoured the landowning classes who still tended to influence the representation of the smaller borough seats. The House of Commons in the 1870s was still dominated by landowners.
- The franchise in the counties was still based on property ownership and was still very restrictive.
- Even in the boroughs, the householder franchise was hedged around with many restrictions. The **one-year residence requirement** discriminated against the significant proportion of working-class males

KEY FACT

The one-year residence requirement This qualification also disenfranchised some middle-class men. Many bank employees and teachers moved from place to place during the course of their progress up the career ladder; Wesleyan Ministers moved as part of their vocation. Each time they moved home they would have to begin the process of registering for the vote over again.

(possibly as high as 30 per cent) who moved frequently from one rented accommodation to another. Some categories of men were specifically excluded from the franchise. These were any man in receipt of poor relief, adult males living with their parents, lodgers paying less than £10 a year rent and servants. The effect of these restrictions was to disqualify up to 40 per cent of adult males from voting in some boroughs. This figure varied from borough to borough because the interpretation of the Act was left in the hands of local officials, some of whom took a more liberal interpretation of the regulations than others.

- Because the basis of the franchise for many was still the ownership of property, 'plural voting' was allowed. Men who owned property were allowed to vote in each constituency in which their properties were situated. It was not uncommon for many owners of businesses to have factories or offices in a borough but to live in a country area near to the town; such people were entitled to vote in both borough and county elections. Some of the more wealthy, owned properties in several constituencies. Plural voting, which in the years after 1867 grew to represent about 7 per cent of the total electorate, gave the middle classes and landowners additional weight in the political system.

In giving the vote to part of the working classes, the 1867 Act did take the electoral system into previously uncharted territory. This is what prompted Lord Derby to describe the reform as a 'leap in the dark'. But Disraeli intended that this step should be a very tentative one, with only the more 'respectable' artisans being given the vote, and the position of property owners within the existing system being protected. Parliamentary representation after 1867 was not based on 'mere numbers' and retained a number of undemocratic features, not the least of which was the fact that the vote was still granted as a privilege, not a right.

'A CHANGE FROM PUBLICITY TO SECRECY': THE SECRET BALLOT ACT, 1872

Support for the secret ballot

The abolition of voting by public declaration and its replacement by a system of voting by ballot was introduced by Gladstone's Liberal government in 1872. Radicals had long campaigned for this reform as a means of preventing the influencing, bribing and intimidation of voters through more discreet means of persuasion by aristocratic patrons. The extension of the franchise in the boroughs in 1867 brought within the electorate working-class men who, it was feared, might be more susceptible to bribery than the more affluent middle-class voters. There was also an element within the Liberal Party, personified by **John Bright**, who believed that the tenant farmers in the counties were obliged to vote for the landlords' candidates through fear of eviction from their farms.

John Bright (1811–89) was a leading radical politician who had been one of the leaders of the Anti-Corn Law League in the 1840s. In the 1850s and 1860s he continued his campaigning against the waste and inefficiency of a governmental system based on aristocratic patronage, and was a leading exponent of the extension of the franchise in 1867. He served in Gladstone's cabinet as President of the Board of Trade, 1868–70.

The secret ballot, therefore, was considered to be an essential first step towards the rooting out of corruption and influence in elections.

Defenders of open voting

The system of open voting was not without its defenders. Lord John Russell, the architect of the First Reform Act of 1832, was adamantly opposed to the secret ballot, which he described as a 'change from publicity to secrecy'. He opposed it, he wrote, because he saw it as 'an obvious prelude from household to universal suffrage' and because it would undermine what he regarded as the exercise of 'legitimate' influence by aristocratic patrons over people who looked to them for leadership. Defenders of the open voting system regarded secret ballots as being in some way 'unmanly' and tainted with cowardice.

The significance of the reform

The secret ballot, therefore, had great symbolic significance for both sides in the debate about democracy. The results of its introduction did not bear out the hopes of its supporters or the fears of its opponents. Corruption of voters was not rooted out and elections continued to be very lively affairs. Those constituencies which had a reputation for a corrupt electorate continued to cause concern after 1872; it seemed that the only difference the secret ballot had made was that voters could now take bribes from both sides of the contest. The election of 1880 was the most expensive to date. It was not until the Corrupt Practices Act of 1883 imposed stiff penalties for bribery and set strict limits on election expenditure that the conduct of elections was, at least partially, cleansed of corruption.

CREATING AN 'UNMODERATED DEMOCRACY'? REFORM AND REDISTRIBUTION, 1884–5

The 1867 Reform Act had established a **household suffrage** in the boroughs; but the franchise in the counties was still based on a narrow property qualification. This was an anomaly that could not survive long, and in 1884 Gladstone, in his second term as Prime Minister, decided to tackle the issue. Although there was very little pressure from the country areas themselves for an extension of the franchise to farm labourers, there was pressure from the radical wing of the Liberal Party to continue with the process of parliamentary reform. Giving the vote to farm labourers, it was assumed, would weaken the influence of the landowners in the county elections and enable the Liberals to gain more seats from the Tories. For this same reason, the Tories opposed the reform in principle, but the party leader, Lord Salisbury, showed great tactical skill in turning the situation to the Tories' advantage. With a permanent Tory majority in the House of Lords Salisbury could have blocked the Franchise Bill,

KEY TERM

Household suffrage The 1867 Act had given the vote to male householders in the boroughs. This meant that even those men who rented their homes could qualify for the vote since they were classified as the 'householder'. In the counties the franchise was still based on the 1832 Reform Act which allowed landowners and tenant farmers the right to vote but did not extend the franchise to agricultural labourers.

but this would have appeared as the actions of a self-serving, reactionary minority. Salisbury therefore let it be known that he would only allow the Franchise Bill to pass if it was accompanied by an extensive Redistribution Bill. Negotiations between the party leaders led to an agreement known as the **Arlington Street Compact** which laid down the principles on which a redistribution of seats was to be based. Together, the 1884 Franchise Act and the 1885 Redistribution Act brought about one of the most radical changes in the parliamentary election system during the nineteenth century.

Franchise Act

The effects of the Franchise Act were very substantial. An extra 2.5 million voters were added to the electorate, most of whom were farm labourers or rural craftsmen. This was a greater number of additional voters than had been created by either the 1832 or the 1867 Reform Acts. The franchise qualification was now the same in both borough and county seats. The establishment of a 'household suffrage' qualification prompted one contemporary writer, Sir Herbert Maine, to describe the new system as an 'unmoderated democracy'. This it quite clearly was not. The qualifying regulations for the franchise still excluded many adult males and all adult females. The same categories of men who were excluded in 1867 were still unable to exercise the right to vote after 1884. The system for registering voters was very complex and bureaucratic; those with low levels of literacy were unlikely to be able to understand the regulations or the procedures for registering as a voter. The result was that, in the decades leading up to the First World War, around one-third of adult males were **disenfranchised** and the vast majority of these were unskilled and casual workers. The effects of this were particularly evident in the large cities, where registration rates were generally lower than in the countryside and the smaller towns.

Redistribution Act

The 1885 Redistribution Act brought about the most far-reaching redistribution of seats of any of the nineteenth century reforms. The traditional pattern of distribution of parliamentary seats was based on each county and borough having two Members of Parliament each. This pattern had been amended in 1832 and 1867 so that some boroughs had been reduced to one member and others had gained additional members. Some counties had also gained extra seats. There had been some redrawing of constituency boundaries in 1867, but parliamentary constituencies were still, in the 1880s, based on historic communities. There were still large variations in the size of electorates between boroughs, and the heavy bias in parliamentary representation in favour of the rural southern part of England continued.

KEY TERM

Arlington Street Compact The agreement between Gladstone and Salisbury over franchise reform was named after Salisbury's London home, where the agreement was finalised.

KEY FACT

Disenfranchisement Tanner (1990) has shown how the franchise qualification was particularly biased against the younger, single men who were not householders. There was a bias in the system against working-class men but in some of the larger cities by the beginning of the twentieth century significant numbers of the poorer slum dwellers had succeeded in registering as voters, e.g. in the East End of London. Younger men had more difficulty in satisfying the registration requirements than older men.

Constituencies of equal size. Under the 1885 Redistribution Act, two major changes were introduced. Firstly, constituencies were made much more equal in size. Taking the figure of 50,000 electors as an average, constituency boundaries were redrawn to bring greater equality of representation. Constituencies which had fewer than 15,000 electors lost their separate representation in Parliament; those between 15,000 and 50,000 lost one of their MPs and those over 50,000 were divided into separate constituencies. Disparities between the size of constituencies continued to exist, but the principle of equal electoral districts had been accepted and an independent Boundary Commission set up to keep constituency boundaries under regular review.

Single-member constituencies. Secondly, most constituencies after 1885 were represented by a single MP. This involved dividing the counties and large boroughs into separate parliamentary divisions. In the process, Parliament lost its connection to those historic communities which had formerly been represented. Thus Bristol, for example, was divided into four constituencies – North, South, East and West – and some of its outlying suburbs were included in the Frome Division of Somerset or the Thornbury Division of Gloucestershire. All other large towns and cities were divided in a similar way.

Not only were these new constituencies rather artificial creations but they were also often dominated by one class or another. Boundaries were drawn with regard to 'the pursuits of the people'. In other words, economic and social factors were taken into account with the result that some constituencies had an overwhelmingly working-class electorate whilst others were dominated by the middle classes. Salisbury was well aware of the trend among the middle classes to move their allegiance away from the Liberal Party to the Conservative Party; in his dealings with Gladstone he took care to ensure that the large towns were divided in such a way as to create distinctly suburban constituencies where the middle classes would be in a majority. The results of redistribution, therefore, were to be a major increase in Conservative MPs returned from the large towns.

TAMING 'MR BALFOUR'S POODLE': THE PARLIAMENT ACT, 1911

The hereditary character of the House of Lords and its power of veto over legislation passed by the House of Commons had long been regarded by radicals as an obstacle to democracy. Abolition of the House of Lords, or its replacement by an elected second chamber, were included in radical programmes during the nineteenth century but never pursued with any great vigour or urgency. For radicals, the priority was to make the House of Commons more representative. Whig and Liberal governments during the nineteenth century had experienced problems with the permanent Tory majority in the Lords. The Lords' attempt to block the 1832 Reform Act was one of a number of occasions when the Upper House used its powers to thwart a reforming government. Gladstone had experienced similar problems when his Irish Home Rule Bill was thrown out by the House of Lords in 1894. The number of occasions when legislation passed by the Commons was actually blocked by the Lords was relatively small, but the very fact that there was an anti-reform majority in the Lords was a factor which all Whig and Liberal governments had to take into account when drafting their legislation.

The Liberal Government, 1906

A Liberal government was elected in 1906 with a large majority and an extensive programme of reforming legislation on its agenda. Right from the beginning there were problems with the House of Lords. In 1906 an Education Bill and a bill to abolish plural voting were vetoed in the Upper House. Other bills suffered a similar fate in 1907. The major clash with the Lords, however, occurred over the budget of 1909. The Chancellor of the Exchequer, **David Lloyd George**, proposed to raise extra government revenue to finance the new Old Age Pension scheme and the expansion of the Royal Navy, by increasing taxes. Much of this increased tax burden would fall on the wealthy, particularly landowners who were faced with increased death duties and a tax on land values. There was an unwritten convention that the House of Lords did not interfere with finance matters but on this occasion the House of Lords, with the assent of the Conservative leader **Balfour**, rejected the budget. Asquith's Liberal government regarded this as an unconstitutional challenge to the authority of the elected government and decided to take on the House of Lords and reduce their powers.

Constitutional crisis

Since this issue had not been raised during the previous election campaign, Asquith decided to call a general election to seek a mandate from the electorate. The result of the January 1910 general election was that the Liberals lost their overall majority but were able to continue in office with the support of Irish and Labour MPs. Asquith then proceeded to introduce a Parliament Bill which would remove the Lords' power of veto and replace it with the power to delay legislation for up to two years. The Lords would also have no power over finance bills, and the maximum period between general elections would be reduced from seven years to five. These limited changes were, inevitably perhaps, rejected by the House of Lords and a full-scale constitutional crisis followed. Attempts at finding a compromise solution came to nothing and Asquith asked the king, George V, to create enough new Liberal peers to swamp the Tory majority in the Lords. This was following the precedent set by

KEY PERSON

David Lloyd George (1863–1945) was Chancellor of the Exchequer in Asquith's government and one of the 'New Liberals' most committed to social reform. Before becoming a minister he had acquired a reputation as a leading radical politician. Coming from a middle-class, nonconformist, Welsh background, he obviously relished the prospect of a clash with the aristocratic House of Lords. He became Prime Minister in 1916, at the head of the wartime Coalition government.

Lord Grey in his clash with the Lords over the First Reform Bill in 1831–2. The king was reluctant to do this and insisted upon another general election before he would agree. The result of the December 1910 general election was almost identical to that in January and the king then agreed to create the Liberal peers if the Bill could not be passed in any other way. Faced with the prospect of not only losing some of their powers but also losing the Tory majority, enough peers changed their minds on the Parliament Bill to allow it to be passed. The Parliament Act became law in 1911.

Parliament Act 1911

The changes made by the Parliament Act to the powers of the Lords were essentially limited. The Lords still kept their power to delay legislation for up to two years; since the period between general elections was reduced to five years, the Lords in practice still had the power of veto over legislation introduced during the last two years of a government's term of office. The Liberal government could have gone further in reforming what Asquith referred to as 'Mr Balfour's Poodle'. Hereditary peers' right to sit in the Upper House could have been removed and the House could have become an elected second chamber, or the House of Lords could have been abolished altogether. Both of these reforms would have been more consistent with a democratic system of government. Asquith, instead, opted for a more limited reform that allowed the Upper House to retain its hereditary character and some of its powers.

A MASS ELECTORATE: THE REPRESENTATION OF THE PEOPLE ACT, 1918

The background to the change in attitudes towards the enfranchisement of women and a large section of the adult male population has already been explained in Chapter 5. What needs to be emphasised here is that the 1918 Representation of the People Act was the most radical and far-reaching of any of the Reform Acts and that the impact of the First World War played a major role in bringing it about. According to **Evans** (2000), 'Britain was jerked into [democracy] by the horrendous discontinuity of the First World War'. The experience of the war rendered old assumptions about the unfitness of women and young, working-class males to participate in political life manifestly untenable. Strong support for manhood suffrage from leading politicians such as Lloyd George was a direct result of the sacrifices being made by young men on behalf of the nation. Once the question of an extension of the franchise was back on the agenda, the issue of 'votes for women' could not be ducked or sidelined by governments any longer, especially as women too were demonstrating their commitment to the war effort in a number of ways. Many politicians and members of political parties, particularly in the Conservative Party, continued to express fears about the dangers of creating an electorate in which working-class males would be in a majority. Some Conservatives viewed the enfranchisement of women, particularly if limited to older women who were assumed to be more likely to vote conservative, as a useful compensatory factor for their party. By 1918 a 'patriotic consensus' in favour of an extension of the franchise had developed and the Representation of the People Act was the result.

Changes in the electorate

The Act resulted in an expansion of the electorate by a factor of almost three. This was the largest extension of the electorate by any of the major Reform Acts; it included about 8 million women, who now made up about 40 per cent of the total electorate. The Act also extended voting rights to those adult males who had been excluded after 1884, the vast majority of whom were from the working classes. The Act therefore completely changed the character of the electorate; it was noticeable that around three-quarters of those who voted in 1918 were doing so for the first time. The Representation of the People Act did not, however, create a system of 'one person, one vote.'

- A large number of adult women were still excluded from the franchise because of their age; younger women – the so-called 'flappers' – were still considered to lack the maturity necessary for exercising political judgment.
- Around 5 per cent of adult males did not register to vote for a variety of reasons.
- Plural voting was allowed to continue; although the exercise of plural voting was now limited to one extra vote, significant numbers of middle-class men had an extra vote in university seats or in a constituency where they owned business premises.

Redistribution of seats

The 1918 Act continued the extensive redistribution of seats which had been started in 1885 and created a system where constituencies were more or less equal in size. The remaining smaller parliamentary boroughs lost their representation and most seats became single-member constituencies. The redistribution also continued the process of dividing constituencies along class lines. More suburban constituencies in which the middle classes predominated were created, providing a boost for the Conservative Party. **Evans** (2000) has calculated that the number of seats dominated by the middle classes increased to around 200. At the same time the Act also created more seats in coal mining areas where the electorate had large working-class majorities.

Many undemocratic features were retained in the electoral system after 1918. The inequality between the voting qualifications for men and for women was redressed in 1928 by the Equal Franchise Act. The anomaly of plural voting was removed in 1948. But it is possible to describe the post-1918 electoral system as 'democratic', in contrast to the pre-war arrangements that manifestly were not.

SECTION 5

Why was the transition to democracy such a lengthy process?

INTRODUCTION

The first change to the electoral system was made in 1832. Equal voting rights were finally achieved in 1948 when plural voting was abolished. During this period the transition to democracy was made in a series of measured, piecemeal changes. Economic and social changes were rendering the political system increasingly unrepresentative and anachronistic. The parties could not ignore the fact that society was changing and that the political system would need to adapt, but they could limit the extensions of the franchise and the redistribution of seats to reduce the impact of their reforms on the stability of the existing political system. Moreover, after 1850, they were rarely under any severe pressure to act in any other way.

Pressures from outside Parliament

The 1832 Reform Act came about as a result of a series of economic and social changes:

- The spread of industrialisation, the growth of large towns and the growing importance of the middle and working classes undermined the claims of the landed aristocracy to be the natural leaders of society.
- The growth of nonconformity in religion undermined the deferential attitudes towards the Anglican landed elite.
- The growth of political clubs and radical newspapers contributed to the development of political awareness among working people.
- Periodic economic crises caused severe distress that swelled the ranks of the radical movement; radical leaders such as Cobbett were able successfully to link distress to the corruption and misgovernment that resulted from the unrepresentative political system.

Pressure from outside Parliament played an important role in persuading MPs who had been elected under the unreformed system to introduce the first reform of the electoral system. The actual terms of the First Reform Act, however, were under the control of the Whig government and were framed in such a way as to strengthen aristocratic control of the parliamentary system. It was a measure designed to prevent a transition to democracy, not to set a course in that direction.

Chartism

The Chartist movement was a direct challenge to the reformed parliamentary system. If implemented, the Six Points of the Charter would have produced a partially democratic political system (women would still have been excluded from the franchise). Chartism was the largest mass political movement during the nineteenth century; leaders such as O'Connor, organisations such as the National Charter Association and newspapers such as the *Northern Star* successfully mobilised large numbers of people, mainly from the working classes and especially at times of severe economic distress. Ultimately, however, the Chartists failed to force governments to concede their demands. Failure was the result of internal weaknesses and the determination of both Whig and Tory governments, supported by the majority of the middle classes, to resist the Chartists' demands. By 1850 the Chartist movement was in decline. Thereafter, during the second half of the nineteenth century and the first decades of the twentieth century, no democratic mass movement on this scale was to re-emerge in Britain. Although there was pressure from outside Parliament in 1866–7 for a widening of the franchise among men and later the suffragist and suffragette movements mobilised support for an extension of the franchise to women, neither of these campaigns were comparable, in size or the radicalism of their demands, to the Chartist movement. Pressure from outside Parliament played a much less significant role in the reforms that happened between 1867 and 1928; the pace of reform was therefore dictated much more by the interests of the main political parties and the people they represented.

An analysis of the reasons why the pace of reform was slow needs to focus on five main themes:

- The extent to which economic changes affected people's satisfaction with the existing system.
- The extent to which the aristocracy were able to retain their power and influence.
- The attitude of the middle classes towards further reforms of the electoral system.
- The extent of working-class support for further extensions of the franchise.
- The effect of the campaign for an extension of the franchise to women.

WHAT WERE THE EFFECTS OF ECONOMIC CHANGE ON THE POLITICAL PROCESS?

In the early phase of the industrial revolution, the concentration of production into large factories in which machinery was driven by steam power was largely confined to the textile industries. These industries were concentrated in South Lancashire and the West Riding of Yorkshire. Most other industries continued to be based on small-scale enterprises using handcraft methods of production. By the 1840s the British economy was entering a second phase of industrial growth during which the impact of industrialisation spread to a wider range of industries and other geographical areas. One of the major factors which caused this transition was the building of the railways.

Railways

After the opening of the Liverpool to Manchester Railway in 1830 there were railway building booms in the 1830s and 1840s which resulted in the completion of 6000 miles of railway track by 1850. During the next 20 years the amount of railway track had increased to 13,000 miles. This involved unprecedented investment that stimulated other sectors of the economy. The iron and steel, engineering and coal mining industries all expanded as a direct result of railway building. New towns were created by the railway companies – Crewe and Swindon are examples of 'railway towns' – and previously inaccessible areas were developed for their mineral resources. Travel between different parts of the country became much easier and quicker; internal trade was increased and companies could begin to expand on the basis of a national market for their products.

Mid-Victorian prosperity

This second phase of the industrial revolution was characterised by a broader range of industries and more balanced economic growth. Although the textile industry continued to expand and cotton exports made a vital contribution to Britain's general prosperity, the expansion of other industries such as engineering and shipbuilding gave a broader base to the economy. The violent swings from boom to depression which had been characteristic of the 1820s, 1830s and 1840s were not a feature of the 1850s and 1860s. Although the trade cycle continued to operate, the downturns in the economy that were experienced in the mid-Victorian period did not result in the mass unemployment and widespread distress that had been evident in the years 1837–42. There were downturns in the economy in 1857 and 1866, the latter helping to fuel the reform agitation which built up before the passing of the Second Reform Act in 1867, but neither of these two events were economic crises on the scale of those experienced in earlier decades. The mid-Victorian period was a time of growing confidence rooted in expanding trade; the absence of any major competitors engendered a feeling that Britain was the pre-eminent

KEY STATISTICS

Percentage of the population living in towns

1870   65%

1901   78%

KEY PEOPLE

Industrialists and entrepreneurs

Alfred Mond and **John Brunner** both came from European Jewish backgrounds. They founded large chemicals companies that were merged with other companies in 1926 to become ICI. Mond was active in politics as a Liberal, but he switched to the Conservatives in 1926.

William Lever was a founder of Lever Bothers, a leading soap manufacturer that produced Sunlight Soap from its Port Sunlight factory in Cheshire. This company merged with a Dutch company in 1929 to become Unilever. William Lever was given a peerage.

Thomas Lipton was the founder of the Lipton grocery chain. By buying his own tea plantations he was able to reduce the price of tea sold in his shops and establish Lipton's Tea as a leading brand name.

Alfred Harmsworth was the founder of the *Daily Mail*. This became one of the leading popular newspapers, catering for a mass readership and supporting the Conservative Party. He received a peerage in 1917, becoming Lord Northcliffe.

industrial nation. Agriculture, too, experienced a period of rising prices and farm incomes.

Late nineteenth-century changes

By the mid-1870s confidence in some sectors was beginning to wane. The large-scale import of American wheat after 1873 reduced corn prices and brought serious problems for British corn farmers. Agriculture generally suffered a decline in prosperity during the last quarter of the nineteenth century, although farmers in some sectors were able to take advantage of the greater ease of access to the growing markets in the towns that the railways offered. Those farmers who concentrated on dairying, fruit growing or market gardening prospered during this period. Traditional industries such as textiles, iron and steel, coal mining and engineering continued to expand and to export a growing proportion of their output but they faced increased foreign competition. New industries also developed, such as chemicals, electrical equipment, bicycle and motor car manufacture; but in all these sectors the British economy lagged far behind its main competitors, the USA and Germany. Living standards, however, did not suffer. Although wages did not increase, food prices came down as a result of the import of cheaper foreign produce. Real wages, therefore, grew by over 30 per cent between 1875 and 1900. Thereafter, rising prices began to pull down real wages but the response of most workers to this was to put pressure on employers through trade unions for wage increases.

Relations between the classes

In the later nineteenth century, the size of industrial enterprises grew considerably. The typical firm of the 1890s employed more workers, in larger factories, than the typical firm of the 1830s. It was also more likely to be owned by shareholders rather than be a family firm, although family-owned enterprises were still very common in British industry. These developments had important consequences for relations between the classes. As firms grew in size and increasingly became run by professional managers, the gulf between employers and employees began to widen. At the other end of the scale, successful owners of large businesses could almost be described as a new 'business aristocracy'. Businessmen such as **John Brunner** and **Alfred Mond** (the founders of ICI), **William Lever**, **Thomas Lipton** and the newspaper 'tycoon' **Alfred Harmsworth**, amassed large personal fortunes that were often greater than those of landowners.

The First World War and after

The First World War marked a watershed in British economic history. Although the war itself brought higher farm prices, bulging order books for industry and full employment, the disruption of international trade led to a loss of export markets for British manufactured goods. After the war, trading conditions had changed and Britain's traditional export industries could not regain their overseas markets. Coupled with the post-war depression which began in 1921, the decline of the 'staple' industries brought mass unemployment to many areas of Britain during the 1920s. Whereas a century earlier, severe economic distress on this scale had led to increased demands for political reform, the situation in the 1920s was very different. Firstly, unemployment benefit had been made available through the National Insurance scheme; secondly, the unemployed had the right to vote and could apply pressure through constitutional channels for improvements in benefits.

KEY TERM

Staple industries
This term refers to the main export industries in Britain in the late 19th and early 20th centuries. These were cotton and woollen textiles, coal mining, iron and steel, shipbuilding and engineering.

HOW SUCCESSFULLY DID THE ARISTOCRACY HOLD ON TO THEIR POWER AND INFLUENCE?

Decline of aristocratic influence?

The landowning aristocracy continued to dominate British social and political life after the passing of the 1832 Reform Act. With agriculture returning to prosperity in the 1850s, landowners continued to thrive. Politically, aristocrats and their relatives still dominated the House of Commons and positions in government. In 1865, about 75 per cent of MPs came from aristocratic or gentry families. After the 1880s, however, there were unmistakable signs of a decline in their position, reflected in the fact that, by 1906, no more than 10 per cent of MPs came from such a background.

There were a number of reasons for this decline:

- The depression in agriculture led to a decline in the landowners' incomes from rent. As farming profits declined, landowners were often faced with a choice between reducing the rent or allowing the farmer to become bankrupt and leave the farm untenanted.
- Increasing taxation added to the pressure on landownership. Death duties on large estates were introduced in 1894, then increased in Lloyd George's 'People's Budget' of 1909 and increased again during the First World War. By 1918 the rate of death duty which had to be paid on estates of over £1 million in value was 30 per cent. Many landowners opted to sell off parts of their estates. Land sales were increasingly common in the years before the war; after the war, millions of acres changed hands. Much of the land was bought by the tenant farmers themselves but successful businessmen were also keen to purchase landed estates, much as the eighteenth-century pioneers of the industrial revolution had done.
- The political power of the aristocracy was also being gradually eroded by the development of more representative forms of government. The introduction of the secret ballot, the Corrupt Practices Act of 1883 and

the 1884 extension of the franchise to rural householders were important stages in the undermining of aristocratic influence in county elections. The introduction of single-member constituencies in 1885 had a dramatic impact on the number of MPs who came from aristocratic backgrounds. Previously, in boroughs which had two or more MPs and in which the Liberals normally had a majority, the selection of Liberal candidates was often shared between the Whig and radical wings of the party. After 1885, Liberal Associations invariably chose only radical candidates for elections in single-member constituencies. The decline of the Whigs was a striking demonstration of the declining political influence of the aristocracy in general. Reform of local government quickly followed. Having successfully resisted the introduction of elected local government in the countryside since the 1830s, the aristocracy had to acquiesce in the introduction of elected county councils in 1888 and elected rural district and parish councils in 1894.

Survival of aristocratic influence

The 1880s can be said to have been a significant turning point in the fortunes of the aristocracy, marking the beginnings of a long-term decline in their wealth, power and status in society. But we must be careful not to exaggerate the extent of this decline, especially in the years before the outbreak of the First World War. There were many ways in which the aristocracy retained at least some of their former status.

- Most aristocratic families remained very wealthy. Investments in shares, the development of mineral wealth under their estates or the exploitation of valuable land in the growing towns were all acceptable means for landowners to maintain or increase their wealth. Even land sales aided survival. Few landowners were forced to sell off all of their land; most managed to hold on to the core of their estates and the post-war land sales happened at a time when land values had risen. Landownership alone, however, had ceased to be the basis of great wealth.
- Aristocrats continued to hold the majority of the positions in cabinets until 1906. Not until **Bonar Law** became Conservative Party leader in 1911 was that party led by a man from the middle classes. The concept of the aristocracy as a governing class that took on the burdens of government out of a sense of duty and self-sacrifice was still very much alive at the beginning of the twentieth century.
- Membership of the aristocratic elite was still very much an aspiration of successful businessmen. The aristocracy did not disappear; it was infused with new blood as wealthy businessmen bought country estates, intermarried with the aristocracy and were **given peerages** themselves. Between 1886 and 1914, 200 new peerages were created; of these, one-third were given to 'plutocrats' and another third to

KEY PERSON

Andrew Bonar Law (1858–1923) was a Glasgow iron merchant. Born in Canada, the son of an Ulster Presbyterian, he was a relatively obscure member of the Conservative Party when he was chosen as leader in 1911. He was selected as a compromise choice because the other leading contenders were too divisive. His style was blunt, vigorous and forthright. (Although the 19th century Conservative leader Peel was the son of a manufacturer, he received the education and upbringing of an aristocrat.)

members of the professions. Thus, even if the character of the aristocracy was undergoing a change, the fact that membership of this elite group was still something to aspire to, shows that the aristocracy still retained a special position in society.

HOW DID MIDDLE-CLASS ATTITUDES TO PARLIAMENTARY REFORM CHANGE?

In his book, *The Forging of the Modern State*, **Evans** (1996) has described the mid-Victorian period as the 'Zenith of the Bourgeoisie'. He puts forward two reasons for his claim. Firstly, the dominant values of society reflected the attitudes of the middle classes and secondly, although most MPs at this time were landowners they had accepted that economic policy had to be based on the needs of industry and commerce. In other words, free trade and laissez-faire economic policies were accepted by governments of both parties. Thus, although it would be incorrect to argue that the 1832 Reform Act had given power to the middle classes, it is equally inaccurate to suggest that reform had done nothing to change the position of the aristocracy vis-à-vis the middle classes. Perhaps a more accurate way of viewing the politics of the mid-nineteenth century is to talk in terms of a partnership between landowning and business interests, a partnership which was expressed in the alliance between Whig aristocrats and middle-class radicals that was the foundation of the emerging Liberal Party.

Middle-class prosperity

The middle classes were growing in numbers, wealth and status. Evans estimates that in the mid-nineteenth century they made up about 15–16 per cent of the total population. As shown in the first part of this book, the middle classes were not a homogeneous or cohesive group. There were wide variations in wealth, occupation and status; the richest manufacturers and merchants had personal wealth which was greater than that of many landowners while, at the other end of the scale, the salaries of many clerks were no higher that those of the better-paid artisans. In general, middle-class incomes were rising. An increase in servant-keeping, which was one of the criteria used to denote membership of the middle classes, was one of the outward signs of middle-class prosperity. This growing wealth was also increasingly spent on the purchase of larger and more spacious homes on the fringes of towns and on a public school education for their children. Both of these were an expression of a keen desire to separate themselves from the working classes.

Middle-class attitudes

Middle-class attitudes increasingly set the tone for the rest of society. One of the basic divisions in Victorian society was that between the

Peerages given to successful businessmen
Arthur Guinness (1880) and Edward Guinness (1891), both from the successful brewing family, were given peerages. Another brewer was Sir Michael Bass (1886). The banker, Nathaniel de Rothschild, was given a peerage in 1885.

'respectable' and the 'non-respectable'. The criteria used to fix the dividing line were essentially derived from middle-class values. Those who were considered respectable were people who provided for themselves through hard work, self-discipline, thrift and sobriety. These values were buttressed by a strong family life in which the father figure was the dominant influence and by regular attendance at church or chapel. The non-respectable were those who relied on the state or charity for their living, were profligate in their spending and did not lead a settled life. This way of defining an individual's social standing had a wide-ranging influence. It underpinned the debate in 1866–7 over which members of the working classes it would be safe to enfranchise; various devices, such as the 12-month residence qualification, were used to ensure that it was only the 'respectable' working classes who would be allowed to vote. Within the working classes, the better-paid artisans, many of whom aspired to a middle-class way of life, were keen to demonstrate their respectability by having regular employment, a settled home life, saving money and attending church or chapel.

National Reform Union

By the mid-nineteenth century, the middle classes had made few inroads into national politics. There was a growing number of MPs from middle-class backgrounds, some of whom followed the lead of Richard Cobden and John Bright in challenging the dominant position of the aristocracy. When the issue of parliamentary reform was revived in the 1860s, a new pressure group, the National Reform Union, was formed. This was an essentially middle-class body that was originally based in Manchester and the South Lancashire cotton towns but grew by establishing branches in other parts of the country. The aims of the NRU were that the franchise should be extended to all ratepayers, voting should be by secret ballot, constituencies should be of equal size and parliamentary elections should be held at least every three years. A ratepayer franchise would, if enacted, give the vote to many artisans, thus extending the franchise into the working classes. This was not a proposal which would commend itself to the bulk of the middle classes but the NRU believed it would serve middle-class interests if the franchise were extended to the 'respectable' working men. Firstly, they believed that an injection of new blood into the electorate would help them to break the aristocratic monopoly on power. Secondly, this would clear the way for further reforms that were being obstructed by the Whig element within the Liberal Party – for example, greater civil and legal equality for nonconformists. The middle-class supporters of the NRU saw artisans as potential allies in their struggle against aristocratic privilege.

Local government

These men were the exceptions rather than the rule, however. Membership of Parliament and of cabinets was still, in the 1860s, dominated by the landowning classes. At the level of local government, on the other hand, the middle classes were beginning to exercise more direct power. Following the Municipal Corporations Act of 1835, local government in the towns came under the control of town councils elected by ratepayers. By the 1850s the local government of the major industrial towns was controlled by the middle classes.

National politics

The 1870s and 1880s were an important turning point in terms of the recognition of the middle classes at national level. Gladstone included John Bright, **Samuel Morley** and **Henry Fawcett** in his cabinet during his first ministry, 1868–74. The Conservative leader, Disraeli, continued this process when he gave cabinet posts to **Richard Cross** and **W. H. Smith**. All of these politicians came from middle-class backgrounds. Thereafter, although cabinets continued to be dominated by aristocrats until the early twentieth century, ministers from middle-class backgrounds became increasingly common. Membership of the House of Commons also came to be dominated by the middle classes in the last decades of the nineteenth century. This period also marked a turning point in terms of middle-class political allegiances. The 1874 election showed early signs that middle-class voters were beginning to switch their allegiance from the Liberal Party to the Conservative Party and each subsequent election during the last quarter of the nineteenth century showed that this trend was gathering momentum. The Conservatives were particularly successful in capturing seats in the suburban areas of the large towns. This was a reflection of the fact that the middle classes were becoming increasingly conservative in their attitudes. They were broadly satisfied with the progress that had been achieved in terms of their status and with the policies that governments were pursuing. An extension of the franchise to the unskilled worker, it was feared, would lead to governments adopting policies that would threaten middle-class interests.

HOW MUCH PRESSURE FOR REFORM CAME FROM THE WORKING CLASSES?

Radicalism and distress

During the period 1815–50 there had been a clear link between economic distress and support for political reform by members of the working classes. Radical activity increased at times of trade depression and poor harvests. The strongest support for political reform came from groups such as the handloom weavers and framework knitters whose craft skills were under threat from the introduction of machinery in the new factories, but artisans were also active in the radical movement. Did this link between distress and reform continue in the period after 1850?

W. H. Smith (1825–91) was a successful newsagent who entered politics when he defeated John Stuart Mill in the election for Westminster in 1868. When Disraeli put his name forward to be First Lord of the Admiralty in 1877 the Queen expressed concern that a man from humble origins should occupy such an exalted position. Lord Randolph Churchill, in a typical show of snobbery, described him as 'one of the lords of suburban villas, the owners of pineries and vineries'.

The first point to make is that there was generally less economic distress among the working classes during the second half of the nineteenth century. The 1850s and 1860s saw a reduction in the severity of trade cycle depressions; even when trade did fall, as in 1866, the impact on living standards was not as devastating as during the depression of 1837–42. Economic growth had become more sustained and there was a wider range of industries to support employment. After the mid-1870s confidence in the strength of the British economy began to decline as foreign competition increased, but growth was maintained and living standards continued to rise. Foreign competition also brought benefits. The import of cheaper foreign food after 1870 generally brought food prices down and this resulted in an improvement in real wages by over 30 per cent between 1875 and 1900. There were, however, periodic bouts of high unemployment, as in the mid-1880s.

Skilled artisans. Secondly, the groups of working people which had figured prominently in the reform movements after 1815 – the handloom weavers and the framework knitters – had all but ceased to exist by the 1850s. The switch to factory-based production in the textile industries was complete by 1850. The industrial revolution was a continuous process of developing and introducing machinery which could perform tasks previously undertaken by craftsmen; across a wide range of industries this process continued through the second half of the nineteenth century. As a result, various groups of craftsmen found their employment under threat at different times. At the same time the introduction of new industrial processes involved the development of new craft skills. The expansion of the engineering and shipbuilding industries, for example, led to an increase in demand for skilled labour. The number of workers employed in these industries almost doubled between 1851 and 1881 and by 1914 they formed the largest single category of British male workers. Overall there was a net increase in demand for skilled workers and this 'labour aristocracy' benefitted more than other workers from the general rise in living standards. Skilled workers in the engineering industry could earn two or three times as much as unskilled labourers, but even the labourers in engineering factories could earn higher wages and have more stable employment than was available in other industries.

Trade unions. During the 1850s various groups of skilled workers established national trade unions. These craft unions proved to be stable and were the main organisations for the defence of the economic interests of artisans in the second half of the nineteenth century. The unions were also a vehicle for asserting the claims of the artisans to greater political equality. The Reform League, established in 1864, had links with the unions. Its aims were more radical than those of the NRU since it campaigned for manhood suffrage, but in the reform crisis of 1866, after

Gladstone's Bill had been defeated, the two organisations co-operated in mounting demonstrations in favour of the Bill. Although the pressure mounted by the two organisations was not a crucial factor in forcing Parliament to pass a Reform Bill, it did help to create a climate in which further reform was seen as inevitable. Once the Second Reform Act had been passed and the artisans had gained the right to vote, there were attempts to build on this foundation by getting working men into Parliament. The Labour Representation League was established in 1869, again with close trade union involvement, and in the general election of 1874 the unions put up 13 candidates. Two were elected. This was a significant development since these were the first working men elected to Parliament. But, as with the middle classes after 1832, further progress was very slow and Parliament continued to be dominated by men from the propertied classes. For their part the artisans and the unions which represented them showed little interest after 1867 in campaigning for further extensions of the franchise, either for unskilled working men or for women. Winning the vote in 1867 was a recognition of the respectability of the skilled worker. As **Checkland** (1964) has written, 'respectability meant establishing a gap between the aspiring family and the great mass who were incapable of any real effort at betterment. In this sense, the working man and his wife who wished for a better life for their children were engaged in a continuous struggle to draw away from other workers'. The right to vote was another means by which artisans drew away from other workers; few wished to devote their energies in a campaign to abolish that dividing line.

Coal miners. Trade union interest in further extensions of the franchise did not end with the 1867 Reform Act. The TUC, which was established in 1868, began to act as a channel for union involvement in political activity. One of its aims was the extension of the franchise to the rest of the adult male population, but in the 1870s and 1880s there were far more pressing items on the trade unions' political agenda. Securing proper legal recognition for the unions, reforming the law on picketing and gaining further reductions in working hours were all considered to be of greater immediate importance than an extension of the franchise. The miners' unions, however, were more active in campaigning for the householder and lodger franchises in the boroughs to be extended to the countryside. Many coal-mining villages were situated in rural areas and miners living there were excluded from the franchise after 1867 even though their counterparts in the towns had gained the right to vote. The Northern Reform Union, based very largely on the mining unions of Northumberland and Durham, continued to campaign after 1867 for the extension of the householder and lodger franchises to the countryside. This was finally achieved in the Reform Act of 1884. After 1885, the unions allowed the subject of manhood suffrage to fade into the background.

The extent of poverty

Although living standards generally were rising after 1850, poverty continued to exist. Surveys carried out by **Charles Booth** and **Seebohm Rowntree** towards the end of the nineteenth century revealed that about 30 per cent of English people lived in severe poverty. It is reasonable to assume that this 30 per cent contained the majority of those adult men who were excluded from the franchise after 1867 and 1884. The poor were mainly the families of unskilled labourers who worked for low wages; their employment was often casual or seasonal and they were more likely to suffer bouts of unemployment than the skilled artisans. Sickness and injury were also common causes of poverty. The poor lived in overcrowded conditions in the unhealthiest parts of the towns. Their dwellings were small, badly drained, damp and insanitary. Life for the urban poor was a daily struggle for the basic necessities of life.

Poverty and radicalism. The existence of continuing distress on this scale did not, however, give rise to political protest movements like those which had emerged in the period 1815–50. In general, the poor did not make a connection between their poverty and their lack of political power. After the 1867 and 1884 Reform Acts had given the vote to male householders and settled lodgers, there was no campaign among the unenfranchised 'residuum' for the right to vote. The connection between distress and radical politics would seem to have been broken. This paradox can be explained by the fact that extreme distress had rarely given rise to political protests. The groups who figured prominently in the pre-1850 radical movements – like the handloom weavers – were those who had known better times and who could identify a clear cause for their current distress. In fighting for the right to vote they were attempting to gain political representation in order to preserve a way of life that was threatened by industrialisation. Those who suffered the worst and most persistent poverty were not much involved in radical politics before 1850 and their apathy towards political activity continued after 1867 when the artisans gained the right to vote. For a family involved in a daily struggle for existence, the right to vote would have very little immediate value or relevance. Moreover, politics and politicians belonged to the society beyond the slum areas which treated the poor with indifference; generally the poor had learned to look after their own and not to seek solutions to their distress in outside help.

New Unionism

Trade union organisation among the unskilled was very difficult to sustain throughout the nineteenth century but the advent of '**New Unionism**' in the late 1880s gave rise to more permanent unions. As with any trade unions, the 'new unions' such as the Dockers' Union and the Gasworkers' Union gave priority to the immediate concerns of their members such as wages and conditions of employment, but political questions were not ignored. Many of the leaders of the 'new unions' were members of socialist organisations and they brought to the union movement a more radical approach than the older generation of trade union leaders from the craft unions. For example, during the 1890s the trade union movement began to debate the issue of a statutory limit of eight hours on the working day. The extension of the franchise, however, was not a priority either for the unions or for the socialists. The unions involved themselves in politics primarily to secure improvements in the laws regulating their activities. The socialists' main priorities were to build their own organisations into an effective political force and to campaign for social legislation such as old age pensions. The achievement of full political democracy was very much a long-term aim, not something to be fought for in the short term.

WHAT WAS THE IMPACT OF THE WOMEN'S SUFFRAGE CAMPAIGN ON THE MOVEMENT FOR DEMOCRATIC CHANGE?

The 1867 Reform Act

Whereas the effect of the 1867 Reform Act was to take the sting out of the campaign for full manhood suffrage, it had the opposite effect on women. The fact that the vote had been given to working men who owned no property and who had received little or no education was an affront to the growing number of well-educated and independent women. The campaign for women's suffrage effectively began with the refusal of Parliament in 1867 to allow women to vote in parliamentary elections on the same terms as men. Using well-tried pressure-group tactics of organising meetings and presenting petitions to Parliament, the women's suffrage campaign grew and developed during the late nineteenth century and gained support among MPs. The full story of the campaign for women's suffrage is told in the second AS part of this book (see Chapters 9–12). A summary of the key points about the tactics of the campaign is all that is required here:

- The case for the enfranchisement of women was based on the fact that women had demonstrated their respectability and responsibility and that it was 'safe' to enfranchise them. Female suffragists demanded the right to vote on the grounds that they were property owners, householders or tax and ratepayers. They were not demanding any radically new definition of the basis on which an individual could qualify for the franchise but they were demanding that the issue of women's suffrage be considered separately from any consideration of extending the vote to more men.
- The campaigners for women's suffrage explicitly accepted the step-by-step approach to the widening of the franchise that Parliament had adopted in 1867.

- Although the campaign was organised on the lines of a pressure group, the strategy adopted by the suffragists was to win support from within the existing political parties. There were close links with the Liberal Party, particularly after 1887 while, early in the twentieth century, socialist suffragists attempted to enlist the support of the Labour Party and the trade unions.

These tactics achieved considerable success in many ways. The legal status of women was improved, women gained increased political rights in local government and a growing number of MPs voted in favour of women's suffrage bills in Parliament. By the beginning of the twentieth century, however, the suffragist campaign had failed to achieve its primary objective – the granting of the right to vote in parliamentary elections for women on the same terms as men. There were two main reasons for this:

- The continuing strength of feeling among many men that women should not have a role in national politics. This view was held by men from all social classes.
- The issue of extending the vote to some women resurrected the issue of extending the franchise to all adult men. Although there was no sustained campaign among disenfranchised men for the right to vote, the fact that a growing number of women were challenging the existing franchise qualification re-opened the debate about who was fit to exercise the franchise. If women were to be allowed to vote, why not extend the franchise to all adults? Full adult suffrage, however, would radically alter the nature of the electorate in class terms, placing working-class voters in an absolute majority. Thus, although the demands of the suffragists were not in themselves very radical it was increasingly apparent that they could not be granted without a more thorough overhaul of the whole franchise system. This in itself was reason enough for Liberal and Conservative politicians to decide to delay serious consideration of the issue.

Party politics

Although the issue of the extension of the franchise had been placed on the political agenda by pressure from outside Parliament, it was the political parties that would have ultimate control over the pace and scope of reform. As on earlier occasions in the nineteenth century when parliamentary reform had been enacted, the parties could not ignore calculations of party political advantage when considering the issues raised by the female suffragists and suffragettes. Both the NUWSS and the WSPU campaigned for a separate women's suffrage bill that would grant the vote to women on the same terms as for men. This gained them support in some political quarters while losing them support in others.

- Many Tory politicians, including the leader from 1911, Bonar Law, could see advantages for the Conservative Party in increasing the proportion of property owners in the electorate. The Conservatives were not in power although they could block any reform they disliked through their majority in the House of Lords.

- Many leading Labour politicians, such as Keir Hardie and George Lansbury, expressed their sympathy for the cause of women's suffrage but the Labour Party and trade unions as a whole were suspicious that an extension of the franchise to women on the same terms as men would merely strengthen propertied interests. When a resolution calling for the TUC to support women's suffrage was put to the annual congress in 1901, the trade union leaders quickly responded by adopting an alternative resolution in favour of full adult suffrage. Soon afterwards the Adult Suffrage Society was formed, led by the female trade unionist Margaret Bondfield; majority opinion within the Labour Party and trade unions in the years before the outbreak of the First World War supported the extension of the franchise to all adults. However, Labour support for adult suffrage was far from wholehearted. Since the Conservative and Liberal parties were unlikely to support complete adult suffrage, a wholehearted campaign for it was not practical politics. The whole issue of the franchise was, therefore, pushed into the background. Support for adult suffrage thus became a reason for doing very little about electoral reform, not an opportunity to campaign on behalf of a fully democratic system.

- Among Liberal MPs there was, by the end of the nineteenth century, steadily growing support for the enfranchisement of women. Moreover, since 1891, the extension of the franchise for adult men had been part of the Liberal Party programme. The Liberal government that took office in 1906, however, was extremely cautious on the issue of franchise reform. Reform on the terms demanded by the suffragists and suffragettes would probably favour the Conservatives. Full adult suffrage might benefit the Labour Party but, in any case, would be resisted by the Tories and involve the government in a major political battle at a time when it was already facing severe difficulties over Ireland and industrial relations. The government could also not afford to be seen to make concessions to the violence of the suffragettes. Prime Minister Asquith's approach to women's suffrage was equivocal and the more pressure he was put under, the more devious he became. When Asquith finally did take action on the franchise issue in 1912 his attempt to attach a female suffrage amendment to a bill which would have given the vote to many of the unenfranchised men proved to be a tactical miscalculation. The Tories would not co-operate in what they regarded as an attempt to change the constitution by stealth while the suffragettes were outraged that the cause of women's suffrage had once again been treated as a by-product of the issue of male suffrage.

The result of these tactical manoeuvrings by the political parties on the suffrage issue was that an impasse had been reached in the years 1912–14. The war changed the political climate and therefore the terms of the debate about extension of the franchise. The contributions made by working-class men and by women to the war effort made the continued denial of their right to vote unsustainable. Practical demonstrations of patriotism removed many of the doubts about their fitness to exercise the franchise. The suspension of the suffragette campaign of militancy enabled consideration of their demands to be made in a calmer atmosphere while the political truce between the parties fostered a willingness to consider the issues in a non-partisan way. Nevertheless, when the Representation of the People Act of 1918 was being drafted, considerations of fitness to exercise the franchise were not abandoned altogether. The exclusion of women aged 21–30, the so-called 'flappers', from the franchise demonstrated that political parties were still determined to control the pace of franchise reform and limit its effects.

SECTION 6

What was the impact on the political parties?

The party labels 'Whig' and 'Tory' were in common use in the eighteenth century but the concept of a political party at that time was very different from the modern usage of the term. Parties in the pre-1832 era were loose groupings of politicians who gathered around wealthy aristocratic patrons. They were primarily concerned with levering themselves into office. Although there were differences between Whigs and Tories on some issues, common policies were not the main factor that united the parties. Party unity and discipline were very loose and parties lacked any formal organisation at both the parliamentary and the constituency levels. By the 1920s political parties had changed out of all recognition. In the place of Whigs and Tories, there were Liberal, Conservative and Labour parties. Parties had national headquarters and local branches with individual members paying subscriptions. Policy differences between the parties were more clear-cut, and policies were the main factors which united party members. Party conferences gave individual members some influence over the policies that each party espoused, although the extent of this influence varied from party to party. As the political system became more democratic and the 'political nation' expanded to include all sections of society, so the parties had to become more professional but also more open in their appeal. This chapter looks at the impact of the parliamentary reforms on political parties and the ways in which they adapted to the emerging democracy.

THE DEVELOPMENT OF A TWO-PARTY SYSTEM, 1832–67

A detailed analysis of how the 1832 Reform Act was 'a point of departure for a new party system' has already been given in the first AS part of this book (see Chapter 5). A summary of the main points will suffice as the starting point for a study of the development of political parties over the period 1832–67.

- Political parties became much more important features of the political landscape. With the decline of royal patronage, governments came to rely much more on their party organisations in Parliament to provide secure majorities in the House of Commons.
- Party organisation in the constituencies also developed as politicians realised the importance of ensuring that their supporters registered as

voters. In the immediate aftermath of the 1832 Reform Act, however, local organisation was usually left in the hands of part-time voluntary agents, most of whom were local solicitors.

- More central co-ordination of policy and strategy was made possible by the establishment of political clubs linked to the main parties. The Whigs established their Reform Club while the Tories founded the Carlton Club. There was no involvement, however, of ordinary party supporters in discussions on policy or the choice of leaders. The parties were far from being democratic in their own internal workings.
- The parties began to recognise that the widening of the electorate meant that they had to broaden the basis of their support. The newly enfranchised middle classes could not control the political parties but they could exercise a strong influence over them. Peel, through his Tamworth Manifesto, attempted to reposition the Tory Party by making it clear that he would be prepared to embrace cautious, limited reform as long as this did not undermine the stability of the constitution. The name **Conservative** was increasingly adopted to describe the party that Peel led. The Whigs entered into an alliance with the Irish Catholic MPs and the small number of radicals – an alliance that was formalised in the Lichfield House Compact. This political grouping became known as the **Liberal Party**.

Development of the Conservative Party

The passing of the 1832 Reform Act had placed the Tory Party in a dilemma. To remain a party of the landed interest and continue to resist reform was the course of action preferred by many Tories, particularly the 'Ultra Tories'. With the middle classes now exercising the right to vote, however, this approach would give the Tory Party very little chance of winning elections. The alternative course, which Peel adopted, was to attempt to appeal to the middle classes by offering cautious reforms and sound, efficient administration. Peel's strategy appeared to have been successful when the Conservatives won the general election of 1841. During the next five years his government introduced a number of reforms, such as the reduction of import and export duties on raw materials and manufactured goods, and a Bank Charter Act that placed the banking system on a sounder foundation. These reforms were generally welcomed by commercial and business interests yet posed no threat to the interests of the landowners and farmers. The Conservative Party's traditional supporters, however, viewed Peel's strategy with suspicion since they were concerned that his pragmatic approach would lead to him making too many concessions to the middle classes at the expense of their own interests. This tension at the heart of Peel's Conservative Party came to a head over the repeal of the Corn Laws in 1846.

The split in the Conservative Party. When Peel introduced a measure to repeal the Corn Laws he was accused of treachery and betrayal by the

KEY TERM

'Ultra Tories' was the name given to that group of Tories who opposed Catholic emancipation in 1829 and who rejected Peel's acceptance of the Reform Act once it had been passed in 1832. They believed that the Tory Party should remain a party exclusively of the landed classes and committed to resisting all concessions to the Catholics, nonconformists and free traders.

majority of MPs in his own party. Led by **Bentinck** and Disraeli, the protectionist wing of the Conservative Party voted against repeal on the grounds that the removal of protective duties on corn would ruin farmers and landowners. Their attacks on Peel were so bitter that the split which opened up in the Conservative Party became a permanent parting of the ways. The majority of Conservative MPs supported Bentinck and Disraeli but a substantial minority, of around 100 MPs, remained loyal to Peel. This Peelite group was never a formal party but the presence of such a substantial body of MPs altered the parliamentary balance. Party politics were thus thrown into a state of flux by the events of 1846.

A weakened Conservative Party. After the split of 1846 the Conservative Party entered a long period of weakness. Although the majority of MPs supported the protectionist cause, most of Peel's cabinet supported repeal. The Peelites, therefore, consisted of the more able and experienced Conservative politicians while the Conservative Party itself was left with a dearth of talent. There were few obvious candidates for the leadership. Bentinck did not have the ability, Disraeli did not have the confidence of his party. His Jewish origins and his ostentatious style aroused prejudice and suspicion, despite the fact that he was by far the ablest politician. The leadership, therefore, fell to Lord Derby who was unable to provide positive leadership. His strategy was to sit back and wait for the Liberals to disintegrate as their differences became more apparent, an approach that did actually give the Conservatives the chance to take office on three occasions as minority governments. None of these governments lasted very long, however, and the Conservatives did not look like a party of government. During the 1850s the Conservatives were forced back onto their traditional strongholds in the English countryside and small towns, and appeared to be the party of reaction and narrow sectional interests. Although Disraeli tried to steer the party towards abandoning its unpopular policy of trade protection, a large section were reluctant to follow him. Until the Conservatives could grasp this particular nettle, however, they were unlikely to appeal to the middle classes.

Development of the Liberal Party

Eventually most of the Peelites coalesced with the Whigs, radicals and Irish to form a new Liberal Party but this process took nearly 20 years to complete. During that time the political situation was characterised by the fluidity of political alliances and the instability of governments. Six times during the 1850s, governments were forced to resign after losing key votes in the House of Commons. General elections between 1847 and 1865 all resulted in an anti-Conservative majority being returned to Westminster. In fact, the Conservatives did not win a single general election between 1841 and 1874. Most of the governments in the period 1846–1868 were either Whig or Whig-Liberal governments, with just three short periods when minority Conservative governments held office.

Lord Palmerston (1784–1865) had a long career in politics, having been associated with the 'Liberal Tories' in the 1820s and then joining the Whig governments of the 1830s as Foreign Secretary. He was Foreign Secretary again, 1846–51, and Prime Minister 1855–8 and 1859–65. Foreign affairs were his main interest, and he brought to the task his skill as a diplomat but also a strong desire to protect national interests. His readiness to use force against weaker powers such as Greece or China played well with public opinion but brought criticism from some of his colleagues.

This points to the fact that there was a natural Liberal majority among the electorate. The question that must be asked, therefore, is why the parliamentary Liberals were unable to build and sustain a stable majority.

Whigs. The key factor here was the inability of Liberal politicians to co-operate. The Whigs were the largest element in the Liberal ranks in Parliament. Between leading figures such as **Lord John Russell** and **Lord Palmerston** there was personal animosity. The Whigs remained a thoroughly aristocratic group who dominated Liberal governments during this period; they still retained their belief in reforming in order to conserve but the pace of reform was too slow for the radical element in the Liberal alliance. Tension between Whigs and radicals was never far below the surface, with the latter complaining that the aristocratic Whigs continued to run the party along the lines of the eighteenth-century family connections. Criticising the way in which Palmerston's government had been formed in 1857, the leading radical Richard Cobden said, 'Half a dozen great families meet at Walmer and dispose of the rank and file of the party'.

Peelites. Another important factor was the behaviour of the Peelites. Unwilling to form a separate party themselves and unable to reunite with the Conservative Party, the Peelites were nevertheless reluctant to commit themselves wholeheartedly to an alliance with the Whig-Liberals. Leading Peelites such as William Gladstone and **Lord Aberdeen** tended to look down on the Whigs as being inferior administrators. There were also sharp disagreements over some areas of policy. Gladstone, for example, disagreed with Palmerston's aggressive defence of British national interests in his foreign policy, partly on moral grounds and partly on the grounds of the increased military expenditure that this policy entailed.

Radicals. Although the number of radical MPs was relatively small, they exercised a disproportionate influence within the Liberal Party. Cobden and Bright, the leaders of the Anti-Corn Law League in the 1840s, became a thorn in the side of Whig-Liberal governments in the 1850s. There was almost constant criticism of Russell and Palmerston over high government expenditure and over the refusal of Palmerston to support any further measure of parliamentary reform. They also showed a fundamental hostility to aristocratic government. Four times in the 1850s Whig-Liberal governments were brought down after losing votes of censure that had been initiated by radical MPs. The regularity with which governments were defeated on crucial votes in Parliament also reflects the looseness of party discipline among MPs at this time. Many backbench MPs resisted pressures to persuade them to vote in accordance with a party line, clinging to the tradition of an MP's independence.

Fusion. There were broad areas of agreement between the various elements in the Liberal Party. Chief among these was their support for free trade, the issue that had divided the Conservative Party in 1846. There was also broad agreement over support for liberal and nationalist movements in Europe, particularly in Italy. When **Italian unification** became a real possibility in 1859–60 it sparked a debate in Britain about the policy this country would adopt towards it. The Liberal factions had been in disarray since 1858 and a minority Conservative government was in power; but the wish among Liberal politicians of all complexions to give support to Italian unification led to an agreement to co-operate once more. The meeting at Willis's Rooms in 1859 led to a firmer collaboration between the Liberal factions and a period of more stable Liberal government. This meeting, as important as the Lichfield House Compact of 1835, laid the foundations for the parliamentary Liberal Party in the period 1859–86.

Rank-and-file Liberalism. Even in the 1860s the majority of Liberal MPs came from landowning and Anglican backgrounds. In 1865 only about one-third of Liberal MPs came from middle-class backgrounds. In the country at large, however, the bulk of the Liberal Party's supporters came from the middle classes and were nonconformist in their religion. Although old Whig families could still use their influence to return MPs to Westminster from county seats, the real strength of the Liberal Party outside London lay in the growing industrial areas, particularly in Lancashire, Yorkshire and the Midlands. In these areas, following the Municipal Corporations Act of 1835, local government had very largely come under the control of the middle classes. Local and provincial newspapers played a crucial role in cultivating a climate of opinion in favour of free trade and cheap government and against aristocratic privileges and the established position of the Church of England. Newspapers like the *Manchester Guardian*, the *Leeds Mercury*, the *Newcastle Chronicle* and the *Sheffield Independent* all enjoyed growing circulations as a result of the removal of the stamp and paper duties and the use of the railways to aid distribution. With a large part of their coverage being devoted to politics, both local and national, these newspapers helped to develop an informed public opinion in the provincial towns.

Nonconformists. Nonconformists continued to play a prominent role in radical Liberal politics at grassroots level. The 1851 Religious Census revealed that nearly half of the church-going population attended the various nonconformist chapels. This was one factor that encouraged nonconformists to become more assertive in their demands for the abolition of church rates and other reforms. Through the unrelenting pressure from the **Liberation Society**, nonconformists gained considerable influence in the Liberal Party at local level. The Society created its own

broke out in northern Italy between the Kingdom of Piedmont and Sardinia, supported by France, and the Austrian Empire. Liberal opinion in Britain supported the Kingdom of Piedmont; Conservative opinion tended to favour Austria as the defender of the status quo.

The **Liberation Society** grew out of the Anti-Church State Association that had been founded by the nonconformist journalist, Edward Miall, in 1844. The Liberation Society championed the cause of nonconformists and campaigned for the abolition of tithes and church rates. Miall became MP for Rochdale in 1852.

system of paid agents and branches in the constituencies at a time when the Liberal Party itself had no such organisation. This enabled the Liberation Society to influence the selection of candidates for parliamentary elections. Other pressure groups linked to the Liberal Party also had close connections with nonconformity. The **United Kingdom Alliance** campaigned for restrictions on the drink trade and the **National Education League** campaigned for free, secular state education. Among the members of the National Reform Union there were people who had been active in the Anti-Corn Law League in the 1840s; and in the Reform League there were many old Chartists. At local level, therefore, the Liberal Party drew together many disparate elements whose one common feature was their dissatisfaction with the present state of things, and their desire for reforms.

Tensions between parliamentary Liberals and the rank and file. Kitson Clark (1962) put forward the concepts of an 'old nation' that consisted of the landed, Anglican elite and a 'new nation' that was largely based on commerce and industry and was nonconformist in religion. For a long time after the Reform Act of 1832, he argued, politics was dominated by the 'old nation', just as had been the case before reform. The 'new nation' continued to be underrepresented through the political system. This was the case during the 1850s and 1860s when the Conservative Party was weak and political life was dominated by the Liberal Party. In Parliament and in government, Liberal politicians were still overwhelmingly drawn from the 'old nation' of landowning Anglicans. Outside Parliament, however, at the grassroots level in the growing industrial towns, Liberal politics had a very different complexion. In these areas the chapel-going businessmen and artisans gave the Liberal Party a distinctly more radical flavour. The frustrations arising from continued aristocratic dominance of politics in general and the Liberal Party in particular led some middle-class radicals to believe that a further instalment of parliamentary reform was needed. This reform, which was finally achieved in 1867, did produce some of the changes anticipated by the radicals but it had many unforeseen consequences as well.

HOW DID THE PARTIES ADAPT TO THE CHANGED POLITICAL CLIMATE AFTER 1867?

The 1867 Reform Act led to a significant widening of the borough franchise, bringing within the 'pale of the constitution' many working-class men who had previously been considered unfit for involvement in political life. During the period when this franchise was in operation there were three general elections, in 1868, 1874 and 1880. Of those elections, the Liberal Party won two with large majorities, in 1868 and 1880, but the Conservatives also won their first election victory in over

30 years when Disraeli led them to victory in 1874. Although the Conservatives were in office in 1867–8, this was a result of Liberal disunity rather than electoral victory by the Conservatives. If, therefore, one of the key features of this period was the continuing dominance of the Liberal Party, it was also the period when Conservative fortunes began to revive.

General elections

Elections began to take on a greater significance during this period. Following the Liberal victory at the general election in 1868, Disraeli immediately resigned from office as Prime Minister. Established precedent was that a government that had lost an election would wait until the first sitting of the new Parliament before tendering their resignations; Disraeli's action in 1868 was a recognition of the changed political climate in which the electorate had the final say in the choice of government.

The election of 1880 was even more significant and has been described by **Pugh** (1982) as the first modern election. Firstly, about 84 per cent of seats were actually contested at this election – a figure that was much higher than in the previous two elections when about half the seats were uncontested. Secondly, the election campaign by the Liberal leader Gladstone was a national campaign. Previously, general elections had been a series of local contests in which local interests and issues predominated and party leaders were careful not to intrude into the constituencies of other candidates. In 1880 Gladstone made a national tour of the large towns to arouse the moral indignation of his audiences against Disraeli's foreign policy. Thirdly, in the election of 1880 Gladstone's campaign presented the electorate with a clear-cut choice between the policies of the two parties. They could either vote for a foreign and imperial policy based on national self-interest and military expansion (Disraeli) or they could choose Gladstone's approach based on moral principles and conciliation of foreign powers.

How did party organisation change?

In Parliament the demands made on MPs were increased and party discipline became much tighter. During the period 1868–76, in particular, there was a large number of reforms introduced by both Liberal and Conservative governments, as both parties strove to appeal to the new electorate. This burst of legislation, similar in scale to that which followed the 1832 Reform Act, involved MPs in longer parliamentary sessions and there was more pressure on them from the party whips to attend parliamentary debates. The imposition of tighter discipline meant that governments suffered fewer defeats at the hands of MPs than the governments of the 1850s.

KEY ORGANISATIONS

The **United Kingdom Alliance** brought together the many temperance societies that had sprung up in the 1850s. Temperance campaigners tried to persuade working men in particular to give up alcohol, and provided Temperance Halls as an alternative to the public house. In 1860 it was estimated that there were 4000 temperance societies with about 3 million members. The Alliance campaigned politically for restrictions on the drink trade.

The **National Education League** was founded in Birmingham in 1869. It campaigned for free, secular (i.e. non-religious) education, paid for from the local rates. One of its leading members was Joseph Chamberlain.

After the extension of the franchise to many working men in the boroughs, the parties recognised that their success in borough elections would depend on the efficiency of their organisation at constituency level. With an enlarged electorate, propaganda and persuasion took the place of influence as the means of enlisting the support of the voters. Equally important, however, was the ability of the parties to ensure that their known supporters were registered as voters. This process had begun after the 1832 Reform Act, but the registration of voters after 1867 became a more complicated business since the franchise qualifications were more open to interpretation and challenge. The 12-month residence qualification, in particular, was interpreted in various ways in different towns; party agents played a crucial role in trying to ensure that their own supporters were placed on the register and their opponents were subject to scrutiny and challenge. So successful were some of the party agents in this aspect of their work that, in many large towns, a person's right to vote depended less on the validity of his claim and more on the efficiency of the local party organisations in maximising voter registration.

The Liberal 'Caucus'. One other feature of the 1867 Reform Act had a direct impact on local party organisation. Under the 'minority clause' of the Reform Act, voters in boroughs represented by three members were given two votes. They could either use both of their votes for one candidate or vote for two candidates. Disraeli inserted this clause into the Act to protect the interests of the Conservative Party. Recognising that most large boroughs would return Liberal MPs, he calculated that a system of two votes for three members would ensure that a minority candidate would be elected. In Birmingham, under the guidance of a leading local Liberal, **Joseph Chamberlain**, the local Liberal Party devised a strategy to counter this. Chamberlain's system involved building an efficient party organisation with accurate lists of supporters and telling Liberal voters which two candidates to vote for. In this way Liberal votes could be spread evenly between all three candidates and the Conservatives would be squeezed out. So successful was this method, known as the Birmingham 'Caucus', that it was adopted by Liberal Parties in other large boroughs.

National organisation. Nationally the parties developed more professional organisations to co-ordinate their activities. A Liberal Registration Association had been established in 1860. This had taken the lead in reviving dormant constituency parties and drawing up lists of candidates, although it could not direct local party organisations on which candidates to adopt. The Conservatives were quick to recognise that the 1867 Reform Act had changed the political atmosphere, and parties needed to respond. In 1867 the National Union of Conservative Constituency Associations was set up with the express purpose of organising Conservative supporters among the newly-enfranchised working men.

Existing Conservative Working Men's Clubs were brought together through the National Union. Although it held an annual conference from 1868, the status of the National Union within the Conservative Party was very weak until Disraeli decided in 1872 to use its conferences as a platform for making major policy speeches. The Conservatives also established a Central Office in 1870 to act as a national headquarters for the party. The Central Office, under the able leadership of the party's principal agent, **John Gorst**, encouraged the creation of new constituency associations, maintained contact with local parties and drew up lists of candidates. Its success pushed the Carlton Club, which had acted as an informal party headquarters since the 1830s, into the background.

National Liberal Federation. Within the Liberal Party a new National Liberal Federation was set up in 1877. Whereas the Conservative Party's national organisations were established under the control of the parliamentary leadership, the NLF was founded on the initiative of Liberal activists in the constituencies, and its relationship with the parliamentary leadership of Gladstone was often strained. The aim of the NLF, in which Joseph Chamberlain was a leading figure, was partly to facilitate the adoption, by other constituency parties, of the Birmingham Caucus methods of election organisation. The success of this strategy was seen in the improved Liberal organisation during the successful election campaign of 1880. But the NLF was also set up as an attempt to radicalise the policy of the Liberal Party. Through the NLF the radical forces in the constituencies hoped to gain more cohesion and more control over the policy of the party. Chamberlain wanted the party to have a clear programme of policies that had been adopted by the annual assembly of the NLF to reflect the views of the constituency activists. Gladstone and the parliamentary leadership were determined to maintain control over policy, not wishing to be committed to a clearly defined set of radical demands. The setting up of the NLF, therefore, represented an attempt by rank-and-file Liberals to establish democratic control over their party.

How did the parties try to win the support of working-class voters?

The political parties were the means by which new groups of voters were drawn into the political system. Although the parties had to adopt new forms of organisation to integrate working-class political activists into their structures and adjust their policies to attract working-class support, it is notable that these changes did not alter the fundamental nature of the Liberal and Conservative Parties. Leadership, the control of policy and the social composition of MPs were all changed very little by the 1867 Reform Act.

Political clubs. Interest in politics was heightened by the widening of the

KEY PEOPLE

Joseph Chamberlain (1836–1914)

From a nonconformist family, Chamberlain made his fortune in brass screw manufacture and then went into politics as a radical Liberal. Active in Birmingham local politics, as Lord Mayor in the 1870s he initiated extensive slum clearance schemes. He entered Parliament in 1876 and rose to prominence when he helped found the National Liberal Foundation in 1877. Although he was given a post in Gladstone's government after 1880, relations between Chamberlain and Gladstone were always strained. Chamberlain tried, through the NLF, to commit the Liberal Party to a programme of social reforms whereas Gladstone refused to be tied to a policy that would involve state intervention and higher expenditure.

Chamberlain broke with Gladstone and the Liberals over Irish Home Rule in 1886 and allied his Liberal Unionist group with the Conservatives. He served as a minister under Salisbury and Balfour from 1895–1903.

John Gorst (1835–1916) was a barrister by profession. An able organiser, he was appointed as the Conservative Party's National Agent in 1870 after losing his parliamentary seat at the general election in 1868. He showed a keen interest in the problems of building Conservative organisation in the towns. Under his leadership the party began to establish a strong base in the urban areas. This bore fruit in the election victory of 1874.

franchise, and the number of party activists increased. Large numbers of working men became involved in political work through membership of the political clubs that were established specifically for them. In most large urban areas there were Conservative Working Men's Associations and Operatives Liberal Associations. In Bristol, for example, a CWMA and an OLA were both established in 1867. Although primarily political clubs, there was a strong social aspect to their activities. For example, they organised annual outings and other social gatherings of members. They were also engaged in the political education of their members through the provision of libraries and speeches from leading politicians. Some clubs went as far as setting up 'Burial Funds' in the same way as Friendly Societies. The aim of providing these non-political benefits was to secure the long-term support of working-class voters but there was also the intention of educating the new voters to ensure that they were 'fit' to exercise political judgement. As the writer of a letter to the *Salford Weekly News* in 1879 put it, the political education provided through these clubs was 'a means by which the non-reading element might be drawn under the influence of the more earnest and thoughtful club members'.

Working-class liberalism. The majority of the new voters were Liberal in their sympathies. Many artisans were nonconformists. They supported the Gladstonian policies of free trade, low taxation, reform of education and limited franchise reform. But many were also members of trade unions which were pressing for trade union reform and the representation of labour interests in Parliament. The establishment of the Labour Representation League was an attempt by the unions to gain more influence within the Liberal Party, not to set up their own independent political party. Success, however, was limited. Gladstone's government, 1868–74, did give the unions legal recognition in the Trade Union Act of 1870, but much of the goodwill gained through this reform was lost when a law banning peaceful picketing was introduced in the following year.

Labour representation. The Labour Representation League also enjoyed only limited success. Few constituencies had a clear working-class majority among the electorate; in most urban areas the local Liberal parties were still dominated by the middle classes, and attempts to persuade them to adopt working-class candidates in parliamentary elections met with little success. During a by-election in Bristol in 1870, for example, a Bristol Industrial, Social and Political Association of Working Men was established in an attempt to persuade the local Liberal Party to adopt a working man as its candidate. The Association argued that since the other Liberal MP for Bristol was the wealthy businessman Samuel Morley (who had received trade union support in his election campaign), the candidate for the vacant seat should be a working man. The Liberal Party, however, adopted another leading local employer as its candidate. Much the same pattern was repeated in other large towns. Only in the mining areas were there constituencies in which working-class voters were in a majority and where one union could exercise a powerful influence over the selection of candidates. Significantly, the first working men elected to Parliament, in 1874, were **Thomas Burt**, a Northumberland coal miner who was elected for Morpeth on the Northumberland coalfield, and **Alexander MacDonald**, the leader of the Miners' Union, who was elected for Stafford. During the period 1874–85, the number of 'Lib-Lab' MPs remained at two. Even in local government elections, local Liberal parties were reluctant to concede places on elected bodies to working men. It was not until 1880 that the Bristol Liberal Party adopted a working-class candidate for the local School Board, after the Bristol OLA had been pressing for this for at least ten years.

Despite the limited concessions made to trade union interests by the Liberals, most working-class voters continued to support the Liberals in elections. There was some evidence of disillusionment with the Liberals in the election of 1874, but in 1880 Liberal support among working-class voters revived. Partly this was because most working-class voters at this time were not motivated by class-consciousness. The lack of progress in getting working men onto local government bodies and into Parliament would only be an issue for the more radical activists. Most Liberal working men were content to give their support to middle-class candidates because they shared the same basic values and supported the same policies. They were also attracted to the Liberals by Gladstone's leadership. With his skill as an orator, his strong moral convictions and his support for policies such as free trade, Gladstone showed himself to be particularly adept at communicating with the new electorate and enlisting their support for his crusading style of politics. Since the 1860s he had been gaining a reputation as the 'friend of the working man'. Gladstone's appeal transcended class divisions and helped the Liberals to remain a broadly-based party.

Working-class conservatism. Around one-third of working-class voters consistently supported the Conservatives after 1867. Support was spread over all areas of the country but was particularly strong in three areas. Liverpool and West Lancashire, Birmingham and the West Midlands and the East End of London all had strong local traditions of working-class conservatism. In each case, local factors combined with national trends to reinforce working-class support for Conservative candidates. In general, working-class conservatism was based on four main factors.

- **Deference.** Respect for their 'social superiors' motivated many working men to vote for the party most clearly associated with the aristocracy.

KEY PEOPLE

Thomas Burt (1837–1922) and **Alexander Macdonald (1821–1881)** were the only two working-class candidates elected to Parliament in 1874 out of a total of 13. Although they made little impact on the parliamentary scene, they have the distinction of being the first two working men elected to Parliament. They supported Gladstone's brand of individualist Liberalism.

This factor was particularly strong in rural areas but was also evident in the East End of London.

- **Patriotism**: the identification of the Conservative Party with the defence of national interests and the Empire. While Palmerston had been leading the Liberals, the Conservatives could not claim to be the only party that could be trusted to preserve the unity of the Empire and defend British interests in Europe, but after his death Gladstone adopted a more moralistic approach to foreign and imperial policy. During the 1870s Disraeli was able to adopt the Palmerstonian mantle and present the Conservative Party as the guardians of the national interest. His appeal to the patriotism of the electorate played particularly well in constituencies where a large proportion of the voters depended on defence industries for their livelihoods. The metal industries of the West Midlands had connections with armaments manufacture; naval dockyard towns were directly dependent for their prosperity on the maintenance of a large navy.
- **Dislike of foreigners** in general, and the Irish in particular, were prejudices that could be played upon in election campaigns. Hostility to Irish immigrants was particularly strong among working-class voters in Liverpool and West Lancashire, and Gladstone's championing of the Irish Catholic peasant farmers lost the Liberals much support in that area. The Conservatives were not slow to exploit these prejudices. When Gladstone took up the cause of Irish Home Rule in 1886, for example, it was argued that Home Rule would bring 'thousands of desperate Irishmen over to England to compete in our markets'. Jewish immigration from Eastern Europe also excited suspicion and hostility among the working-class population of the East End of London, the area in which many immigrants settled.
- **Liberal weaknesses.** The Conservatives, traditionally the party of resistance to reform, adopted the strategy of waiting for the Liberals to run into difficulties over their own reforming efforts. Drawing their support from such a disparate range of interests, the Liberals were almost bound to disappoint some of their supporters. Liberal reforms were based on compromises between conflicting and competing interests; when disillusionment with the results of reform occurred, the Conservatives could expect to reap the benefits. The Licensing Act of 1872 is a good example of this. Pressure for restrictions on the sale of alcohol had come particularly from the largely nonconformist temperance movement, but the Act of 1872 did not satisfy their demands. Indeed, in introducing a system of regulation for public houses, it appeared to legitimise the sale of alcohol. On the other hand, the introduction of even mild regulations outraged the drinkers among working-class voters and pushed the brewers closer to the Conservative Party.

Policy. The Conservatives made few adjustments in policy in order to attract the new working-class voters. Disraeli's ministry, 1874–80, did introduce a number of social reforms that were designed to improve living and working conditions. His government also reversed the law banning peaceful picketing which Gladstone's government had passed. But the reforms of Disraeli's ministry did not amount to a coherent Conservative programme of social reform designed to win working-class votes. Disraeli himself showed very little interest in the reforms, leaving the detailed work to his Home Secretary, Richard Cross. Many of the reforms were already in the process of being drawn up when the Conservatives took office in 1874 and would have been implemented even if a Liberal government had been in power. There is a received Disraeli myth that he showed remarkable forethought in seeing that the future of the Conservative Party depended on its ability to attract support from the urban working classes and that he steered the party in the direction of a new **'One-Nation Toryism'**. The reality was that Disraeli had no such insight. His views on the future direction of the Conservative Party were rooted in the past. The party remained firmly committed to preserving the power of the landowners and the privileged position of the Church of England. His main strategy for attracting support from other classes was to present the Conservative Party as the national party.

Impact on party organisation. The influx of working-class members into the Conservative political clubs also made very little impact on the way the party was run. Gorst, the principal agent, gave priority to the task of building up Conservative organisation in the towns; and in 1874 the party made significant gains in urban constituencies. Working Men's Conservative Associations were set up in all the major towns. In an effort to secure membership and foster loyalty, Conservative clubs often provided social activities such as drinking and billiards; clubs often had their own brass bands and football teams and the party often sponsored sickness and burial societies. In these ways the new urban conservatism can be seen to have embraced working-class culture; but control over the choice of candidates and over policy remained firmly in the hands of traditional Conservatives. When the Bristol WMCA tried to persuade the local Conservative Party to adopt a working man as a candidate in a School Board election in 1870, it was ignored. A second attempt was made in 1880 and a working-class Conservative was elected to the School Board, but only after the WMCA had defied the local party. The Conservative Party offered few opportunities for working men to advance in local government and no opportunities for them to enter Parliament. Unlike working-class Liberals, most Conservative working men were not members of trade unions and did not have the benefit of the pressure that union organisation could bring to bear on the party.

KEY TERM

'One-Nation Toryism' has been used both as a slogan and as a rallying cry for a particular faction within the Tory Party. Put simply, it was a brand of Conservatism that stressed the need to avoid class warfare through the party of the upper classes adopting policies, i.e. social reforms, that would benefit the working classes. Although later exponents of this style of Conservatism have seen Disraeli as their inspiration, Disraeli himself did not view social reforms in this light. His recipe for uniting the classes was to appeal to patriotism.

What was the impact of the 1867 Reform Act on the political allegiances of the middle classes?

When the Liberal politician Lord Granville was visiting Manchester in 1867 he reported that middle-class Liberals were 'frightened out of their wits at the borough franchise' and they felt 'that the power of the middle class was gone'. In the 1868 general election a majority of middle-class voters continued to support Liberal candidates, much as they had done for the previous 20 years, although the defeat of John Stuart Mill by the middle-class Conservative W. H. Smith in Westminster was a harbinger of things to come. By 1874 a significant change had become apparent. The Conservatives won a number of urban constituencies and closer analysis revealed that the main reason for Conservative success was a change in the voting behaviour of the middle classes. At each subsequent election during the last quarter of the nineteenth century, the swing to the Conservatives among middle-class voters became more marked. Evidence of this change can be seen in the changing pattern of elections in London. In 1859 and 1865, the Conservatives had failed to win a single seat in the capital. After winning three seats in London in 1868, the Conservatives went on to take ten seats in 1874.

Much of this change occurred without the Conservatives having to make any special effort to attract middle-class voters. Disraeli remained rooted in a pre-industrial landed society and showed little interest in the middle classes. The main factor was that the middle classes began to be alarmed by the increasingly radical tone of Gladstonian Liberalism. Despite the fact that Gladstone's ministry, 1868–74, did more to promote middle-class interests through its reforms than to appease working-class demands, the middle classes began to feel that a Conservative government would do more to check the political advance of the working classes than the Liberals. Under Disraeli's leadership the Conservatives had quietly dropped their policy of trade protection, thereby removing a major obstacle to middle-class support. Disraeli's appeal to the patriotism of the electorate won middle-class as well as working-class support. As many of the middle classes became wealthier, they tended to move into the suburbs, become less attached to the nonconformist faith of their parents and grandparents, and to identify more closely with the landed classes. The basis for a Conservative Party built on an alliance of property interests was being laid in the 1860s and 1870s and would come to full fruition in the 1880s and 1890s.

HOW DID POLITICAL PARTIES DEVELOP AFTER THE REFORMS OF THE 1880s?

The major changes that were made in the conduct of elections (1883), the franchise (1884) and the distribution of seats (1885) remained the basis of electoral law until the end of the First World War in 1918. During this period the fortunes of the parties underwent significant changes.

- The Liberal Party went into decline after it split over Irish Home Rule in 1886. During the period 1886–1906, the Liberal Party held office for a mere three years, between 1892 and 1895.
- The character of the Liberal Party changed significantly. Most of the Whigs who had dominated the parliamentary party and Liberal cabinets for so long left the party in 1886 and allied with the Conservatives. The Liberal Party in Parliament became more radical in policy and middle class in social background, thus more closely mirroring the Liberal Party in the constituencies.
- The Conservatives were the most successful party in the period 1886–1906. The trend among the middle classes to vote Conservative was consolidated during this period whilst the Conservatives also enjoyed some success in appealing to working-class voters through pursuing an expansionist imperial policy.
- The Liberal Party faced a new challenge after 1900 with the formation of the Labour Representation Committee, dedicated to promoting independent Labour representation in Parliament. From 1906, when 29 Labour MPs were elected, this group adopted the title of the Labour Party. The growth in trade union support for the new Labour Party threatened the links that the Liberal Party had been developing with the unions since the 1870s. However, the threat from the Labour Party was contained by a 'Lib-Lab' electoral pact that the two parties agreed in 1903.
- The Liberals' fortunes revived after 1903, resulting in a Liberal landslide victory in 1906. A programme of social and welfare reforms, known as 'New Liberalism', was introduced by the Liberal government between 1906 and 1914.
- The First World War had a major impact on the fortunes of the political parties. The Liberals suffered another split in 1916, causing them to appear weak and divided when peacetime politics returned in 1918. Both the Conservative and the Labour parties gained support on the basis of their wartime records.

These changes in the parties' fortunes were related to the broad social, economic and political trends of the time. Major events such as the First World War also had an impact on the parties. The electoral changes made in 1883–85 formed the framework in which political parties were operating in this period but it is also possible to identify some features of the political scene that derived directly from the reforms.

What were the effects of the Corrupt Practices Act?

The restrictions on campaign spending produced two apparently contradictory results. Firstly, the parties needed more professional election agents who were well versed in the law. Secondly, the parties also needed more volunteer workers, who could undertake much of the more mundane work involved in election campaigns at no cost to the candidates or the party organisations. The Liberal Party had large numbers of voluntary activists, although Liberal decline after 1886 resulted in some constituency parties finding difficulty in holding on to their volunteers. The Conservatives set up the Primrose League in 1883 as their vehicle for recruiting party volunteers.

Primrose League. The Primrose League was dedicated to promoting the Tory principles of maintaining the established church, the power of the landed classes and the Empire. Founded by Lord Randolph Churchill and named after Disraeli's favourite flower, the League elevated Disraeli to the position of a Tory icon who had, in the eyes of its founders, rebuilt the Tory Party on the basis of a 'True Union of the Classes'. The League adopted a romantic style in the names given to its members. Male members were 'Knights', female members 'Dames'. Branches were known as 'Habitations'. The organisation had a hierarchical structure, designed not only to mirror but also to celebrate the hierarchical nature of society that the Tories sought to defend.

The League was very successful. From a membership of 237,000 in 1886, it had grown to over 1 million by 1891 and to over 2 million by 1910. It enabled the Conservative Party to recruit women members as well as men and involve them in the work of the party. Loyalty was maintained between elections by developing an extensive range of social activities. It is estimated that half of the League's members were women.

The Primrose League proved to be an ideal vehicle for encouraging popular participation in the Conservative Party without exposing the traditional leadership to demands for greater involvement in decision-making. Lord Salisbury, and his successor as Conservative Party leader Arthur Balfour, felt uncomfortable with rank-and-file organisations such as the constituency associations and the National Union when they tried to influence policy. Despite the talk of 'Tory democracy' that came from leading Conservatives like Lord Randolph Churchill in the 1880s, the Conservative Party preferred to keep democracy at arm's length. The value of the Primrose League was that it gave the Conservative Party a broad membership base but it was never a threat to the leadership. Control over policy and over the choice of leader remained firmly in the hands of leading politicians.

What were the effects of the Third Reform Act?

The granting of the vote to farm labourers in 1884 forced the parties to develop new ways of reaching rural voters. Although the Conservatives were traditionally the strongest party in the countryside they could not take the new voters for granted, particularly after the secret ballot had reduced the opportunities for landowners to exert their traditional influence. The Primrose League had many rural as well as urban branches to consolidate the Conservatives' base in the countryside. What seats the Liberals had previously won in the countryside had mainly been those secured by Whig landowners; otherwise the Liberals had been largely an urban political force. This was also true of the new Labour Party that was beginning to emerge in the 1890s. Both the Liberal Party and later the Labour Party did give more attention to winning support in the countryside but their success depended on a number of factors. In 'closed' villages the opportunity for independent political action among farm labourers, even after the secret ballot and extension of the franchise, was very limited. 'Open' villages, however, offered greater scope for radical politics, particularly where nonconformist chapels had been established. The emergence of trade unionism among farm labourers in the 1870s also gave more scope for the development of radical politics in areas where the union was strongest, such as Norfolk. Without a firm organisational base in the coutryside, however, the Liberal Party had to rely on political 'missionaries' from the towns to carry the radical message to country villages. Mobile vans bringing speakers, leaflets and lantern shows were sent to the countryside by many political organisations, including the **Land Nationalisation Society** and the **Land Restoration League**. The use of cycling clubs was another device. Primrose League 'Dames' could combine exercise with political missionary work by joining the Primrose Cycling Corps. Among socialist pioneers, the same opportunities were provided by the **Clarion Cycling Clubs**, which were especially popular in northern industrial areas.

Rural issues. After the Third Reform Act the Liberals gave more attention to rural issues in an attempt to win farm labourers' votes. Radical Liberals believed that farm labourers would not be able to exercise independent political judgement unless they had the economic independence that would come with being small farmers in their own right. Joseph Chamberlain was one of the first Liberals to raise the banner of land reform in his 'Unauthorised Programme' of 1885. In this he advocated state help for farm labourers to acquire smallholdings – a policy dubbed 'Three Acres and a Cow'. His proposals were rejected by Gladstone but Liberal efforts in the countryside were rewarded in the 1885 general election when the party secured a number of rural seats.

The Conservatives also introduced a number of reforms of landholding and local government in the countryside after 1886. Elected county

KEY ORGANISATIONS

Little is known about the **Land Nationalisation Society** or the **Land Restoration League**, other than that they were radical organisations campaigning for land reform. The idea of establishing an independent class of small peasant farmers who would be a counterweight to the influence of wealthy landowners had attracted parts of the radical movement since the early part of the century. **Clarion Cyclists** were socialist 'missionaries' from the industrial towns who took copies of *The Clarion* newspaper to country villages in the hope of gaining supporters.

councils were introduced in 1888, a concession to the democratic principle that was long overdue although landowners continued to exercise influence in many councils. The Conservatives also introduced an Allotments Act in 1887 and a Smallholdings Act in 1892 under which local councils could purchase land and lease it in small plots at economic rents. The amount of land that was redistributed under these Acts, however, was very small.

What were the effects of the 1885 Redistribution Act?

The Redistribution Act had immediate and far-reaching consequences for both the Conservative and Liberal parties.

- An unforeseen consequence of the establishment of single-member constituencies was that the Whigs suffered serious damage. In the large urban constituencies that had returned two or three members before 1885, the Whigs often shared the Liberal candidacies with the radicals. With single-member constituencies, middle-class-dominated local Liberal parties were less inclined to give preference to Whig candidates. Far fewer Liberal MPs after 1885 came from landowning backgrounds or identified with the Whig element within the party. Most Whigs broke with the Liberal Party in 1886 over the issue of Irish Home Rule; but even before their defection to the Liberal Unionists the Whigs were in decline. The loss of the Whigs was a major factor in the radicalisation of the Liberal Party that occurred after 1886.
- The Conservatives made significant gains of seats in the large urban areas in elections after 1885. Salisbury's insistence on a Redistribution Act was motivated by his understanding that the Conservatives had been gaining ground among the middle classes in the suburbs since 1874 – the so-called 'Villa Toryism' – and that by dividing the towns along class lines, to create new single-member constituencies, the Tories could convert votes into seats. One of the major factors in the electoral success of the Conservative Party in the period 1886–1906 was its ability to win extra seats in the former Liberal heartlands of the industrial areas.

KEY TERM

Villa Toryism
Many of the affluent middle-class families who moved to the suburbs lived in large, detached houses that were described as 'villas'. 'Villa Toryism' was the term used to describe the trend of the suburban middle classes to become Conservative voters.

Impact on the Labour Party. In the longer term, the Redistribution Act gave some assistance to the new Labour Party. As a party that aimed its appeal mainly at the working classes, the Labour Party struggled to win seats in constituencies with a socially mixed population. The Redistribution Act did create, however, some 89 constituencies which had a clear majority of working-class electors and many of these constituencies were targeted by the Labour Party in its early attempts to win seats. Many of these constituencies were in mining areas, others were in the cotton towns of South Lancashire, the woollen towns of West Yorkshire and in the East End of London. The mere fact of having a working-class majority, however, did not mean that the Labour Party would become a major political force in these constituencies, still less that it would win the seats. Other factors came into play, not the least of which was the attitude of the trade unions towards independent labour representation. The Miners' Union had, since the 1870s, been gradually sponsoring more MPs from mining constituencies under the auspices of the Liberal Party. The success of this strategy made the Miners' Union reluctant to abandon its '**Lib-Labism**' and it was not until 1909 that the union decided to affiliate to the Labour Representation Committee.

There is an argument that the Labour Party's early development suffered from the fact that a large proportion of the working classes were unable to vote after the extensions of the franchise in 1867 and 1884. The first Independent Labour MP was elected in 1892 when Keir Hardie was returned to Parliament for West Ham. Thereafter progress was slow; Hardie was defeated in 1895 but re-elected in 1900 together with another LRC candidate. With growing trade union support after 1900 and the signing of an electoral pact with the Liberals in 1903 – the '**Lib-Lab pact**' – the LRC was able to make a significant breakthrough into parliamentary politics in 1906 when 29 LRC (Labour) candidates were elected. This marked the high point of the Labour Party's pre-war success because, although in the 1910 elections some 42 Labour MPs were elected, the increase was entirely due to the Miners' Union switching its support from the Liberal Party in 1909. Before 1914, therefore, the Labour Party did not pose a serious threat to the Liberal Party but it seems unlikely that its fortunes would have been significantly different if more of the adult male working classes had been able to vote. Among those who were disenfranchised under the 1867 and 1884 rules were servants and soldiers who would probably have voted Conservative if they had had the chance. The bulk of the remainder of the approximately 40 per cent of adult males who could not vote was from the most impoverished section of the population who had shown no inclination towards radical politics. Labour had difficulty in building its organisation in the poorest parts of the East End of London. Labour's strength lay in the industrial areas among the comparatively stable, skilled, unionised and politically conscious members of the working-class population. In other words, the Labour Party was seeking to appeal to the same groups of 'respectable' working men as the Liberal Party, and Labour did not see an extension of the franchise as the key to its success. Although the Labour Party included adult suffrage among its policy objectives, the issue was never given a high priority.

How did the composition of the House of Commons change?
The gradual reduction in the number of MPs from landowning backgrounds and the increase in the numbers who came from middle-class backgrounds continued after 1885. The trend was more marked

KEY TERM

'**Lib-Labism**' was the term used to describe the policy of unions that sponsored labour representation in Parliament under the auspices of the Liberal Party.

KEY FACT

The Lib-Lab pact
In 1903 the Liberal Party Chief Whip, Herbert Gladstone, and the Secretary of the LRC, Ramsay MacDonald, agreed an electoral pact under which the two parties would not put up candidates against each other. The risk of an election with both Liberal and Labour candidates was that the anti-Conservative vote would be split and the Conservatives could win many constituencies on a minority vote. Under this arrangement, LRC candidates were not opposed by the Liberals in 30 constituencies.

among Liberal MPs than among the ranks of the Conservatives. Whereas in 1868, 26 per cent of Liberals came from landowning backgrounds, this figure had fallen to a mere 7 per cent by 1910. In the same period, the proportion of MPs from middle-class backgrounds had grown from 67 per cent to 89 per cent. Among the middle-class MPs, the number of lawyers in particular increased.

Change was much slower in the Conservative Party. Although in each new group of Conservative MPs elected after 1885 there was a substantial majority from the middle classes, landowners still made up over 38 per cent of the parliamentary party in 1900. In 1910, 26 per cent of Conservative MPs came from landowning backgrounds. Moreover, aristocratic landowners continued to dominate Conservative cabinets and not until 1911 was a leader chosen who came from an industrial background.

The first working men had been elected to Parliament in 1874. Until 1885 the number of 'Lib-Labs' in Parliament did not rise above two but with the radicalisation of the Liberal Party after 1886, and the growth of the unions, this number had increased to 12 by 1895. The 1906 Parliament saw the first significant increase in the numbers of working men entering Parliament, with 29 Labour and 24 Lib-Lab MPs being elected. Not all of the new MPs came from working-class backgrounds but the majority were trade unionists. The presence of working-class MPs, however, did not make much impact on the 'gentleman's club' atmosphere of the House of Commons. Indeed, the new Labour MPs were more likely to be absorbed into this atmosphere than to challenge it.

WHAT WAS THE IMPACT OF THE 1918 REPRESENTATION OF THE PEOPLE ACT ON THE PARTIES?

The reforms of the parliamentary system introduced in 1918 had far-reaching consequences for the political parties. The new electorate was radically different from that which had existed before the war in terms of class, age and gender. The working classes now formed a majority of the new electorate; many of those voting in the 1918 general election were young men and women who could vote for the first time. The Representation of the People Act also instituted a major redistribution of seats, with the remaining small boroughs losing their representation in Parliament and many more seats being given to the large urban areas. Apart from the continuing discrimination against women, the electoral system was now to all intents and purposes democratic and the parties would have to be able to appeal to the mass electorate if they were to have any chance of success.

The political situation between 1918 and 1931 contained the following key features:

- There was a sustained rise in support for the Labour Party after 1918. Labour replaced the Liberals as the main progressive force in British politics, and the first Labour government took office in 1924 – albeit as a minority government. Labour reached its peak of post-war achievement in 1929 when it won 37 per cent of the popular vote and the second Labour government took office.
- The split in the Liberal Party that had occurred in 1916 continued after the war and proved a serious handicap to Liberal efforts to contain the threat from Labour. Lloyd George continued his **Coalition Government** with the Conservatives until they ditched him in 1922. Asquith attempted to maintain an independent Liberal Party in opposition to Lloyd George. The Liberals reunited in 1923 but the damage by then was irreparable. Liberal strength in the House of Commons dropped dramatically, particularly after 1923. In 1929 the party won only 59 seats, although this was an improvement on its 1924 result.
- The Conservatives were the most successful party during the period 1918–31. Either in coalition with Lloyd George, or in government on their own account, they were in office for ten of those 13 years.

Clearly the Conservative and Labour parties were more successful in appealing to the mass electorate than the Liberals, although we should exercise some caution in making these judgements. Conservative success in the election of 1922 was achieved on the support of little more than 38 per cent of the electorate, while the combined Labour and Liberal votes amounted to over 58 per cent. Conservative strength was at least partly due to the division in the anti-Conservative vote between Asquith Liberals, Lloyd George Liberals and Labour. As late as 1923, the Liberals' share of the vote, at 29.6 per cent, was less than a single percentage point behind that of Labour, at 30.5 per cent; yet the Liberals won 159 seats compared with Labour's 191. The appeal of a party's policies and the competence of its leadership were only part of the explanation for its success or failure during this period. The working of the electoral system and the way each party operated within that system were also critical factors.

How did the electoral system help the Conservative Party?

- The Conservatives gained a number of seats as a result of redistribution. Shifts in population since 1885 resulted in the growth of the suburban areas, and the creation of many new suburban seats in 1918 benefited the Conservatives.
- The granting of votes to women over 30 was, on balance, of greater benefit to the Conservatives than to Labour or the Liberals.

KEY TERM

Coalition Government
The first wartime Coalition government was formed by Asquith in 1915, involving ministers from all three main parties. A new Coalition was formed in 1916 when Asquith was forced to resign and Lloyd George took over, at the cost of splitting the Liberal Party. Lloyd George and the Conservatives agreed to continue in a Coalition after the war, and Coalition candidates swept the board in the general election of December 1918. Labour then withdrew from the Coalition. Within the post-war Coalition, the Conservatives were the largest party although Lloyd George was retained as Prime Minister because of his prestige as the man who had led the country to victory.

KEY PERSON

Stanley Baldwin (1867–1947)
became party leader in 1923 after the retirement of Bonar Law. He came from a middle-class, manufacturing background in the Midlands but liked to cultivate the image of a country gentleman. After an unspectacular early career in politics, he rose to prominence after he took a leading role in forcing the party leadership to withdraw from Lloyd George's Coalition government in 1922. Baldwin was not a charismatic or dynamic leader. His great strengths were his integrity and his conciliatory style, together with his ability to use the new medium of radio to talk directly to the voters in their own homes. Baldwin was Conservative leader until 1937 and served as Prime Minister during eight of those years.

The Conservatives took care, especially under **Baldwin's** leadership, to cultivate women voters. Only in 1923, however, did women voters make a significant impact on an election result, when large numbers of women voted against the Conservatives after Baldwin campaigned for the abandonment of free trade.

- A significant number of the new working-class voters also supported the Conservatives for the reasons outlined earlier (see pages 240–2). Possibly as many as one-third of the working-class voters were regular or intermittent Conservative voters. The result was that the Labour Party never, during the whole of the period 1918–31, achieved a popular vote that was higher than that for the Conservatives.

Few of these benefits, however, were automatic results of the changes in the electoral system. It was the success of the Conservative Party in adapting its organisation to the changed electoral situation that converted opportunities into achievements. The success of the Conservatives was built on the following foundations.

- A large mass membership giving the party access to an army of volunteer helpers. The Conservatives built a larger membership base than the Labour Party and were particularly successful in recruiting and involving women. Former members of the Primrose League and disillusioned middle-class women from the Liberals were given an active role in canvassing and the many other tasks associated with election campaigns. By the late 1920s the women's side of the Conservative Party organisation claimed over 1 million members.
- An efficient party organisation ensured that election campaigns were run in a professional manner. Full-time agents were provided with training. The Conservative Party had more full-time agents than the other two, partly because it had the money to maintain a professional organisation but also because the party recognised the need.
- The ability to adapt its policy to the changed complexion of the electorate. Although the Conservatives continued to present themselves as the national party and a bulwark against the dangers of socialist revolution, there was also a willingness to embrace more positive themes of social reform. Baldwin's government, 1924–9, introduced a number of progressive social reforms that addressed some of the concerns of working-class and female voters.

During election campaigns the Conservatives were usually more successful than the other parties in identifying their supporters through an efficient canvass and in ensuring that those supporters actually voted on polling day. 'Getting the vote out' became as important as finding the right policies in the new political era.

How did the Labour Party benefit?

- The advent of full adult suffrage did benefit the Labour Party in the long term but in the first election held under the new franchise, in 1918, Labour made only modest gains over its position in 1910. As outlined in the previous section, there was no automatic correlation between extending the franchise and increasing the Labour vote.
- The creation of more constituencies in the industrial areas, particularly in the coalfields, benefitted the Labour Party because much of its support was concentrated in these areas.

As with the Conservatives, however, it was up to the Labour Party to take advantage of the new opportunities presented by the changed electoral system. The Labour Party did this in a number of ways.

- A new party structure was introduced in 1918. The LRC had been an unwieldy alliance of trade unions with the ILP which was not well suited to building a strong and efficient party machine at constituency level. The new Labour Party had individual membership in constituency parties, linked together by a strong central organisation. The actual task of establishing new constituency party organisations could not be completed quickly and it was not until 1923 that many constituency parties had been created.
- Women's sections drew female supporters into the work of the party.
- Labour leaders placed great emphasis on large public meetings and rallies as a means of reaching the mass electorate, following the example of Gladstone in the nineteenth century. They also made effective use of poster campaigns.
- Links with the trade unions were essential as the main source of finance for the Labour Party but the unions were also an important vehicle for the party to convey its message to the ordinary members. Union membership had grown dramatically during the First World War and by 1920 a majority of the manual labour force belonged to unions.
- The failure of Coalition and Conservative governments to deal effectively with unemployment was an issue that Labour politicians could exploit in their election campaigns.

Both Conservative and Labour parties took full advantage of another aspect of the electoral system, at the expense of the Liberals. With single-member constituencies in a 'first past the post' electoral system, there was an inbuilt bias against third party candidates. In many constituencies by the early 1920s the Liberals found themselves in this position. The Conservatives had their safe seats in the countryside and the middle-class suburbs; Labour was beginning to establish this position in predominantly working-class constituencies, particularly in the coalfields. The Liberal vote, which at over 29 per cent in 1922 and 1923 was still significant, tended to be more evenly spread across a number of areas. It was therefore difficult for the Liberals to convert votes into seats. As the Liberals acquired the image of a party in decline their vote was squeezed even further since the other parties could claim that a vote for a Liberal candidate would be wasted. Middle-class Liberals tended to transfer their votes to the Conservatives and working-class Liberals to Labour. A system of proportional representation, which was under consideration in the consultations prior to the 1918 Act, would have benefitted the Liberals by giving them more seats. It would also have prevented the Conservatives from forming a government in 1922 on the basis of less than 40 per cent of the total vote. The idea was, however, opposed by the Conservatives and not pursued with any conviction by the other two parties.

What was the impact on the role of the state?

INTRODUCTION

During the 1820s the involvement of local and central government in the affairs of ordinary people was very limited. The responsibilities of government were largely confined to the maintenance of law and order, the administration of justice and the defence of the realm. Most law-abiding subjects of the Crown would rarely be affected by the actions of the state. Few were in the state's employ; in the 1780s, the Crown employed only about 16,000 people in total. Local government had an essentially regulatory role. Justices of the Peace licensed ale-houses and supervised the administration of the Poor Law but, apart from the local provision of outdoor relief for the poor, local government provided no services for people.

By the late 1920s the role of the state at both national and local levels had expanded. A few examples of this expanded role will help to illustrate this point.

- Most of the nation's children were educated in state-run schools and attendance was compulsory up to the age of 14.
- Hours of work for the majority of workers, together with safety standards at work, were regulated by law; places of work were subject to inspection by factory inspectors.
- People who contributed to the National Insurance scheme were able to claim unemployment and sickness benefits when the need arose. There were other forms of assistance available from local Public Assistance Committees.
- Many people lived in housing which they rented from the local council. These houses were built to standards laid down by law.
- In some industries, basic minimum wages were laid down by law.
- Many people bought their water, gas and electricity from publicly-owned companies. Sewage, drainage and refuse collection were also the responsibility of local authorities.
- The state was involved in the reorganisation of a number of industries, including the railways and coal mining.

Laissez-faire

This list of activities in which the state was involved by the 1920s is by no means exhaustive but will suffice to illustrate the point that during this

KEY TERMS

Laissez-faire
This French phrase, meaning literally 'allow to do', is the term used to describe the policy of allowing individuals to make their own decisions about their social and economic activities, free from state interference or regulation. In the nineteenth century it was particularly associated with the followers of Adam Smith and with the 'Manchester School' of economic thought. The 'Manchester School' were the leading exponents of a free market and free trade.

Collectivism is used to describe an approach to social and economic questions that is the opposite of individualism. It involves society acting 'collectively', through political institutions, to tackle social problems. Socialism is a form of collectivism, but not the only possible interpretation of this approach.

period the state had undertaken responsibility for the health and welfare of its citizens in ways that would have been inconceivable during the 1820s. Not only did central and local government in the early nineteenth century not possess the administrative machinery that would have been needed to take on these functions, but the prevailing climate of opinion at this time would not have tolerated such an extension in the powers of the state or the increases in taxation that were needed to finance it. Scepticism about the role of the state and resistance to any extension in its powers remained strong throughout the nineteenth century and into the twentieth. **Evans** (1996) has written that the prevailing ethos in the mid-nineteenth century 'remained one of rugged individualism'. Belief in individual self-help, a **laissez-faire** approach to social and economic questions and a free market are often seen as defining characteristics of the Victorian era. Yet it was precisely during that era that the first steps were taken towards a more **collectivist** approach to social problems. Clearly, therefore, we must avoid such simplistic interpretations of this period as 'an age of laissez-faire' or 'an age of state intervention'. Furthermore, although there were connections between extensions of the franchise in 1832, 1867, 1884 and 1918 and growing state involvement in social questions, we must be careful not to present these connections in terms of a simple cause and effect relationship. As we shall see, the picture was a complex one.

WHAT WAS THE ROLE OF THE STATE IN THE 1820S?

The Lord Lieutenant was the monarch's representative in each county. Usually the greatest nobleman, he led the county militia (part-time soldiers) and was responsible for official appointments, e.g. Justices of the Peace, within the county.

As we have seen above, central and local government barely touched the lives of ordinary people in the early nineteenth century. At local level, administration was in the hands of Justices of the Peace who were appointed by the **Lord Lieutenants** of the counties from among the local squires and parsons. They were responsible for the licensing of ale-houses, the supervision of poor relief and the administration of justice. In the towns, unelected corporations performed few of the functions that later town councils were to take on. At national level, ministries employed relatively few civil servants. Most of those who were employed were appointed through the patronage of ministers; the most important criteria used in the selection of civil servants, therefore, were family and political connections, not the competence of the person appointed.

Repeal of paternalist legislation
Since the sixteenth century a series of laws had been passed which regulated various economic activities, such as wages, prices, employment and trade. These laws had been designed to protect particular interests – the Navigation Laws, for example, protected British shipowners by giving them a monopoly over the carriage of goods between Britain and the colonies – or to offer a form of paternalistic protection for working

people. By the early nineteenth century, however, state regulation was coming under increasing criticism. Influential economists such as **Adam Smith** argued that state controls promoted inefficiency, special privileges and monopolies, and that the operation of the market should be freed from outdated restrictions. His arguments were not only taken up by many manufacturers and traders but also by politicians. Accordingly, many old laws were repealed or reformed.

- In 1813 and 1814, the Elizabethan Statutes of Artificers were repealed. These were laws that allowed JPs the power to regulate wages and the employment of apprentices.
- In the 1820s, the Navigation Laws were modified to allow foreign shipowners to use British ports.
- Controls on the export of machinery were relaxed in the 1820s.
- Many onerous taxes, such as the salt tax and beer tax, were abolished.

In these ways the state was beginning to withdraw from the regulation of trade and industry. It is significant that this process, which had begun at least partly in response to pressure from commercial interests, was happening even before the middle classes were given the right to vote in 1832. Lack of representation in Parliament did not necessarily preclude particular groups from pressing their case on the legislators. For example, in 1815 the Assize of Bread in London was abolished after 800 master bakers petitioned Parliament. This had been a device by which the price of bread in the capital could be fixed. Its abolition heralded the complete withdrawal of the state from the regulation of prices.

The beginnings of intervention

These changes were symptomatic of the growing influence of laissez-faire ideas among politicians. Other reforms in the same period, however, give a different picture. The first two Factory Acts were passed in 1802 and 1819, largely because of pressure from Sir Robert Peel and Robert Owen, both leading cotton manufacturers. These laws attempted to protect children employed in cotton factories but were ineffective because inspection of factories was rarely carried out, being the responsibility of JPs. Nevertheless, ineffective though they were, the Factory Acts were a sign that laissez-faire was not universally accepted as the only sensible approach to social questions.

TO WHAT EXTENT DID STATE INTERVENTION INCREASE IN THE PERIOD 1832–67?

After the passing of the First Reform Act in 1832 the middle classes had been admitted to the 'political nation'. Although the landowning aristocracy still retained power over central government and dominated

Adam Smith (1723–90)
The author of *The Wealth of Nations*, Smith is considered to have been the founder of the modern science of economics. His writings became the basis for free market, free trade and laissez-faire policies. His influence still lives on, particularly through the activities of the Adam Smith Institute, a political think-tank.

the parliaments of this period, the middle classes had gained influence as a result of the Reform Act. Political parties had to appeal to middle-class voters if they were to win elections. At local government level, the new municipal corporations in the larger towns were controlled by local middle-class interests. Leading spokesmen for the middle classes in this period, such as Edward Baines, Richard Cobden and John Bright, all pressed strongly the case for minimal state interference in social and economic questions, for free trade and for cheap and efficient government. Although this 'rugged individualism' was not shared by all the middle classes, there was a general presumption in favour of a laissez-faire approach by governments. For their part, both Whig-Liberal and Conservative governments in this period adopted policies that reflected the prevailing mood. This was particularly evident in the free trade policies implemented by governments in the 1840s and 1850s.

Free trade
- In his budgets of 1842 and 1845, Peel reduced or abolished import and export duties on a wide range of raw materials and manufactured goods.
- In 1846 Peel took the policy of free trade further by repealing the Corn Laws, in the face of fierce opposition from landowners and farmers.
- The Navigation Acts were repealed in 1847 and 1854.
- Gladstone carried on Peel's work during the 1850s. As Chancellor of the Exchequer he completed the task of removing import and export duties and of reducing taxes.

By the early 1860s British overseas trade was, to all intents and purposes, free of duties and other restrictions. This policy was successful in stimulating trade and employment and it also reduced taxes on consumption – therefore prices of many basic commodities came down – so it was generally popular.

State intervention
Notwithstanding the success of the campaign for free trade, this period also saw significant extensions of state regulation in a number of ways.

- The 1834 Poor Law Amendment Act established an element of central government control over the local Poor Law Guardians. The Poor Law Commission, appointed by ministers, was given the task of supervising the administration of poor relief by the locally-elected Guardians.
- Factory and Mines Acts in 1833, 1842, 1844, 1847 and 1850 established the principle that women and children working in textile factories and coal mines should have their hours and conditions of work regulated by law. The Acts also established the important principle that places of work should be subject to inspection by

professional inspectors who had the power to prosecute factory and mine owners who were found to be in breach of the law.

- All births, deaths and marriages had to be officially registered after 1837.
- Although elementary schooling was still provided only by religious charities, the payment of state grants after 1833 was followed by the establishment of a system of school inspections.
- Legislation to improve public health in the growing towns was first passed in 1848. Although the Act placed the onus for improving water supplies, sewage systems and street cleansing onto the local authorities, a central Board of Health was set up to oversee their work.
- Vaccination of all infants against smallpox was made compulsory in 1853.
- A Railway Act of 1844 began the process of state regulation of this new industry by giving railway commissioners the power to inspect companies and to investigate accidents.

This is by no means an exhaustive list of the legislation, passed during this period, that established an unprecedented level of state regulation and inspection. There appears to be a contradiction here. In an age when the newly enfranchised middle classes showed a strong preference for minimal state interference, and when governments had to show some sensitivity towards public opinion, there was a major expansion in the role of the state. In attempting to explain this paradox, three main points need to be made.

1. Governments were subject to a variety of conflicting pressures. The radical spokesmen for the 'Manchester School', Cobden and Bright, and Edward Baines were not the only voices that ministers listened to, nor were they necessarily the most influential. The Benthamites exercised an influence over policy that was out of all proportion to their numerical strength since they offered ministers a method for investigating a problem and for framing legislation. When applying their 'utilitarian test' to a law or institution, the Benthamites did not make a prior judgement that a laissez-faire or an interventionist solution would be the most appropriate. On some issues the Benthamites came down in favour of a laissez-faire approach; on others they concluded that a system of regulation and inspection was required. The Benthamites had an important influence over Poor Law reform, factory legislation and public health reform.

There were other voices and other pressures also. A leading campaigner for factory and mines legislation was Lord Shaftesbury, an aristocrat who was also an evangelical Christian. He was supported by a number of manufacturers who acted partly from humanitarian motives and partly out of self-interest – factory legislation would limit the ability of their competitors to reduce prices by forcing their employees to work longer hours. Finally, factory and mine workers themselves were involved in the campaign for protective legislation. Although they did not have the right to vote they were able to influence legislation through effective propaganda and through enlisting the support of influential figures such as Lord Shaftesbury.

2. The reforms were a necessary response to the problems of an industrialising society. Although there was, at all levels of society, a deep scepticism about the role of the state, collectivist solutions came to be regarded as the only practicable way of dealing with the problems created by the growth of towns and the expansion of industry. This grudging acceptance of state intervention was particularly evident in the debates over public health reform. Rising levels of infectious disease, high death rates and the terrifying experience of major cholera epidemics in 1831 and 1848 finally led to the 1848 Public Health Act. This Act was only passed after a mass of evidence had been accumulated through local and national studies, particularly Edwin Chadwick's Report into the Sanitary Condition of the Labouring Population in 1842. However, even with this evidence the reformers were unable to persuade Parliament to legislate until the cholera outbreak of 1848 shook the middle classes out of their complacency. Chadwick produced overwhelming evidence that private companies had failed to ensure an adequate supply of clean water and to remove sewage and other refuse from the towns efficiently and effectively. Where private enterprise had failed, publicly-financed solutions were required. Thus in the 1860s a new sewerage system for London was begun with public money.

3. The powers of the state were limited. Since the reform legislation was passed, in the face of fierce opposition to expanding the role of the state, severe limits were placed on the effectiveness of the system of regulation and inspection.

- The Poor Law Commission had the power merely to establish general principles governing the relief of poverty; it was left to local Guardians to interpret these principles.
- The implementation of the Public Health Act of 1848 by local authorities was only compulsory in towns where the death rate exceeded 23 per 1000. In other towns the Act was only implemented after the presentation of a petition signed by at least 10 per cent of the ratepayers. The powers of the central Board of Health were limited and the Board was abolished in 1858 after encountering stiff resistance.
- The effectiveness of factory inspection was limited by the fact that only four inspectors were employed to cover the entire country.

Thus, although the principle of state intervention in many areas of social and economic life was established by legislation passed during this period, the prevailing mood of scepticism towards the role of the state and of preference for laissez-faire solutions, limited the scope and effectiveness of this intervention.

HOW DID THE ROLE OF THE STATE CHANGE IN THE PERIOD 1867–1914?

The 1867 Reform Act brought within the 'political nation' a large proportion of the male working-class population. In 1884 the numbers of working-class voters were increased when the franchise was extended to rural male householders and their lodgers. The enlarged electorate thus contained men who had first-hand experience of long working hours, poor housing, disease, the lack of educational provision for their children and the ever-present threat of poverty. These were the people who might be expected to benefit the most from increased state intervention in social problems and therefore to cast their votes in favour of candidates who promised more reforming legislation. A superficial glance at the period 1868–80, when first a Liberal government led by Gladstone and then a Conservative government led by Disraeli introduced a number of reforms, would seem to support this view. Closer inspection, however, will reveal a number of flaws in this analysis.

What were the main reforms introduced in the period 1868–80?

- An Education Act in 1870 established state-run schools for the first time. These new Board Schools, run by locally-elected School Boards, provided an elementary education to children whose parents could not afford to pay for private education. Attendance at school was made compulsory in 1880.
- Factory Acts in 1874 and 1878 extended regulation and inspection to all large factories, although most of the legislation amounted to little more than a codification of existing rules into one law.
- An Artisans' Dwellings Act of 1875 gave local authorities the power to undertake slum clearance schemes.
- Public Health Acts of 1872 and 1875 divided the country into sanitary districts, each of which was to have a sanitary authority with powers to improve sanitation and control the spread of infectious diseases. Unlike the 1848 Act, the 1875 Act compelled local authorities to implement the legislation.

The legislation of the 1870s, then, can be seen to have taken the powers of the state into new areas and to have extended the principles of compulsion and collective action. The results were mixed. In education, the provision of compulsory (and, by 1891, free) education helped to raise standards of literacy. In public health, the last quarter of the nineteenth century saw major efforts in the large towns to lay new deep drains and improve the water supplies, with the result that death rates in the urban areas fell more rapidly. This period also saw a major switch from privately owned utilities to local authority owned water, gas and electricity companies. By 1900, two-thirds of water companies and electricity companies were publicly owned. The powers given to local authorities under the Artisans' Dwellings Act, however, were largely ineffective because there was no compulsion on local authorities to act.

Were these reforms the result of pressure from working-class voters?

The balance of the evidence seems to show that working-class voters had just as negative a view of state intervention into social problems as the middle classes. This is hardly surprising in view of the fact that, for most working-class families, their main experience of state intervention would have been the punitive Poor Law and its hated workhouse system. Working-class families also resented much of the legislation that was ostensibly passed for their benefit. Many families felt keenly the loss of children's earnings that was a result of compulsory schooling and did not welcome the attentions of truant inspectors when children did not attend. Compulsory vaccination was unpopular. Slum clearance often had the negative effect of reducing the supply of cheap housing. **Pugh** (1999) has written that, 'From the perspective of the working-class family, "improvement" was invariably intrusive or humiliating; it brought interference, inspection, regulation and taxation'.

There is little evidence, therefore, that working-class voters were pressing for these reforms in an organised or sustained way, or that the parties believed that social reforms were a way of appealing to working-class voters. Gladstone's government concentrated more on legal, administrative and religious reforms. The Liberal policies that appealed most to the working-class voters were free trade and low taxation, both of which helped to reduce the cost of living for working-class families. Disraeli's emphasis was on a patriotic, nationalistic approach to foreign policy, one that had an emotional appeal for working-class voters.

It is also significant that the pace of reform slowed down considerably in the 1880s and 1890s, and yet the largest extension of the franchise in the nineteenth century was made in the 1884 Reform Act. Clearly there was no direct or simple connection between the extension of the franchise to working-class men and an increase in state intervention.

If not pressure from the new working-class voters, what then were the main reasons why state intervention increased during this period?

Among the many pressures that governments were under, two main factors stand out:

- **Administrative momentum.** Once the state had begun to legislate on working conditions in factories and mines and on public health, the process developed its own internal dynamic. Factory Inspectors, Medical Officers of Health and Inspectors of Nuisances submitted regular reports on their work which highlighted the weaknesses in the legislation they were charged with enforcing. Further legislation, therefore, became almost inevitable.
- **The needs of the economy.** The gradual loss of Britain's economic supremacy after the 1870s had many causes; but some politicians and business leaders focused on the weaknesses of Britain's educational system, in comparison with Germany and the USA, as an underlying cause. Educational reform after 1870 was partly a response to these concerns.

What reforms were introduced between 1906 and 1914?

In 1906 a Liberal government was elected with a large majority. After 20 years of Conservative domination in which the pace of reform had slackened, the Liberal government introduced a wide-ranging programme of social and economic reform. Some of their reforms were an extension of Victorian social legislation but in a number of key respects the 'New Liberal' legislation was qualitatively different from what had gone before. Firstly, many reforms involved a greater degree of compulsion than would have been acceptable in the nineteenth century. Secondly, the reforms took the role of the state into areas of economic and social activity that had hitherto been considered beyond its scope. Thirdly, the increase in state intervention brought a vast increase in bureaucracy.

The main reforms were as follows:

- The provision of school meals and medical inspections of children at school in 1906.
- The introduction of old age pensions in 1908.
- The establishment of a compulsory and contributory National Insurance system in 1911 which provided unemployment and sickness benefits for those workers covered by the scheme.
- The establishment of Labour Exchanges in 1908 to help the unemployed find work.
- A Trade Boards Act of 1909 and the Miners' Minimum Wage Act in 1912, both of which established the principle of a statutory minimum wage, albeit for selected groups of workers. There was also an act in 1908 that established an eight-hour working day for miners. This was the first attempt by the state to control wages and hours for adult workers since the repeal of the Statute of Artificers in 1813.

To what extent were these reforms the result of pressure from working-class voters?

By 1906 class had become one of the major factors in determining voter behaviour, and the Liberal Party had become more aware of the extent of its dependence on working-class votes. The working classes had begun to make their presence felt within the political system, either through the ballot box or through the direct action that could be exerted through the trade unions. The explosion of trade union militancy among the unskilled that occurred in the years 1889–92 was to be repeated with even greater force in the years 1910–14. Through trade union pressure, the Liberals had been obliged to concede more seats to Lib-Lab candidates during the 1890s. The emergence of the Labour Party posed a potential long-term threat to the Liberals' ability to hold on to their working-class supporters. Both the trade unions and the Labour Party campaigned for extensive programmes of social reform including free secondary education for all, old age pensions, the abolition of the Poor Law and action to create jobs for the unemployed. There would appear, therefore, to be a clear and direct connection between pressure from the labour movement and the Liberal government's introduction of welfare reforms. There was also a direct connection between the pressure that the Miners' Union was able to exert through strike action and through its sponsoring of MPs, and the concessions made to the miners in 1908 and 1912.

There are, however, a number of problems with this analysis.

- Social reform was not a major issue in the election of 1906. The election was fought mainly on the issue of free trade versus 'tariff reform'; many working-class voters were keenly aware of the benefits they enjoyed as consumers from the free trade policy and gave their votes to Liberal or Labour candidates on this basis.
- The Conservative and Liberal parties avoided entering into a competitive auction on social reforms in order to attract working-class voters.
- Although old age pensions were very popular, many of the other Liberal reforms were not given an unqualified welcome by working-class voters. National Insurance, for example, was roundly criticised for being a contributory scheme, thereby excluding those who could not afford the contributions.

Undoubtedly, the presence of working-class voters among the electorate and the pressure that could be exerted through the labour movement were important factors in the Liberals' decision to extend state intervention. Many other factors, however, were also involved.

- **Concern for national security.** There had been considerable alarm at the time of the Boer War when a high proportion of the working-class youths who volunteered for military service had failed medical inspections. In some towns as many as six out of every ten volunteers were declared unfit for military service. Generations of poverty and poor medical care had left their mark on the nation's youth.

- **Concern over Britain's economic performance.** By 1900 the British economy had fallen behind the USA, and British manufacturers were having increasing difficulty in competing in world markets. One of the explanations put forward for this was that British workers could not match the productivity of those in competing economies because the effects of poverty made them unfit. The Liberal politician Herbert Asquith belonged to the '**National Efficiency**' **group** which advocated state action to deal with poverty as a prerequisite to improving Britain's economic performance.

- **The growing acceptance of collectivist ideology.** Although policies such as free trade were still overwhelmingly popular, and few in the early twentieth century advocated a greater role for the state in managing the economy, there was a growing body of opinion in favour of collectivist solutions to social problems. The spread of 'gas and water socialism' in the late nineteenth century offered a practical demonstration of what could be achieved through public rather than private enterprise. Surveys by Booth and Rowntree (see page 225) revealed the extent of poverty and underlined the extent to which the laissez-faire approach had failed. Gradually a more positive view of the role of the state was beginning to take hold, particularly among some civil servants, politicians and opinion-formers.

The Liberal reforms did not create a welfare state. They dealt with specific aspects of the problem of poverty as it affected children, the unemployed, the sick and the old. The Victorian Poor Law was left in place to provide a comprehensive safety net for those who did not qualify for assistance under any other scheme. In one important respect, however, the Liberal welfare reforms broke new ground. Unlike the Poor Law system under which recipients of relief forfeited their political rights, benefits such as old age pensions and unemployment benefit did not involve any loss of political rights. Indeed, pensions were presented as a 'right conferred by citizenship' rather than a stigma resulting from poverty. The connection between political rights and social welfare had been established.

HOW DID THE ROLE OF THE STATE CHANGE IN THE PERIOD 1914–31?

During the First World War the role of the state expanded out of all recognition. Under the pressure of total war, the state needed to maximise production of essential war materials and to maintain the morale of the civilian population. Ideological objections to interference with the free market were brushed aside as the state began to regulate and control many aspects of economic and social activity.

- Many key industries, such as the railways, coal mines and merchant shipping, were brought under government control.
- The government set up its own munitions factories to supplement the production efforts of privately-owned companies.
- Rents were subject to legal controls after 1915.
- Food rationing and control of food supply and distribution was introduced in 1917.
- The introduction of conscription in 1916 inevitably led to growing control over the labour market.
- New ministries were established for Labour, Pensions, Food, Health, Shipping, etc. All of these new ministries involved a massive expansion in the number of civil servants.

Many of these wartime controls were temporary. Businessmen, in particular, were keen that the controls and regulations should be removed as soon as peace returned, and to some extent this is what happened. By 1921 government control over the railways, mines and shipping had been dismantled. The expansion of the role of the state during wartime, however, left a permanent mark on society. In the post-war world, the role of the state in social and economic affairs was much greater than it had been before the war.

- During the period 1918–31 the state was closely involved in promoting the reorganisation of the railways, the coal mining and the shipbuilding industries.
- A state-owned company, the Central Electricity Generating Board, was set up in 1927 to generate electricity and run the national grid. A state-owned Forestry Commission was also established.
- The 1918 Education Act raised the school-leaving age to 14 and established state-run secondary schools.
- The 1919 Housing Act began the process of building council houses. The scheme was extended by a further Housing Act in 1924.
- The 1918 Maternity and Child Welfare Act compelled local authorities to implement national standards of health care by establishing maternity clinics and health visitors.
- The Unemployment Insurance scheme was extended to cover the majority of workers and a 'dole' was introduced for unemployed workers who did not qualify for benefit.
- Widows' pensions were introduced in 1925.

One of the most significant features of the post-war legislation was that it was introduced by governments of all political hues. Post-war political debate showed a remarkable degree of consensus about the need for, and the efficacy of, state intervention. Once again, the impact of the extension of the franchise in 1918 was an important factor in bringing about this change. The social legislation designed to improve the health and welfare of specific groups of women and the extension of unemployment benefit were clearly aimed at winning the support of the newly enfranchised. As in earlier periods, however, a range of factors led to the change.

- **The impact of the war.** The war changed the terms of the debate about state intervention. For many there was no longer a question about whether state intervention was desirable. Wartime controls and state-run enterprises had been instrumental in directing the nation's resources and maximising production, thereby making a decisive contribution to the final victory. The war had also generated a climate in which people expected some reward for their sacrifices, and when the debate about post-war reconstruction began in 1917, social improvement through state intervention was assumed to be the way forward. Lloyd George's promise of 'Homes fit for heroes to live in', made during the election campaign in 1918, captured this mood.

- **The impact of the Labour Party and the trade unions.** The rise in support for the Labour Party between 1918 and 1929 caused both established parties to give serious thought to how the rise of socialism could be contained. Similarly, the massive growth of the trade unions between 1914 and 1921, together with the post-war rise in direct action and trade union militancy, heightened the fears of a descent into class conflict and revolution. Social reforms passed by Coalition and Conservative governments were, in this context, partly an attempt to avert class conflict. We must be careful, however, not to carry this analysis too far. When a trade depression hit the British economy in 1921 the government's response was to cut expenditure. This involved stopping the building of council houses and attempting to place strict limits on the payment of benefits, especially by local Poor Law Guardians which had come under Labour control. The operation of the systems of welfare benefits could still generate sharp divisions between the parties, even if the underlying principle of state intervention had been accepted by all.

SECTION 8

CONCLUSION

The transition from a political system controlled by an exclusive aristocratic elite to one in which every adult over the age of 21 was entitled to vote was a long and protracted process. Even in the 1920s the British political system retained many traditional features that sat uneasily alongside the democratically-elected House of Commons. Membership of the House of Lords, for example, was still based overwhelmingly on the hereditary principle and, although the powers of the House of Lords had been reduced, the second chamber still retained the ability to delay legislation and frustrate the wishes of an elected government. The fact that women were not permitted to exercise the franchise on the same terms as men until 1928 illustrates another very important feature of the transition to democracy. Plural voting, which gave the middle classes a disproportionate influence, was still allowed. Each time the franchise was extended, the opportunity to vote was conceded as a privilege rather than a right. As **Vincent** (1972) has pointed out, 'The vote was discussed chiefly as a kind of personal reward or certificate of good character, never as an instrument for changing the social condition of the people'. Extensions of the franchise in 1832, 1867, 1884, 1918 and 1928 were conceded by the governments of the day on the basis that the beneficiaries of the reforms had proved their 'fitness' to be admitted to the political nation and it was therefore safe to grant them the right to vote. This was a far cry from the aims of those eighteenth-century radicals who had first raised the cry for universal suffrage on the basis of abstract notions of 'The Rights of Man'.

The transition to democracy was a protracted process for a number of reasons:

- The landed aristocracy showed a remarkable ability to retain their social and political leadership, despite the gradual erosion of their economic position. The Conservative Party continued to be led and dominated by aristocrats until the early twentieth century. The Whigs retained a strong position within the parliamentary Liberal Party until 1886.
- The aristocracy also showed the ability to accommodate and absorb successful, upwardly-mobile members of the middle classes. In the mid-nineteenth century, the Liberal Party was founded on an alliance between the industrial and commercial middle classes and Whig aristocrats. By the end of the nineteenth century, this position had very

largely been achieved by the Conservative Party. Few among the middle classes, even at the height of the mid-Victorian Liberal Party, had much interest in the calls by Cobden and Bright for an assault on aristocratic privilege. A country estate, a title and acceptance into the ranks of the landed classes were still ambitions that motivated many successful business and professional men.

- Generally, rising living standards after the 1850s drew the sting from agitation for radical reform among the working classes. The Chartist movement represented the last serious attempt to force Parliament to concede thoroughgoing reform of the political system and the immediate adoption of full democracy. Following the defeat of Chartism there was a general acceptance that reform could only be achieved in a piecemeal, step-by-step fashion. This implied an acceptance that the political parties, and their aristocratic leaderships, would control the pace of change. Symptomatic of this new climate was the fact that many former Chartists became active among the rank and file of the Liberal Party, and agitation for reform in 1867 and 1884 had close links with the Liberals.

The political parties themselves showed a remarkable degree of flexibility in adapting their organisations to the changes in the political climate after each successive reform. Until the 1870s the Liberals proved to be more flexible, and therefore more successful, than the Conservatives, but the fact that the Conservatives survived at all reflects a degree of flexibility. New forms of organisation were developed to accommodate and absorb the newly enfranchised groups. In this way the parties broadened the basis of their support and membership and became mass political parties by the 1880s. They also became more professional in the way they organised themselves for election campaigns. Broadening the basis of membership, however, caused increasing tensions within the parties since, although the old aristocratic elites were prepared to accept the new groups as allies, they were not prepared to welcome them as equal partners. The Liberals suffered more from this tension than the Conservatives mainly because, as the party of reform, they attracted the very groups who were campaigning for a wider democracy in society at large. The Conservatives faced fewer challenges to the control of established leaders. This was partly because conservatism placed greater stress on deference and loyalty, and partly because the Conservatives showed consummate skill in attaching a mass membership to the party without conceding any role for that membership in the choice of leaders or discussions over policy.

Superficially there appears to be a connection between the gradual transition towards political democracy and the expanding role of the state in social welfare, if only because the timing of the major extensions in the role of the state seems to follow the timing of the extensions in the franchise. Many historians have argued that the social welfare reforms in

Britain were the inevitable result of the extension of political democracy. This simple view does not stand up to detailed examination, however. Firstly, there was no simple or direct correlation between the granting of the vote to particular groups and the introduction of reforms that were designed to help them. Effective factory and mines legislation began in the 1830s, long before the workers who would benefit from this protection were enfranchised. The 'New Liberal' welfare reforms were not introduced until 30 years after working men had been admitted to the franchise. Reforms specifically aimed at helping women were introduced before women gained the vote.

This is not to deny that political parties were calculating the impact of social reforms on their popularity with the electorate. But we should be careful not to conclude that, by the end of the nineteenth century, Liberals and Conservatives had abandoned the doctrines of laissez-faire and embraced the ideology of collectivism. Politicians and, it must be stressed, the majority of middle-class and artisan voters, made a presumption in favour of individualist, self-help approaches to social problems although this was increasingly modified in the light of experience. Just as the transition to political democracy was made in a piecemeal, step-by-step manner, so the move towards what may be termed a 'social democracy' was made in a cautious, piecemeal, empirical way. As evidence mounted of the scale of the problems created by industrialisation and urbanisation, politicians and administrators tried new approaches based on state intervention in an attempt to cope. Once started, the process of state intervention developed a momentum of its own. Sometimes, as with factory reform, it was the workers themselves who were campaigning for legal protection – although it is significant that they did not achieve all of their demands. Sometimes, as with old age pensions, the reforms proved popular with the people who were the recipients of the state support, but this was by no means always the case. This merely emphasises the point that the reasons why the state intervened more in social questions between 1830 and 1931 are many and various. There is no simple, mono-causal explanation that will fit every reform in every circumstance.

A2 ASSESSMENT: REPRESENTATION AND DEMOCRACY IN BRITAIN, 1830–1931

STRUCTURED, SOURCE-BASED QUESTIONS IN THE STYLE OF EDEXCEL

Study Sources 1–3 below and answer the questions which follow:

Source 1. *The growth of the electorate as a result of parliamentary reform, 1831–1928*

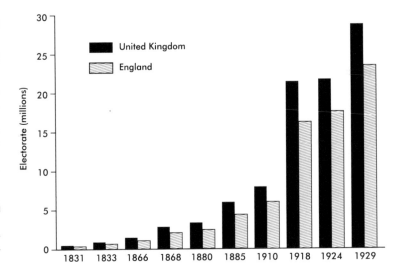

Source 2. *An extract from* The Economist, *December 1884, analysing the changes being brought about by the 1884 Third Reform Act and the proposed redistribution of seats.*

[The Bills] disturb all personal interests in a way no previous bill has ever done. With the exception of the sixty or so seats in the boroughs with between 50,000 and 165,000 voters, no seat in the country is unaffected . . . Most [existing] political organisations perish under the Bill. There will no longer be a Liverpool, but nine Liverpools, often singularly apart in feeling.

[Members of Parliament] will rarely or never be unopposed, for the new Bribery Act makes elections relatively cheap.

Source 3. *From Eric Evans,* Parliamentary Reform, 1770–1918 *(2000).*

What was essentially a reformist creed remained undemocratic. Democracy, as one Whig supporter said, was 'fatal to the purposes for which government exists'. Throughout the nineteenth century, therefore, the key reform question was 'Whom is it safe to enfranchise?' It was the definition of 'safe' which changed, rather than the ultimate objective. The enfranchisement clauses of the so-called Great Reform Act were carefully designed to include the fearfully conservative lower middle classes and to exclude working people, many of whose leaders called stridently for democracy.

(a) Study Sources 1, 2 and 3.

Use these sources to outline how the electorate changed in the period, 1832–1928. (4)

(b) Use your background knowledge to answer this question.

The following Reforms were all made between 1832 and 1918.

1) The Reform Act of 1832

2) The Reform Act of 1867

3) The Secret Ballot Act, 1872

4) The Representation of the People Act, 1918.

Choose **one** of the Acts listed above which you think represents a key turning point in the development of democratic politics in Britain. Explain why you think it was a turning point. (10)

(c) Study all the sources and use your own knowledge.

Explain the main reasons why each of the Reform Acts of the years 1832–1918 increased the numbers of voters. (16)

Reading

In order to answer these questions you will need to read sections 3, 4 and 5 of this book.

How to answer these questions

Question (a). Note that this question refers you to three sources and you will be expected to cross-reference between all three. The question is also about change over a long period of time. Be careful not to make the assumption that the question is solely about the changing size of the electorate, although this is clearly a part of the question. You should interpret the question to be about the changing composition and nature of the electorate. From the sources, you can see that the electorate grew in size (give figures from the bar graph), that the changes were greater at some times than at others and that the social composition of the electorate changed as different classes were enfranchised. Source 2 also refers to the changes in constituencies and in the conduct of elections.

Question (b). In this question you have a free choice of any of the four Acts. You do not have to select the Act which you think was the most important turning point, although you could do so if you wish. The key requirement here is to show that you understand the concept of a historical turning point and can produce a reasoned argument about the importance of the Act you have selected. Note that the question is about 'the development of democratic politics' in Britain; your analysis of the significance of the Act you choose should be related to that.

Any discussion of historical turning points must do the following:

• Show accurate knowledge of the Act itself.
• Demonstrate an understanding of the situation before the Act was passed and of the pressures which led to its passing.
• Analyse the significance of the Act in terms of the changes which happened as a result of its passing. This should include long-term as well as short-term consequences.

Question (c). This question is worth the most marks and requires an essay-style answer. The question is about change over a period of time. There are five Reform Acts to cover in your answer and it would be sensible to deal with each in turn; but it is also important that you make links between the different reforms in order to give the essay an overall coherence. The focus will be on the reasons why the franchise was extended on each of the five occasions, and you will therefore need to demonstrate good knowledge of the circumstances surrounding the passing of each of the Reform Acts and the actual terms of those reforms. Try also to identify any common threads in the story. Source 3 is particularly useful here. You could refer to Evans's argument that the 'key reform question was "Whom is it safe to enfranchise?" ' and use this as a unifying theme throughout the essay by applying the same line of argument to each of the five reforms. 'Whom was it safe to enfranchise?' remained the key question asked by governments, but the answers changed as circumstances changed. Remember to look at the immediate circumstances surrounding the passing of each reform but also give due weight to the underlying, long-term social and economic changes.

A2 ASSESSMENT: THE DEVELOPMENT OF DEMOCRACIES – PART 1: GREAT BRITAIN, 1867–1918

STRUCTURED SOURCE-BASED QUESTIONS IN THE STYLE OF AQA

Study Sources A, B and C below and then answer the questions which follow:

Source A. *From* The Age of Improvement *by Asa Briggs, in which the author is summarising some of the predictions of Robert Lowe on the consequences of the proposals for parliamentary reform in 1867.*

Reform would lead to the canvassing and carrying out of policies which would undermine national union and prosperity. The working classes were interested in the vote not in itself but as a means to an end, and were already looking beyond political democracy to 'socialism'. The machinery of government might be used to assist strikes – Lowe was very conscious of the 'dangers' of trade union rule. 'Once give working men the vote, and the machinery is ready to launch these votes in one compact mass upon the institutions and property in this country.'

Source B. *From a speech by Lord Derby, Prime Minister, at the time of the Second Reform Act.*

No doubt we are making a great experiment and 'taking a leap in the dark', but I have the greatest confidence in the sound sense of my fellow countrymen, and I entertain a strong hope that the extended franchise which we are now conferring upon them will be the means of placing the institutions of this country on a firmer basis, and that the passing of the measure will tend to increase the loyalty and contentment of a great portion of Her Majesty's subjects.

Source C. *From* British Political History, 1867–1995 *by G. Stewart and M. Pearce.*

The whole concentration on legislation is in many ways a distortion of perspective. Law-making was not what mattered to Disraeli or anyone else . . . The social legislation that history books make so much of did not figure in the 1880 election campaign. It was, in short, the sort of non-controversial things all governments did. There was little that a Liberal government would not have done, and in fact much arose from Royal Commissions set up under the previous Gladstone government. Only the trade union legislation was radical. The Education and Licensing Acts can be seen as reactionary. As to the rest, they were, as one Tory MP put it, 'suet-pudding legislation, wholesome but not very interesting'.

(a) Study Sources A and B and use your own knowledge to explain how the two sources differ in their views on the consequences of the Second Reform Act. **(10)**

(b) Study all the sources and use your own knowledge.

To what extent can the reforms introduced between 1868 and 1880 be explained as an attempt by Liberal and Conservative governments to attract the support of the newly enfranchised voters? **(20)**

Reading

In order to answer these questions you need to read sections 3, 4 and 7 of this book.

How to answer these questions

Question (a). Note the instruction to refer to the sources and to use your own knowledge.

There is clear disagreement between the two sources on the likely consequences of reform. Source A is pessimistic while B is cautiously optimistic. A argues that reform will undermine the institutions of the country while B argues that it will place them on a firmer basis. Note, however, that despite his apparent optimism about reform, Derby still refers to it as 'a leap in the dark'; in other words, he is not entirely confident.

Use your background knowledge to explain the origins of these sources. Who were Robert Lowe and Lord Derby? Why would Lowe have been opposed to the Bill – bearing in mind that he was a Liberal politician – and why would Derby have been more supportive – given that he was the Conservative Prime Minister at the time when the Second Reform Act was passed? What was there in the Second Reform Act that was put forward by the Conservatives that Derby found reassuring from a Conservative point of view?

Question (b). This question requires an essay-style answer. Remember that an essay needs to be well structured with a clear line of argument running through it. The essay needs to be broken down into paragraphs, in each of which you make a separate point and support that point with well-selected, relevant factual examples.

There are a lot of reforms to cover in this answer and there is a danger that your essay could become a mere list of the main reforms passed by Gladstone's and Disraeli's governments. This would not make for a successful answer. A better approach would be to identify all the factors that led to the burst of reforms during this period and deal with them on a factor-by-factor basis. Clearly, the enfranchisement of part of the male working-class population in 1867 did have some connection with the reforms which followed. For example, the Education Act of 1870 and the Trade Union Act of 1870 were clearly linked to the enfranchisement of artisans. There were, however, many other factors that led to the reforms of this period as section 7 of this book makes clear. You need to show an awareness of the range of factors involved to gain higher marks.

There is scope here for discussion about the motives of the Conservative government, 1874–80, in introducing many social reforms. Source C is particularly useful here as a starting off point for your discussion. It is also important that you can differentiate between the reforms of Gladstone's government and those of Disraeli's. Can you detect any difference in emphasis and motive between the two? Finally, you should address the issue of the aspirations and interests of the new working-class voters. To what extent were they looking to governments for more state intervention in social problems?

BIBLIOGRAPHY

WORKS PARTICULARLY RELEVANT TO AS STUDENTS

Parliamentary Reform 1815–50

Aydelotte, W. O. 'The House of Commons in the 1840s', *History*, **39**, 1954

Briggs, A. (ed) Chartist Studies, 1959

Brock, M. *The Great Reform Act*, Cambridge University Press, 1973

Cannon, J. *Parliamentary Reform 1640–1832*, Cambridge University Press, 1980

Epstein, J. and Thompson, D. (eds) *The Chartist Experience*, Macmillan, 1982

Evans, E. J. *The Forging of the Modern State 1783–1870*, Longman, 1996

Evans, E. J. *Parliamentary Reform, 1770–1918*, Longman, 2000

Gash, N. *Aristocracy and People 1815–65*, Arnold, 1979

Jones, D. *Chartism and the Chartists*, Lane, 1975

Lang, S. *Parliamentary Reform 1785–1928*, Routledge, 1999

Pugh, M. *The Evolution of the British Electoral System*, Historical Association, 1988

Royle, E. *Chartism*, Longman, 1996

Thompson, E. P. *The Making of the English Working Class*, Penguin, 1968

Wright, D. *Democracy and Reform 1815–85*, Longman, 1970

Votes for Women 1867–1928

Bartley, P. *Votes for Women 1860–1928*, Hodder & Stoughton, 1998

Evans, E. J. *Parliamentary Reform, 1770–1918*, Longman, 2000

Lang, S. *Parliamentary Reform 1785–1928*, Routledge, 1999

Liddington, J. and Norris, J. *One Hand Tied Behind Us*, Virago, 1978

Marwick, A. *The Deluge*, Penguin, 1967

Pugh, M. *Women's Suffrage in Britain 1867–1928*, Historical Association, 1980

Purvis, J. and Holton, S. (eds) *Votes for Women*, 2000

Smith, N. *The British Women's Suffrage Campaign 1866–1928*, Longman, 1998

Walker, L. *The Women's Movement*, Routledge, 1999

WORKS PARTICULARLY RELEVANT TO A2 STUDENTS

Representation and Democracy 1830–1931

Adelman, P. *The Rise of the Labour Party 1880–1945*, Longman, 1972

Blake, R. *The Conservative Party from Peel to Churchill*, Fontana, 1972

Checkland, S. *The Rise of the Industrial Society in England 1815–85*, Longman, 1964

Evans, E. J. *The Forging of the Modern State 1783–1870*, Longman, 1996

Evans, E. J. *Parliamentary Reform, 1770–1918*, Longman, 2000

Gash, N. *Aristocracy and People 1815–65*, Arnold, 1979

Kitson Clark, G. *The Making of Victorian England*, Methuen, 1962

Lang, S. *Parliamentary Reform 1785–1928*, Routledge, 1999

McKibbin, R. *The Evolution of the Labour Party 1910–24*, 1974

Midwinter, E. *Victorian Social Reform*, Longman, 1968

Pugh, M. *The Making of Modern British Politics, 1867–1939*, Blackwell, 1982

Pugh, M. *The Evolution of the British Electoral System*, Historical Association, 1988

Pugh, M. *State and Society, 1870–1997*, Arnold, 1999

Ramsden, J. *An Appetite For Power*, 1999

Robbins, K. *The Eclipse of a Great Power, 1870–1975*, Longman, 1983

Sykes, A. *The Rise and Fall of British Liberalism, 1876–1988*, 1997

Ramsden, J. *An Appetite For Power*, 1999

Tanner, D. *Political Power and the Labour Party, 1900–18*, 1990

Vernon, J. *Politics and the People: A Study in English Political Culture 1815–67*, Cambridge University Press, 1993

Vincent, J. *The Formation of the British Liberal Party, 1857–68*, Penguin, 1972

INDEX

HEINEMANN ADVANCED HISTORY